# A GIFT FOR:

_____

# FROM:

2020
_____

# faith
# THAT
# MATTERS

## 365 DEVOTIONS
## FROM CLASSIC CHRISTIAN LEADERS

DALLAS WILLARD | HENRI J. M. NOUWEN

FREDERICK BUECHNER | A. W. TOZER

N. T. WRIGHT | JAMES BRYAN SMITH

EUGENE PETERSON | BRENNAN MANNING

HarperOne
*An Imprint of* HarperCollins*Publishers*

**HarperOne**

# January

# THE SPIRITUAL WORK OF GRATITUDE

## Henri J. M. Nouwen

He said:
"Naked I came from my mother's womb,
And naked shall I return there.
The LORD gave, and the LORD has taken away;
Blessed be the name of the LORD."

JOB 1:21 NKJV

To be grateful for the good things that happen in our lives is easy, but to be grateful for all of our lives—the good as well as the bad, the moments of joy as well as the moments of sorrow, the successes as well as the failures, the rewards as well as the rejections—that requires hard spiritual work. Still, we are only truly grateful people when we can say "Thank you" to all that has brought us to the present moment. As long as we keep dividing our lives between events and people we would like to remember and those we would rather forget, we cannot claim the fullness of our beings as a gift of God to be grateful for.

Let's not be afraid to look at everything that has brought us to where we are now and trust that we will soon see in it the guiding hand of a loving God.

Consider your moments of joy and sorrow, your successes as well as failures, the times God gave, and the times he took away. Can you join Job in proclaiming, "Blessed be the name of the LORD"?

*Lord, cultivate within me a spirit of gratitude for all you've given and all you've taken away. Blessed be your name, Lord. Amen.*

# IN THE MORNING, TRUST GOD

## Eugene Peterson

O Lord, in the morning thou dost hear my voice;
in the morning I prepare a sacrifice for thee, and watch.

PSALM 5:3 RSV

The work of God begins while we are asleep and without our help. He continues to work through the day in our worship and obedience. A sacrifice is the material means of assembling a life before God in order to let God work with it. Sacrifice isn't something we do for God but simply setting out the stuff of life for him to do something with. On the altar the sacrificial offering is changed into what is pleasing and acceptable to God. In the act of offering we give up ownership and control, and watch to see what God will do with it. With a deep awareness that the God who speaks life into us also listens when we speak, we put into words the difficulties and delights that we foresee in the hours ahead. We assemble fears and hopes, apprehensions and anticipations, and place them on the altar as an offering.

---

A pivotal word in the morning is the word *watch*. We watch to see what God will do with the array of concerns we set before him. Morning prayer places us before the watchful God, readying us to enter the day watchful for dangers to recede, for the dangerous day to fill with God's angels.

*Lord, this early hour I bring to you all of my apprehensions—trusting you, watching you. Amen.*

# MADE FOR EACH OTHER

## N. T. Wright

> As iron sharpens iron,
> so one person sharpens another.
>
> PROVERBS 27:17

We are made for each other. Yet making relationships work, let alone making them flourish, is often remarkably difficult. We all know that justice matters, yet it slips through our fingers. We mostly know that there is such a thing as spirituality, and that it's important, yet it's hard to refute the charge that it's all wishful thinking. In the same way, we all know that we belong in communities, that we were made to be social creatures. Yet there are many times when we are tempted to slam the door and stomp off into the night by ourselves, simultaneously making the statement that we don't belong anymore and that we want someone to take pity on us, to come to the rescue and comfort us. We all know we belong in relationships, but we can't quite work out how to get them right. The voice we hear echoing in our heads and our hearts keeps reminding us of both parts of this paradox, and it's worth pondering why.

"We were made for each other" is a profound ſtatement of reality, echoed in the proverb—for it's in community that we are shaped and find our sharpened selves. It's also a signpost of a deeper reality, telling us there is a road ahead that leads to goodness.

*Lord, thank you for making me for community; may I
become more like you through others' help. Amen.*

# DO YOU KNOW THAT GOD LOVES YOU?

## James Bryan Smith

See what great love the Father has lavished on us,
that we should be called children of God!

1 JOHN 3:1

I have come to believe that God is madly in love with us. God loves us with a passionate love. It is too great for us to comprehend; we do not have the words to describe it fully. It is too vast to grasp completely. *But we can know it. And we can feel it.* It is in his hands as he holds us. It is in his gentle words as he comforts us. It is written all over his face.

And yet many of us feel alienated from God. We are a technologically advanced society, but our souls are sick. We seek help in psychotherapy, support groups, tarot cards, crystals—anything that will relieve the pain. But we find that these supposed sources of help are helpless. The emptiness will not be filled.

What we long to know is that we are loved. To be more specific, we hunger to know that we are accepted as we are, forgiven for all we have done, and cared for by a gracious, loving God. When we know this, we walk away well.

———⚭———

God is telling his people that when he looks at us, he smiles in love—as a father smiles at his child. He wants us to know that, deep down. Do you?

*Lord, I receive this day your acceptance, forgiveness, and care, believing you love me—like a Father. Amen.*

# LIBERATION FROM TIME'S TYRANNY

## Brennan Manning

> "I am the Alpha and the Omega, the first and
> the last, the beginning and the end."
>
> REVELATION 22:13 NRSV

Whether the end-time is imminent or not, the lordship of Jesus Christ extends over the cosmic continuum. Authentic prayer puts us in touch with this reality and liberates us from the tyranny of time. Jesus' word calls us to conscientious conduct in the world today; tomorrow's survival is his responsibility.

The New Testament knows only the linear concept of time. Creation marked the beginning, the death/resurrection of Christ is the decisive mid-point, and his Second Coming determines the end-time. But this latter, future event is no longer the center of redemptive history. Regardless of the precise date of the Parousia, we are living in the last days, or, in theologian Oscar Cullman's oft-quoted phrase, in "the *is*ness of the shall be."[1] The final stage of salvation-history was inaugurated on Easter Sunday.

In the Christian view of history, the end-time is coming, but the world is already ruled by Christ by virtue of his decisive Easter victory.

The one who launched creation is responsible for its beginning and for its end. Trust him with everything in between.

> *Lord, the Alpha and Omega of time, may I be*
> *liberated from feeling responsible for it. Amen.*

# WHY HAS JESUS' RELEVANCE ENDURED?

## Dallas Willard

*In him was life, and that life was the light of all mankind.*

JOHN 1:4

And what is it, really, that explains the enduring relevance of Jesus to human life? Why has he mattered so much? Why does he matter now? Why does he appear on the front covers of leading newsmagazines two millennia later? Why, even, is his name invoked in cursing more than that of any other person who has lived on earth? Why do more people self-identify as Christians—by some estimates 32 percent of the world population[2]—than any other world religion? How is it that multitudes today credit him with their life and well-being?

I think we finally have to say that Jesus' enduring relevance is based on his historically proven ability to speak, to heal, and to empower the individual human condition. He matters because of what he brought and what he still brings to ordinary human beings, living their ordinary lives and coping daily with their surroundings: he promises wholeness for their lives. In sharing our weakness he gives us strength and imparts through his companionship a life that has the quality of eternity.

He comes where we are, and he brings us the life we hunger for.

---

The secret of the enduring relevance of Jesus is that he is the light of life, and he delivers God's life to the world, to you.

*Jesus, the life and light of all mankind, continue to speak to, heal, and empower my human condition. Amen.*

# WHO IS GOD TO YOU?

## A. W. Tozer

> You, Lord, are a compassionate and gracious God,
> slow to anger, abounding in love and faithfulness.
>
> PSALM 86:15

The history of mankind will probably show that no people has ever risen above its religion, and man's spiritual history will positively demonstrate that no religion has ever been greater than its idea of God. Worship is pure or base as the worshiper entertains high or low thoughts of God.

Always the most revealing thing about the church is her idea of God, just as her most significant message is what she says about him or leaves unsaid, for her silence is often more eloquent than her speech. She can never escape the self-disclosure of her witness concerning God.

Were we able to extract from any man a complete answer to the question, "What comes into your mind when you think about God?" we might predict with certainty the spiritual future of that man. Were we able to know exactly what our most influential religious leaders think of God today, we might be able with some precision to foretell where the church will stand tomorrow.

What comes to mind when we think about God is the most important thing about us. Is he compassionate and gracious, slow to anger and abounding in love, or something else?

*Lord, give me a right idea about who you are and what you are up to in the world, so I can rightly worship you in fullness. Amen.*

# JESUS' GOOD NEWS OF THE KINGDOM

## N. T. Wright

*Jesus went throughout Galilee, teaching in their synagogues
and proclaiming the good news of the kingdom.*

MATTHEW 4:23 NRSV

There is very little in the Bible about "going to heaven when you die" and not a lot about a postmortem hell either. The medieval pictures of heaven and hell, boosted though not created by Dante's classic work, have exercised a huge influence on Western Christian imagination. Jesus' sayings in the other gospels about the "kingdom of God" are rendered as "kingdom of heaven"; since many read Matthew first, when they find Jesus talking about "entering the kingdom of heaven," they have their assumptions confirmed and suppose that he is indeed talking about how to go to heaven when you die, which is certainly not what either Jesus or Matthew had in mind. Many mental pictures have grown up around this and are now assumed to be what the Bible teaches or what Christians believe.

But the language of heaven in the New Testament doesn't work that way. "God's kingdom" in the preaching of Jesus refers not to postmortem destiny, not to our escape from this world into another one, but to God's sovereign rule coming "on earth as it is in heaven."

---

How should your grasp of God's sovereign heavenly rule coming on earth affect how you understand Jesus' good news about the kingdom?

*Lord, give me a proper understanding of your kingdom
to ground my present and future hope. Amen.*

9

# EXTRAORDINARY GRACE-GIFTS

## Frederick Buechner

> To each one the manifestation of the Spirit
> is given for the common good.
>
> 1 CORINTHIANS 12:7

Most of the time when we say people are charismatic, we mean simply that they have presence. You don't have to be famous to have it either. You come across it in children and nobodies.

On the other hand, if you took Mother Teresa, or Francis of Assisi, or Mahatma Gandhi, or the man who risked his neck smuggling Jews out of Nazi Germany, and dressed them up to look like everybody else, nobody would probably notice them. These are the true charismatics, from the Greek word *charis* meaning "grace." According to Saint Paul, out of sheer graciousness God gives certain men and women extraordinary gifts or *charismata* such as the ability to heal, to teach, to perform acts of mercy, to work miracles.

These people are not apt to have presence, and you don't feel any special vibrations when they enter a room. But they are all in their own ways miracle-workers.

---

What extraordinary grace-gifts has God given you for the purpose of working ordinary miracles? How can you exercise them each day for God's glory and the common good?

*Lord, remind me of the extraordinary gifts you've given me;*
*empower me to use them for others' good. Amen.*

# TIME IS ON OUR SIDE

## A. W. Tozer

I trust in you, O LORD;
I say, "You are my God."
My times are in your hand.

PSALM 31:14–15 NRSV

Because God's nature is infinite, everything that flows out of it is infinite also. We poor human creatures are constantly being frustrated by limitations imposed upon us from without and within. The days of the years of our lives are few, and swifter than a weaver's shuttle. Life is a short and fevered rehearsal for a concert we cannot stay to give. Just when we appear to have attained some proficiency we are forced to lay our instruments down.

How completely satisfying to turn from our limitations to a God who has none. Eternal years lie in his heart. For him time does not pass, it remains; and those who are in Christ share with him all the riches of limitless time and endless years. God never hurries. There are no deadlines against which he must work. Only to know this is to quiet our spirits and relax our nerves. The foe of the old human race becomes the friend of the new, and the stars in their courses fight for the man God delights to honor.

⸺∞⸺

Time is on our side because the God of time is on our side. For the sons and daughters of the new creation, time isn't a devouring beast; it's our pet.

*Lord, I'm thankful to know that you hold my time safely in your hands. Amen.*

# SHOW FORTH NEIGHBOR-LOVE

## Dallas Willard

> "Which of these three, do you think, was a neighbor to the man who fell into the hands of the robbers?" He said, "The one who showed him mercy." Jesus said to him, "Go and do likewise."
>
> LUKE 10:36–37 NRSV

The word *neighbor* comes out of older English, where it referred to "the boor that is nigh thee." Here I want you to think of your neighbors as simply those we are intimately engaged with in life. The Samaritan found himself in intimate engagement with a victim of violence, and he responded accordingly.

A common usage of the word *neighbor* today locates the neighbor as one who lives "next door" or close by. A "next-door" neighbor is one with a special degree of intimacy, in this understanding, and there is something to that. But in this understanding my most important neighbor is overlooked: the one who lives with me—my family, or others taken in by us. They are the ones I am most intimately engaged with in my life. They are the ones who first and foremost I am to love as I love myself. If only this were done, nearly every problem in families would be resolved, and the love would spread to others.

---

How have you defined *neighbor*? How would you define one now, especially in light of Jesus' teachings?

*Lord, open my eyes to the needs of those who live "next door"; empower and embolden me to go and show forth neighbor-love. Amen.*

# ALL KNOWING IS A GIFT FROM GOD

## N. T. Wright

*He has made known to us the mystery of his will, according
to his good pleasure that he set forth in Christ.*

EPHESIANS 1:9 NRSV

Though the historical arguments for Jesus' bodily resurrection are truly strong, we must never suppose that they will do more than bring people to the questions faced by Thomas, Paul, and Peter, the questions of faith, hope, and love. What the candles of historical scholarship will do is show that the room has been disturbed, that it doesn't look like it did last night, and that would-be normal explanations for this won't do. Maybe, we think after the historical arguments have done their work, maybe morning has come and the world has woken up.

But to investigate whether this is so, we must take the risk and open the curtains to the rising sun. When we do so, we won't rely on the candles anymore, not because we don't believe in evidence and argument but because they will have been overtaken by the larger reality from which they borrow, to which they point, and in which they will find a new and larger home. All knowing is a gift from God, historical and scientific knowing no less than that of faith, hope, and love; but the greatest of these is love.

❦

Whether historical or scientific knowledge, faith-, hope-, or love-filled knowledge—it's all given by a gracious God.

*Lord, thank you for gifting humankind with
the knowledge of your mysteries. Amen.*

# WELCOME THE EVENING

## Eugene Peterson

> In peace I will lie down and sleep,
> for you alone, LORD, make me dwell in safety.
>
> PSALM 4:8

We begin our lives asleep in the womb, formed by another. Passive in the darkness, we are made. When we finally venture into daylight action, we are not done with the passivities of sleep but return to them at once. In our early days we are more asleep than awake, as another, and others nourish us into the wholeness that we have neither the wisdom nor the strength to fashion ourselves. Gradually our waking hours lengthen and we take up for ourselves tasks others did for us, entering into the work of the world—loving, helping, feeding, healing, building, teaching, making.

But we never arrive at a condition where we are beyond sleep, self-sufficient in twenty-four-hour control. Daily we give up consciousness, submitting ourselves to that which is deeper than consciousness in order to grow and be healed, be created and saved. Going to sleep is a biological necessity; it can also be an act of faith. People who live by faith have always welcomed the evening hour of prayer, disengaging themselves from the discordant, arrhythmic confusion of tongues, and sinking into the quiet rhythms of God's creating and covenanting words.

Are you able to go to sleep in peace, believing deep down that the Lord keeps you secure during the night hour?

*Lord, now I lay me down to sleep,*
*believing that my soul you'll keep. Amen.*

# THE BASIS OF OUR SECURITY

## Henri J. M. Nouwen

He made my feet like the feet of a deer,

and set me secure on the heights.

PSALM 18:33 NRSV

What is the basis of our security? When we start thinking about that question, we may give many answers: success, money, friends, property, popularity, family, connections, insurance, and so on. We may not always *think* that any of these forms the basis of our security, but our *actions* or *feelings* may tell us otherwise. When we start losing our money, our friends, or our popularity, our anxiety often reveals how deeply our sense of security is rooted in these things.

A spiritual life is a life in which our security is based not in any created things, good as they may be, but in God, who is everlasting love. We probably will never be completely free from our attachment to the temporal world, but if we want to live in that world in a truly free way, we'd better not belong to it.

───✸───

What is the basis of your security? Is it success or money, property or popularity, friends or family, connections or insurance? Or is it the Lord your God, who has set you securely on the high places?

*Lord, may my spiritual life be rooted not in the fleeting security of created things, but in the steadfast security of your will, flowing from your everlasting love for me. Amen.*

# BLESSED EXPECTATIONS

## Eugene Peterson

> Blessed is the one
> who does not walk in step with the wicked
> or stand in the way that sinners take
> or sit in the company of mockers.
>
> PSALM 1:1

*B*lessed is a directional antenna, a mind-set for picking up signals we would otherwise miss. We get ready to pray. What are we getting into? We are on the outskirts of God's ways, about to enter the deep interiors. What is the appropriate attitude before this unknown?

Apprehension will make us cautious, crippled for taking risks, if risks need to be taken. Stoic dutifulness will make us heavy-footed, clumsy in the dance, if the dance is scheduled. The *blessed* arouses expectation, readiness for a more that is also a good. We don't know the contents of the *blessed*, or the difficulties—how could we, we are not there yet?—but we sense that we are entering a way on which we will become more of ourselves, not less, not other. The anticipation of being blessed works changes in us that make us capable of being blessed.

Living in the way God intended brings blessing both from this life and from God, for he blesses the way of the righteous.

*Lord, may I experience all the blessings that
come from living as you intend. Amen.*

# PUT THE WORLD TO RIGHTS

## N. T. Wright

The LORD works . . . justice for all the oppressed.

PSALM 103:6

Throughout history we have witnessed extravagant examples of human actions that have outraged our sense of justice. For example, powerful generals sent millions to die in the trenches in the First World War, while they themselves lived in luxury behind the lines or back home. When we read the poets who found themselves caught up in that war, we sense behind their poignant puzzlement a smoldering anger at the folly and yes, the injustice of it all.

You only have to mention Hitler or the Holocaust to awaken the questions: How did it happen? Where is justice? How can we put things right? And, in particular, how can we stop it from happening again?

All people know that this strange thing we call *justice*, this longing for things to be put right, remains one of the great human goals and dreams. Christians believe that this is so because all humans have heard, deep within themselves, the echo of a voice that calls us to live like that. And they believe that in Jesus that voice became human and did what had to be done to bring it about.

*Justice* is another way of saying we long for the world to be put to rights. What do you wish to see put back together again?

*Jesus, show me how I may contribute to establishing justice on earth. Amen.*

# GOD'S WHOLE LAW: LOVE

## James Bryan Smith

> "'Love the Lord your God with all your heart and with
> all your soul and with all your strength and with all your
> mind'; and, 'Love your neighbor as yourself.'"
>
> LUKE 10:27

When Jesus was asked to sum up the whole of the Law, he answered by coupling the great Deuteronomy edict about loving God (6:5) and the seemingly lesser law of Leviticus about loving your neighbor (19:18).

Why did Jesus combine them? Because he knew that they were essentially one law. Love comes from one source: God. We love, said John, because God first loved us (1 John 4:19). In the face of God's magnificent love for us, we cannot but love in return.

When that love is known and felt by us, it affects how we view ourselves and ultimately how we view one another. God's love for us results in a proper love for ourselves, and then extends to love for our neighbors.

—————

Paul summarized the whole of the Christian life in his letter to the Galatians when he wrote, "The only thing that counts is faith expressing itself through love" (Galatians 5:6). How does your faith measure up to this summary? Is yours a faith that loves?

*Lord, teach me what it means and how it looks to love you and love my neighbor wholly, so I can live a faith that matters. Amen.*

# HOPE IN CHRIST

## Frederick Buechner

Now hope does not disappoint, because the love
of God has been poured out in our hearts.

ROMANS 5:5 NKJV

For Christians, hope is ultimately hope in Christ. The hope that he really is what for centuries we have been claiming he is. The hope that despite the fact that sin and death still rule the world, he somehow conquered them. The hope that in him and through him all of us stand a chance of somehow conquering them too. The hope that at some unforeseeable time and in some unimaginable way he will return with healing in his wings.

No one in the New Testament calls a spade a spade as unflinchingly as Saint Paul. "If Christ has not been raised, your faith is futile," he wrote to the Corinthians. "If for this life only we have hoped in Christ, we are of all people most to be pitied" (1 Corinthians 15:17, 19). That is the possibility in spite of which Saint Paul and the rest of us go on hoping even so. That is the possibility that led Dostoyevski to write to a friend, "If anyone proved to me that Christ was outside the truth, and it really was so that the truth was outside Christ, then I would prefer to remain with Christ than with the truth."

What if you learned somehow that the resurrection of Jesus never happened? Would you choose the Savior over the "truth"?

*Lord Jesus, thank you for proving that your resurrection—as well as your whole life—happened through my relationship with you. Amen.*

# THE SEARCH FOR SIGNIFICANCE

## Dallas Willard

"Come, follow me," Jesus said, "and I will send you out to fish for people."

MATTHEW 4:19

The drive to significance that first appears as a vital need in the tiny child, and later as its clamorous desire for attention, is not egotism. Egotistical individuals see everything through themselves. They are always the dominant figures in their own field of vision.

Unlike egotism, the drive to significance is a simple extension of the creative impulse of God that gave us being. It is not filtered through self-consciousness any more than is our lunge to catch a package falling from someone's hand. It is outwardly directed to the good to be done. We were built to count, as water is made to run downhill. We are placed in a specific context to count in ways no one else does. That is our destiny.

Our hunger for significance is a signal of who we are and why we are here, and it also is the basis of humanity's enduring response to Jesus. For he always takes individual human beings as seriously as their shredded dignity demands, and he has the resources to carry through with his high estimate of them.

The search for significance is hardwired into us by our Creator. Jesus takes that natural drive, calls us to follow, and uses it for his own significant ends.

*Lord, may my life be a significant one—directed outwardly toward you and others. Amen.*

# THE GOSPEL AND OUR VIEW OF GOD

## A. W. Tozer

Hear, O Israel: The LORD our God, the LORD is one. Love the LORD your God with all your heart and with all your soul and with all your strength.

DEUTERONOMY 6:4–5

The man who comes to a right belief about God is relieved of ten thousand temporal problems, but even if the multiple burdens of time may be lifted from him, the one mighty single burden of eternity begins to press down upon him with a weight more crushing than all the woes of the world piled one upon another. That mighty burden is his obligation to God. It includes an instant and lifelong duty to love God with every power of mind and soul, to obey him perfectly, and to worship him acceptably. And then when the man's laboring conscience tells him that he has done none of these things, but has from childhood been guilty of foul revolt against the Majesty in the heavens, the inner pressure of self-accusation may become too heavy to bear.

The gospel can lift this destroying burden from the mind, give beauty for ashes, and the garment of praise for the spirit of heaviness.

Low views of God destroy the gospel; high views leave room for the gospel to work.

*Lord, let me see you high and lifted up
that I may love you with all I am. Amen.*

# SHARE JESUS' KINGDOM

## Dallas Willard

> "Go and make disciples of all nations."
>
> MATTHEW 28:19

Those who have found their way into Jesus' kingdom will inevitably want to share the new reality they have found with those around them. When we discover something great, we naturally want all those we really care about to be in on it. We would no more want to leave the sharing of the kingdom only to "full-time workers" than we would anything else we were really enthusiastic about.

The directions Jesus gave to his people when he last met with them in his familiar visible form was that they should "make disciples." Although the language may seem somewhat intimidating, and our contemporary practice is almost unrecognizably different from what his earliest people did, there is no reason to think he has changed his expectations and hopes for us. Our only question is a practical one: How do we do it?

The answer comes in three parts: we must, of course, be disciples, we must intend to make disciples, and we must know how to bring people to believe that Jesus really is the one.

---

What steps can you take to help people to belief in Jesus the Son and move beyond mere faith and obedience into disciple-making?

*Jesus, show me how I myself can fulfill your command to share and enlarge your kingdom. Amen.*

# DON'T FOLLOW KING AGRIPPA

## Frederick Buechner

Agrippa said to Paul, "You almost persuade me to become a Christian."
ACTS 26:28 NKJV

When Saint Paul was on his way to Rome to stand trial, King Agrippa granted him a hearing, and Paul, who was seldom at a loss for words, put up a strong defense. He described how on the road to Damascus he had come to believe Jesus was the Messiah and how all he had been doing since was trying to persuade other people to believe he was right. After Paul finished, Agrippa came out with the only remark he ever made that has gone down in history.

*Almost* is apt to be a sad word under the best of circumstances, and here, on the lips of the last of his line the last time you see him, it has a special poignance. If only Paul had been a little more eloquent. If only Agrippa had been a little more receptive, a little braver, a little crazier. If only God weren't such a stickler for letting people make up their own minds without forcing their hands. But things are what they are, and *almost* is the closest Agrippa ever got to what might have changed his life.

It's sad enough to miss God's invitation. But to *just* miss it is sadder still, especially when an apostle is trying to help you discover it! May *almost* never mark our spiritual journeys.

> Lord, make me alert to all of your divine invitations. Amen.

# ENOUGH LIGHT FOR THE NEXT STEP

## Henri J. M. Nouwen

> Come now, you who say, "Today or tomorrow we will go to
> such and such a town and spend a year there, doing business
> and making money." Yet you do not even know what tomorrow
> will bring. What is your life? For you are a mist that appears
> for a little while and then vanishes. Instead you ought to
> say, "If the Lord wishes, we will live and do this or that."
>
> JAMES 4:13–15 NRSV

Often we want to be able to see into the future. We say, "How will next year be for me? Where will I be five or ten years from now?" There are no answers to these questions. Mostly we have just enough light to see the next step: what we have to do in the coming hour or the following day. The art of living is to enjoy what we can see and not complain about what remains in the dark. When we are able to take the next step with the trust that we will have enough light for the step that follows, we can walk through life with joy and be surprised at how far we go. Let's rejoice in the little light we carry and not ask for the great beam that would take all shadows away.

All we're guaranteed is today. Tomorrow is the Lord's to give as well as reveal.

> Lord, thank you for today. Enable me to trust
> you for the steps into tomorrow. Amen.

# EARTHY AND DIVINE DEALINGS

## Eugene Peterson

Samuel took the horn of oil and anointed him
in the midst of his brothers; and the Spirit of the
LORD came upon David from that day forward.

1 SAMUEL 16:13 NKJV

The David story, like most other Bible stories, presents us not with a polished ideal to which we aspire but with a rough-edged actuality in which we see humanity being formed—the God in the earth/human condition. The David story immerses us in a reality that embraces the entire range of humanness, stretching from the deep interior of our souls to the farthest reach of our imaginations. No other biblical story has this range to it, showing the many dimensions of height, depth, breadth, and length of human experience as a person comes alive before God—aware of God, responsive to God. We're never more alive than when we're dealing with God. And there's a sense in which we aren't alive at all (in any uniquely human sense of "alive") until we're dealing with God.

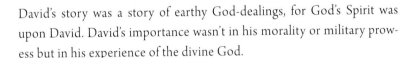

David's story was a story of earthy God-dealings, for God's Spirit was upon David. David's importance wasn't in his morality or military prowess but in his experience of the divine God.

*Lord, may my life mirror David's dealings with
you, so that we commune and relate to one
another in earthy honesty and love. Amen.*

# TWO IMPORTANT QUESTIONS

## N. T. Wright

> If anyone is in Christ, the new creation has come:
> The old has gone, the new is here!
>
> 2 CORINTHIANS 5:17

First, what is the ultimate Christian hope? Second, what hope is there for change, rescue, transformation, new possibilities within the world in the present? And the main answer can be put like this: as long as we see Christian hope in terms of "going to heaven," of a salvation that is essentially *away from* this world, the two questions are bound to appear as unrelated. Indeed, some insist angrily that to ask the second one at all is to ignore the first one, which is the really important one. This in turn makes some others get angry when people talk of resurrection, as if this might draw attention away from the really important and pressing matters of contemporary social concern. But if the Christian hope is for *God's new creation*, for "new heavens and a new earth," and if that hope has already come to life in Jesus of Nazareth, then there is every reason to join the two questions together.

Hope offers a clear and motivating reason for our work in today's world.

*Lord, thank you for my present and future hope in your new creation; may it transform me and then those around me. Amen.*

# GOD'S NATURE IS ESSENTIALLY LOVE

## James Bryan Smith

God is love.

1 JOHN 4:16

Many of us find it difficult to believe that God could look at us and smile. For years I viewed God as a judge, as do most of the people I know. The god I served was angry with me, ready to punish me for a slight infraction. I never knew where I stood with this god. If I lived flawlessly, I might, for a few moments, feel secure, but for the most part I did not. Much of the problem was that I viewed God as a person much like myself. I created this god in my own image. Like me, this god was capable of love, but it was a conditional love.

This god was mostly cold and distant, exact with his judgment and severe with his punishment. This god of my religious imagination was eventually replaced by the real God, the God of Abraham, the Father of Jesus. But the change did not occur overnight. The false idol I had created had to be slowly melted down by the fire of God's furious love.

While we're capable of loving and not loving, God is not. Love is God's very nature. How can we learn to love as God does?

*Lord, deepen my understanding of your loving nature that I may know and reflect you, the true God. Amen.*

# MORALISM MEANS NOTHING

## Brennan Manning

> Whatever were gains to me I now
> consider loss . . . that I may gain Christ.
>
> PHILIPPIANS 3:7–8

The habit of moralizing spoils religion. Personal responsibility to an inviolable moral code replaces personal response to God's loving call. Moralism and its stepchild, legalism, reduce the love story of God for his people to the observance of burdensome duties and oppressive laws. The legalist deformation of religion concerns itself with shadow, not substance.

At the funeral home, a well-intentioned friend eulogized the deceased: "John was a wonderful Christian. He never missed church, was married only once, and never told a dirty joke." Here the criterion for holiness and the ultimate sign of religious surrender is observance of the Law. The Pharisees did as much!

Let the Christian community cry out in anger against the lying moralistic slogans that pile up with impunity! Salvation cannot be earned or merited but only humbly and gratefully received as a loving gift from the Father's hand.

Religious rituals and laws are a complete loss compared to our righteousness through intimately knowing Jesus.

*Lord, help me rely on nothing more for my spirituality than knowing Christ and being found in him. Amen.*

# SET YOUR MIND ON THINGS ABOVE

## Dallas Willard

> Set your minds on things that are above, not on things that are on earth, for you have died, and your life is hidden with Christ in God.
>
> COLOSSIANS 3:2–3 NRSV

The ultimate freedom we have as human beings is the power to select what we will allow our minds to dwell upon. It is in our thoughts that the first movements toward the renovation of the heart occur. Thoughts are the place where we can and must begin to change. There the light of God first begins to move upon us through the word of Christ, and there the divine Spirit begins to direct our will to God and his way. We are not totally free in this respect, but we do have great freedom here. We still have the ability and responsibility to try to retain God in our knowledge. And those who do so will surely make progress toward him; for if we truly do seek God as best we can, he, who always knows what is really in our hearts, will certainly make himself known to us.

⋙○⋘

Through the course of your day, how often do you use your God-given freedom to set your mind on him and his way?

*Lord, direct my mind, attention, and will toward you.*
*Let the light of your presence shine on me. Amen.*

# YOUR CALLING

## Frederick Buechner

> Confirm for us the work of our hands.
>
> PSALM 90:17 NASB

*Vocation* comes from the Latin *vocare*, "to call," and means the work a person is called to by God.

All different kinds of voices call you to all different kinds of work. Which is the voice of God? A good rule for finding out is this: the kind of work God usually calls you to is the kind of work (a) that you need to do and (b) that the world needs to have done. If you really get a kick out of your work, you've presumably met requirement (a), but if your work is writing cigarette ads, the chances are you've missed requirement (b). On the other hand, if your work is being a doctor in a leper colony, you have probably met requirement (b), but if most of the time you're bored and depressed by it, the chances are you have not only bypassed (a), but you probably aren't helping your patients much either.

Neither the hair shirt nor the soft berth will do. The place God calls you to is the place where your deep gladness and the world's deep hunger meet.

———∞———

Your calling is located at an intersection of joy and need. Does your work qualify as a calling?

*Father, show me how to function where you most need me and I'm most delighted. Amen.*

# LIFE ITSELF IS GRACE

## Frederick Buechner

The LORD is gracious and full of compassion.
He has given food to those who fear Him.

PSALM 111:4–5 NKJV

I discovered that if you really keep your eye peeled to it and your ears open, if you really pay attention to it, even such a limited and limiting life as the one I was living in Rupert Mountain opened up onto extraordinary vistas. Taking your children to school and kissing your wife good-bye. Eating lunch with a friend. Trying to do a decent day's work. Hearing the rain patter against the window. There is no event so commonplace but that God is present within it, always hiddenly, always leaving you room to recognize him or not to recognize him, but all the more fascinatingly because of that, all the more compellingly and hauntingly.

If I were called upon to state in a few words the essence of everything I was trying to say, it would be something like this: Listen to your life. See it for the fathomless mystery that it is. In the boredom and pain of it no less than in the excitement and gladness: touch, taste, smell your way to the holy and hidden heart of it because in the last analysis all moments are key moments, and life itself is grace.

---

Every life-moment is touched by God's grace in tangible ways. How does he touch yours?

*Lord, thank you for all the ways your grace touches my life. Amen.*

# A LESSON IN EARTHY SPIRITUALITY

## Eugene Peterson

> By you I can crush a troop,
> and by my God I can leap over a wall.
>
> PSALM 18:29 NRSV

I've always had an aversion to what I call "boutique" spirituality, the "nice" religion that Henry James once criticized as "little more than cathedrals and mild social convenience."[3] I've found the David story, as so many have before me, a major means for recovering an earthy spirituality that's exuberantly holy. David attracts attention by his vigor, his energy, his wholeheartedness, his God-heartedness.

The image of David vaulting the wall catches and holds my attention. David running, coming to a stone wall, and without hesitation leaping the wall and continuing on his way—running toward Goliath, running from Saul, pursuing God, meeting Jonathan, rounding up stray sheep, whatever, but running. And leaping. Certainly not strolling or loitering.

David's is a most exuberant story. Earthy spirituality characterizes his life and accounts for the exuberance. Earthy: down-to-earth, dealing with everydayness, praying while doing the laundry, singing in the snarl of traffic. Spiritual: moved and animated by the Spirit of God and therefore alive to God.

Would you say your spirituality is earthy, or is it the boutique kind that trades in religious rituals and respectability?

*Lord, I need a spirituality that connects to my everyday doings; I seek that in you. Amen.*

February

# THE FORCES BEHIND IDEAS

## Dallas Willard

> Our struggle is not against enemies of blood and flesh, but against . . . the spiritual forces of evil in the heavenly places.
>
> EPHESIANS 6:12 NRSV

Ideas are very general models of our assumptions about reality. They are ways of thinking about and interpreting things. They are so pervasive and essential to how we think about and how we approach life that we often do not even know they are there or understand when and how they are at work.

Christian spiritual formation is inescapably a matter of recognizing in ourselves the idea systems of evil that govern the present age and respective culture, as well as those that constitute life away from God. The needed transformation is largely a matter of replacing those idea systems of evil with the idea system that was embodied and taught by Jesus Christ. These higher-level powers and forces are spiritual agencies that work with the idea systems of evil. These systems are their main tool for dominating humanity.

---

How do systemic spiritual forces influence ideas in pop culture, politics, and social media?

> *Lord, give me eyes to see the ways in which systems of evil work with the ideas of the day; remind me that the spiritual forces behind them are my true enemy. Amen.*

# PAUL'S PIVOT

## Frederick Buechner

*As he neared Damascus on his journey, suddenly a light from heaven*
*flashed around him. He fell to the ground and heard a voice.*

ACTS 9:3–4

It was about noon when he was knocked flat by a blaze of light that made the sun look like a forty-watt bulb, and out of the light came a voice that called him by his Hebrew name. "Saul. Why are you out to get me?" And when he pulled himself together enough to ask who it was he had the honor of addressing, what he heard to his horror was, "I'm Jesus of Nazareth, the one you're out to get."

If Jesus of Nazareth had what it took to burst out of the grave like a guided missile, he thought, then he could polish off one bowlegged Christian-baiter without even noticing it, and Paul waited for the ax to fall.

Only it wasn't an ax that fell. "Those boys in Damascus," Jesus said. "Don't fight them. Join them. I want you on my side," and Paul never in his life forgot the sheer lunatic joy and astonishment of that moment. He was blind as a bat for three days afterward, but he made it to Damascus anyway and was baptized on the spot. He was never the same again, and neither, in a way, was the world.

───❧───

When has God knocked you flat, figuratively speaking? What was the result in your life?

*Father, use light, wind, confrontation—whatever you*
*have to—to keep me walking in your way. Amen.*

# STUFF THAT TRULY LASTS

## Dallas Willard

> "Do not lay up for yourselves treasures on earth . . .
> but lay up for yourselves treasures in heaven."
>
> MATTHEW 6:19–20 NKJV

Jesus tells us that to treasure things that are "upon the earth" is not a smart strategy. Treasures of the earth, by their very nature, simply cannot be held intact. This can be very depressing to think about if you know of no alternative. Leo Tolstoy fell into a lengthy, suffocating depression because of the vision that everything he valued would die or otherwise pass away. This was after he had become one of the most successful authors the world has ever known. But the worldview that imposed itself on him was one of utter hopelessness, much as it is today. Through the teachings of Jesus he found an alternative, and such an alternative as soon delivered him from hopelessness about life and from the meaninglessness of human work.

So the wisdom of Jesus is that we should direct our actions toward making a difference in the realm of spiritual substance sustained and governed by God. Invest your life in what God is doing, which cannot be lost.

Tolstoy realized an essential truth: a materialistic worldview is hopeless, for the stuff of this world disappears. May we find hope in Jesus' perspective instead: the stuff of heaven is everlasting.

*Jesus, shift my energy from storing treasures from the stuff of earth to accumulating the stuff of heaven—the materials that truly last. Amen.*

# LET GOD'S LAW TARGET YOUR LIFE

## Eugene Peterson

His delight is in the law of the LORD,
And in His law he meditates day and night.

PSALM 1:2 NKJV

Torah (law) comprises God's words that hit the target of the human condition. The noun *torah* comes from a verb, *yarah*, that means to throw something, a javelin, say, so that it hits the mark. The word that hits its mark is *torah*. In living speech, words are javelins hurled from one mind into another. The javelin word goes out of one person and pierces another. Not all words are javelins; some are only tin cans, carrying information from one place to another. But God's word has this aimed, intentional, personal nature. When we are spoken to this way, piercingly and penetratingly, we are not the same. These words get inside us and work their meaning in us.

As we prepare to pray, to answer the words God addresses to us, we learn that all of God's words have this characteristic: they are *torah* and we are the target.

Prominent in Psalm 1 is the act of Torah-meditation, for blessing comes to the one who allows these words to hit him or her squarely in the chest. God's Word isn't a reference book for information; it isn't inert or bookish. Instead, these creating and saving words hit us where we live.

> *Lord, may your Word target every area of my life,*
> *penetrating where I need guidance. May I delight in*
> *that Word, meditating on it day and night. Amen.*

# JESUS IS LORD OVER DEATH

## N. T. Wright

> Death has been swallowed up in victory.
>
> 1 CORINTHIANS 15:54 NRSV

Because of the early Christian belief in Jesus as Messiah, we find the development of the very early belief that Jesus is Lord and that therefore Caesar is not. Already in Paul the resurrection, both of Jesus and then in the future of his people, is the foundation of the Christian stance of allegiance to a different king, a different Lord. Death is the last weapon of the tyrant, and the point of the resurrection, despite much misunderstanding, is that death has been defeated.

Resurrection is not the redescription of death; it is its overthrow and, with that, the overthrow of those whose power depends on it. Resurrection was never a way of settling down and becoming respectable; the Pharisees could have told you that. It was the Gnostics, who translated the language of resurrection into a private spirituality and a dualistic cosmology, thereby more or less altering its meaning into its opposite, who escaped persecution. Resurrection was always bound to get you into trouble, and it regularly did.

---

"Jesus is Lord, Caesar is not" was an important belief for early Christians precisely because Jesus was Lord over death itself, having conquered it by the resurrection. It still is for the same reason.

*Lord Jesus Christ, Son of God, I worship you as Lord because you live, having conquered death triumphantly. Amen.*

# CREATION IS PROOF OF GOD'S LOVE

## James Bryan Smith

Rejoice always, pray continually, give thanks in all
circumstances; for this is God's will for you in Christ Jesus.

1 Thessalonians 5:16–18

All around us are hints and evidences of God's desire for us to be full of joy. These signs show us that God's love surpasses what we can know. The first sign is creation itself. We live in a world that is magnificent and beyond our understanding. For many years I did not have the eyes to see the glory of creation. Nature was never majestic; it was just a hunk of matter and molecules spinning endlessly in a pattern of evolution. But a single statement by G. K. Chesterton changed the way I look at the world around me. He pointed out that nature is not a system of necessity. Yes, the sun will probably come up tomorrow, but it need not. Perhaps each day God says to the sun, "Arise! Go forth!"

I remember walking out in my backyard after reading those words, looking at the grass and the trees and the birds, and thinking, *Wow!* Instead of seeing them as some kind of dead prop in the drama of my life, I saw them as wondrous gifts spoken forth from the mouth of God.

If we look at creation carefully and meditate on its goodness, we will discover ourselves crying out, "You really love me, don't you, God?"

*Lord, when I consider creation, I better
understand the love you have for me. Amen.*

# FREED FROM LEGALISM TO LOVE

## Brennan Manning

If you died with Christ from the basic principles of the world, why, as though living in the world, do you subject yourselves to regulations . . . according to the commandments and doctrines of men?

COLOSSIANS 2:20, 22 NKJV

Unfortunately, religion readily lends itself to legalistic misunderstanding. A reliance on ceremonies and the observance of commandments too easily leads to a false trust in the external elements of religion and creates a mystique of spiritual superiority. Does the neutral onlooker identify a Christian by his pious practices and cultic regularity or by the loving quality of his everyday presence in the workaday world?

From another perspective, legalism attempts to determine every moral choice on the basis of existing regulations. Law thus tends to become an end in itself rather than a means to an end. The result is the frustration of the very motive that brought religious law into being. Jesus resolutely insisted that law was the expression of the love of God and neighbor and that piety that stands in the way of love stands in the way of God himself.

Jesus said the highest expression of our spirituality is not legalism but love—of God and people.

> Lord, free me from a legalistic focus so that I can love you and others more deeply. Amen.

# WHAT DOES THE CROSS MEAN TO YOU?

## Dallas Willard

May I never boast except in the cross of our Lord Jesus Christ, through which the world has been crucified to me, and I to the world.

GALATIANS 6:14

Images are always concrete or specific, as opposed to the abstractness of ideas, and are heavily laden with feeling. They have a powerful emotional linkage to governing idea systems. They mediate the power of those idea systems into the real situations of ordinary life.

Jesus understood the great significance of images. He intentionally selected an image that would brilliantly convey himself and his message: the cross. The cross represents the lostness of man, as well as the sacrifice of God and the abandonment to God that brings redemption. No doubt it is the all-time most powerful image and symbol in human history. Need we say he knew what he was doing in selecting it? He planned it all, for he is also the master of images. For our own benefit, we as followers need to keep the image of the cross vividly present in our minds.

What significance does the cross—those boards of execution that held the limp, lifeless body of our Savior—mean to you?

*Lord Jesus Christ, Son of God, thank you for the cross!*
*Thank you for selecting it as a symbol of your love, the mode*
*of my redemption, and the gift of my salvation. Amen.*

# IDOLATRY: UNWORTHY IDEAS OF GOD

## A. W. Tozer

> Although they knew God, they neither glorified him as
> God nor gave thanks to him, but their thinking became
> futile and their foolish hearts were darkened.
>
> ROMANS 1:21

Among the sins to which the human heart is prone, hardly any other is more hateful to God than idolatry. The idolatrous heart assumes that God is other than he is and substitutes for the true God one made after its own likeness. Always this god will conform to the image of the one who created it and will be base or pure, cruel or kind, according to the moral state of the mind from which it emerges.

Let us beware lest we in our pride accept the erroneous notion that idolatry consists only in kneeling before visible objects of adoration, and that civilized peoples are therefore free from it. The essence of idolatry is the entertainment of thoughts about God that are unworthy of him. It begins in the mind and may be present where no overt act of worship has taken place.

Wrong ideas about God are not only the fountain from which the polluted waters of idolatry flow; they are themselves idolatrous. The idolater simply imagines things about God and acts as if they were true.

How has humanity crafted unworthy ideas about God, raising up an idol for worship and adoration?

*Lord, give me a right understanding of you, so that I entertain thoughts worthy of you and worship you in truth. Amen.*

# GOD'S JUSTICE-LOVE REQUIREMENT

## N. T. Wright

Do justice, . . . love kindness.

MICAH 6:8 NASB

It is important to see, and to say, that those who follow Jesus are committed, as he taught us to pray, to God's will being done "on earth as it is in heaven." And that means that God's passion for justice must become ours too.

When the slave trade was at its height, with many people justifying it on the grounds that slaves are mentioned in the Bible, it was a group of devout Christians, led by the unforgettable William Wilberforce in Britain and John Woolman in America, who got together and made it their life's business to stop it. When, with slavery long dead and buried, racial prejudice still haunted the United States, it was the Christian vision of Martin Luther King Jr. that drove him to peaceful, but highly effective, protest. Wilberforce was grasped by a passion for God's justice on behalf of the slaves, a passion which cost him what might otherwise have been a dazzling political career. Martin Luther King's passion for justice for African Americans cost him his life. Their tireless campaigning grew directly and explicitly out of their loyalty to Jesus.

When Christians use their belief in Jesus to escape from the demands of justice, they abandon a central element in their own faith.

*Lord, help me join Wilberforce and King*
*in passionate pursuit of justice-love. Amen.*

# LISTEN FOR HIM

## Frederick Buechner

> I am always with you;
> you hold me by my right hand.
>
> PSALM 73:23

The question is not whether the things that happened to you are chance things or God's things because, of course, they are both at once. There is no chance thing through which God cannot speak—even the walk from the house to the garage that you have walked ten thousand times before, even the moments when you cannot believe there is a God who speaks at all anywhere. He speaks, I believe, and the words he speaks are incarnate in the flesh and blood of our selves and of our own footsore and sacred journeys. Sometimes we avoid listening for fear of what we may hear, sometimes for fear that we may hear nothing at all but the empty rattle of our own feet on the pavement.

He says he is with us on our journeys. He says he has been with us since each of our journeys began. Listen for him. Listen to the sweet and bitter airs of your present and your past for the sound of him.

To live without listening to the Lord is to live deaf to the fullness of the music of God. The Lord speaks to us reassuring words of his presence, his protection, his provision. Are you listening?

> *Heavenly Father, give me ears to hear your voice of hope*
> *and reassurance, of comfort and peace. Amen.*

# GROWING BEYOND SELF-REJECTION

## Henri J. M. Nouwen

"Since you are precious and honored in my sight,
and because I love you,
I will give people in exchange for you,
nations in exchange for your life."

ISAIAH 43:4

One of the greatest dangers in the spiritual life is self-rejection. When we say, "If people really knew me, they wouldn't love me," we choose the road toward darkness. Often we are made to believe that self-deprecation is a virtue called *humility*. But humility is in reality the opposite of self-deprecation. It is the grateful recognition that we are precious in God's eyes and that all we are is pure gift. To grow beyond self-rejection we must have the courage to listen to the voice calling us God's beloved sons and daughters, and the determination always to live our lives according to this truth.

———∞∞———

Two voices compete for our hearts' attention: one voice is from within, the one of self-loathing, self-rejection, self-deprecation; the other is the voice of the Lord, who says we're precious and honored and loved. May we have the courage to reject the voice within and listen instead to the voice of the Lord.

*Lord, tune my heart to listen to you so I may grow beyond the debilitating curse of self-rejection. Amen.*

# NOT "JUST" A LAYPERSON

## Eugene Peterson

> Samuel saw Eliab and thought, "Surely the LORD's anointed
> stands here before the LORD." But the LORD said to Samuel, "Do
> not consider his appearance or his height, for I have rejected
> him. The LORD does not look at the things people look at."
>
> 1 SAMUEL 16:6–7

The choice of David, the runt and the shepherd, to be the anointed, to be a sign and representative of God's working presence in human life and history, is surely intended to convey a sense of inclusion to all ordinary men and women, the plain folk, the undistinguished in the eyes of their neighbors, those lacking social status and peer recognition. Which is to say, the overwhelming majority of all who have lived on this old planet earth. Election into God's purposes isn't by popular vote. Election into God's purposes isn't based on proven ability or potential promise.

It's of considerable moment to realize that the centerfold account in Scripture of a human being living by faith comes in the shape of a layperson. But there isn't a hint in the narrative that his status is evidence of inadequacy. This is humanity burgeoning and vital, bold and extravagant, skillful and inventive in love and prayer and work.

———

We may feel plain and undistinguished, yet we are anointed to God's purposes. Don't ever say you're "just" a layperson. Your identity is extravagant and vital.

> *Lord, help me see my identity as you've purposed
> it: burgeoning, bold, and skillful. Amen.*

# PROFOUND SPIRITUAL EXPERIENCES

## N. T. Wright

> I know a person in Christ who fourteen years
> ago was caught up to the third heaven.
>
> 2 CORINTHIANS 12:2 NRSV

Rich and deep experiences of the type we call "spiritual" often—indeed, normally—engage the emotions in very profound ways. Sometimes such experiences produce such a deep sense of inner peace and happiness that people speak of having been for a while in what they can only call "heaven." Sometimes they even laugh out loud for sheer happiness. Sometimes the experience is of a sharing in the suffering of the world which is so painful and raw that the only possible response is to weep bitterly.

I am speaking of those widely reported times in which people have had the sense of living for a while in multiple dimensions not normally accessible to us, in one of which they experienced either such a wonderful resolution and joy, or such anguish and torment, as to make them react as though they were really undergoing those things for themselves. Such experiences, as every seasoned pastor or spiritual guide knows, can have a lasting and profound effect on one's life.

When have you had a deep spiritual experience in which you experienced the joy of heaven? What effect did it have on your life?

*Lord, I ask for profound spiritual experiences*
*that further my life in you. Amen.*

# GOD WOOS US

## James Bryan Smith

Your love is better than wine.

SONG OF SONGS 1:2 NRSV

Philosophy tries to reduce God to a first mover and science attempts to remove God entirely. But God looms quietly in the wings and allows us such silly speculation. Contemporary author Frederick Buechner once noted that our attempts at theology are akin to a dung beetle looking up at a human and trying to do humanology.[4] Whatever we are allowed to discover about God, he is more.

When God revealed himself to me it blew my belief system to bits. Like Thomas Aquinas, I knew that all of my speculation was like straw compared to the reality of God. And like the lover in the Song of Solomon I could only respond, "Draw me after you." God woos us like a lover who seeks his beloved. The torrid passion sometimes felt between two human beings is a pale reflection of the burning desire God has for us. It was love, not a theory of redemption, that made the martyrs sing praise while being tortured. It was love, not a doctrine of the atonement, that kept Jesus on the cross.

───❧───

It's God's love that attracts us, like the tender kisses of a lover. How has God drawn you to himself?

*Lord, thank you for your love, which always draws me to you. Amen.*

# EMBRACE AND RECEIVE ABBA'S LOVE

## Henri J. M. Nouwen

God sent the Spirit of his Son into our hearts,
the Spirit who calls out, *"Abba*, Father."

GALATIANS 4:6

Calling God "Abba, Father" is different from giving God a familiar name. Calling God "Abba" is entering into the same intimate, fearless, trusting, and empowering relationship with God that Jesus had. This relationship is called Spirit, and this Spirit is given to us by Jesus and enables us to cry out with him, "Abba, Father."

Calling God "Abba, Father" is a cry of the heart, a prayer welling up from our innermost beings. It has nothing to do with naming God but everything to do with claiming God as the source of who we are. This claim does not come from any sudden insight or acquired conviction; it is the claim that the Spirit of Jesus makes in communion with our spirits. It is the claim of love.

*Abba* is a very intimate word. The best translation for it is "Daddy." The word *Abba* expresses trust, safety, confidence, belonging, and most of all, intimacy. It does not have the connotation of authority, power, and control that the word *father* often evokes. On the contrary, *Abba* implies an embracing and nurturing love.

---

The Spirit reveals to us that God is *our* Abba—for we are his beloved children.

*Abba, I come to you as my heavenly Daddy,
ready to embrace and receive your love. Amen.*

# THINK LIKE MARTIN LUTHER

## Dallas Willard

> The Berean Jews were of more noble character than those in
> Thessalonica, for they received the message with great eagerness and
> examined the Scriptures every day to see if what Paul said was true.
>
> ACTS 17:11

What is thinking? It is the activity of searching out what must be true, or cannot be true, in light of given facts or assumptions. It is a powerful gift of God to be used in the service of truth.

Martin Luther, thinking and standing in the power of God before his examiners at Worms, said, "Unless I am convicted by Scripture and plain reason . . . my conscience is captive to the Word of God. I cannot and will not recant anything, for to go against conscience is neither right nor safe. God help me. Amen."[5]

And so we must apply our thinking to the Word of God. We must thoughtfully set it into practice. In doing so, we will be assisted by God's grace in ways far beyond anything we can understand on our own. Then the ideas and images that governed the life of Christ through his thought life will possess us.

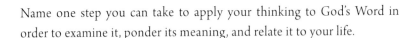

Name one step you can take to apply your thinking to God's Word in order to examine it, ponder its meaning, and relate it to your life.

*Heavenly Father, assist me in exploring your Word in order to search its riches for practical insight into your ways for my life. Amen.*

# GOOD TO BE IN COMPANY

## James Bryan Smith

The LORD God said, "It is not good that the man should
be alone; I will make him a helper as his partner."

GENESIS 2:18 NRSV

God has made us interdependent. From the moment of our creation God felt it was important for us to live in community. He looked at Adam and said, "It is not good that the man should be alone." At the core of our being is a need to love and be loved by others. The great wonder of our existence is the fact that God has made us incomplete. Only by living in community can we find the fulfillment for which we hunger.

Our need to love and be loved is an inescapable fact of our existence. God has designed us this way because God values human community. He could have dispensed all of our necessities directly to us, so that we would have had no need of each other. Instead, he gives us all of the resources we need to care for one another and encourages us to share those resources.

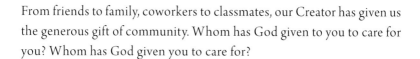

From friends to family, coworkers to classmates, our Creator has given us the generous gift of community. Whom has God given to you to care for you? Whom has God given you to care for?

*Lord, I recognize that it is not good for me to be alone, for you have made me for community. Ignite in me a love for my community as I in return receive their love. Amen.*

# GOD LOVES OUR ENEMIES

## Dallas Willard

> "Love your enemies, do good to them."
>
> LUKE 6:35

Bertrand Russell, a well-known British philosopher of this century, was raised a Christian, though he later adopted atheism. He was familiar with the teachings of Jesus, if not their actual meaning. In one place he comments, "The Christian principle, 'Love your enemies' is good. . . . There is nothing to be said against it except that it is too difficult for most of us to practice sincerely."[6]

Russell's fallacy is the fallacy of the Pharisee. The Pharisee takes as his aim keeping the law rather than becoming the kind of person whose deeds naturally conform to the law. Jesus knew the human heart better than Bertrand Russell did. Thus he concludes his exposition of the kingdom kind of goodness by contrasting the ordinary way human beings love, loving those who love them, with God's *agape* love. This is a love that reaches everyone we deal with. It is not in their power to change that. It is the very core of what we are or can become in his fellowship, not something we do. Then the *deeds* of love, including loving our enemies, are what that *agape* love does in us and what we do as the new persons we have become.

Love for one's enemies seems impossible, but it isn't. We're able to love our enemies because God loves them, a love he has given us to share.

*Lord, help me access your ocean of love*
*for even those who hurt me. Amen.*

# THE HEART OF RELIGION, THE HEART OF THE CHILD

## Frederick Buechner

*"Truly I tell you, anyone who will not receive the kingdom of God like a little child will never enter it." And he took the children in his arms, placed his hands on them and blessed them.*

MARK 10:15-16

Unless you become like a child, Jesus said, you will never enter the kingdom of heaven, and maybe part of what that means is that in the long run what is good about religion is playing the way a child plays at being grown-up until he finds that being grown-up is just another way of playing and thereby starts to grow up for himself. Maybe what is good about religion is playing that the kingdom will come, until—in the joy of your playing, the hope and rhythm and comradeship and poignance and the mystery of it—you start to see that the playing is itself the firstfruits of the kingdom's coming and of God's presence within us and among us.

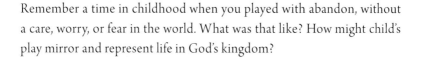

Remember a time in childhood when you played with abandon, without a care, worry, or fear in the world. What was that like? How might child's play mirror and represent life in God's kingdom?

*Lord Jesus Christ, Son of God, give me the heart of a child so that I receive the kingdom of your Father in all its fullness. Amen.*

# WATCH OUT FOR WOLVES

## Dallas Willard

> "I am sending you out like sheep among wolves. Therefore
> be as shrewd as snakes and as innocent as doves."
>
> MATTHEW 10:16

These are the instructions Jesus gave to his apprentices when, on one occasion, he sent them out to minister the kingdom of the heavens to the needs of human beings. These homely images begin to open up the positive side of an association with others that will help them without condemning them or forcing upon them good things that they simply cannot benefit from.

What is the wisdom of the snake? It is to be watchful and observant until the time is right to act. It is timeliness. One rarely sees a snake chasing its prey or thrashing about in an effort to impress it. But when it acts, it acts quickly and decisively. And as for the dove, it does not contrive. It is incapable of intrigue. Guile is totally beyond it. There is nothing indirect about this gentle creature. It is in this sense "harmless." The importance scriptural teaching places on guilelessness is very great.

These are qualities we must have to walk in the kingdom with others, instead of trying to drive them to change their ways and attitudes and even who they are.

———⚬✖⚬———

When we approach people, what matters is not only what we say and do, but also how we say and do it.

*Lord, teach me how to use the best qualities of
snakes and doves to reach people for you. Amen.*

# OPERATION RESCUE: JESUS CHRIST

## N. T. Wright

Apart from law, the righteousness of God has been disclosed,
and is attested by the law and the prophets, the righteousness
of God through faith in Jesus Christ for all who believe.

ROMANS 3:21–22 NRSV

Christianity is all about the belief that the living God, in fulfillment of his promises and as the climax of the story of Israel, has accomplished all this—the finding, the saving, the giving of new life—in Jesus. He has done it. With Jesus, God's rescue operation has been put into effect once and for all. A great door has swung open in the cosmos which can never again be shut. It's the door to the prison where we've been kept chained up.

We are offered freedom: freedom to experience God's rescue for ourselves, to go through the open door and explore the new world to which we now have access. In particular, we are all invited—summoned, actually—to discover, through following Jesus, that this new world is indeed a place of justice, spirituality, relationship, and beauty, and that we are not only to enjoy it as such but to work at bringing it to birth on earth as in heaven.

From the beginning of God's story, God has been on a mission to rescue and restore the world—which he put into final effect in and through Jesus. In listening to Jesus, we discover what God has been up to all along.

*Lord, show me how I can participate in your
rescue operation through Jesus. Amen.*

# LIVE WITHIN GOD'S ETERNAL PURPOSES

## Dallas Willard

> "The time has come. . . . The kingdom of God has come
> near. Repent and believe the good news!"
>
> MARK 1:15

Having established a beachhead of divine life in an ordinary human existence, Jesus finally stepped into the public arena to expose his life publicly and to make it available to the world. Mark's Gospel reports that "Jesus then came into Galilee announcing the good news from God. 'All the preliminaries have been taken care of,' he said, 'and the rule of God is now accessible to everyone. Review your plans for living and base your life on this remarkable new opportunity'" (Mark 1:14–15).

In Matthew's account of Jesus' deeds and words, the formulation repeatedly used is the well-known "Repent, for the kingdom of the heavens is at hand" (3:2; 4:17; 10:7). This is a call for us to reconsider how we have been approaching our life, in light of the fact that we now, in the presence of Jesus, have the option of living within the surrounding movements of God's eternal purposes, of taking our life into his life.

Jesus announced God's eternal purposes, his rule and reign, had arrived. This is good news, for it means they are accessible to everyone, and we can take our lives into his. Are you living your life in his life?

*Lord, as I reconsider how I've been approaching my life, I pledge to live it within your eternal purposes from this day forward. Amen.*

# ARE YOU PREPARED FOR GOD'S REVELATION?

## A. W. Tozer

> What can be known about God is plain to them,
> because God has shown it to them.
>
> ROMANS 1:19 NRSV

What is God like? What kind of God is he? How may we expect him to act toward us and toward all created things? Such questions are not merely academic. They touch the far-in reaches of the human spirit, and their answers affect the life and character and destiny. When asked in reverence and their answers sought in humility, these are questions that cannot but be pleasing to our Father which art in heaven.

To our questions God has provided answers; not all the answers, certainly, not enough to satisfy our intellects and ravish our hearts. These answers he has provided in nature, in the Scriptures, and in the person of his Son.

Though God in this threefold revelation has provided answers to our questions concerning him, the answers by no means lie on the surface. They must be sought by prayer, by long meditation on the written Word, and by earnest and well-disciplined labor.

———— ∞ ————

God can be seen only by those who are spiritually prepared to receive him. Are you prepared?

*Lord, help me see, apprehend, and understand
the light of your glorious revelation. Amen.*

# WHAT HAS JESUS USHERED IN?

## N. T. Wright

> Christ has indeed been raised from the dead, the firstfruits of
> those who have fallen asleep. For since death came through a
> man, the resurrection of the dead comes also through a man.
> For as in Adam all die, so in Christ all will be made alive.
>
> 1 CORINTHIANS 15:20–22

The resurrection of Jesus offers itself, to the student of history or science no less than the Christian or the theologian, not as an odd event within the world as it is but as the utterly characteristic, prototypical, and foundational event within the world as it has begun to be. It is not an absurd event within the old world but the symbol and starting point of the new world. The claim advanced in Christianity is of that magnitude: Jesus of Nazareth ushers in not simply a new religious possibility, not simply a new ethic or a new way of salvation, but a new creation.

Through Jesus' resurrection something entirely new was born. Jesus was the first of the harvest of new creation resulting from the new resurrected life that burst forth from the grave when he arose.

> *Heavenly Father, thank you for raising your Son
> to new life so I could share in his harvest of
> resurrection life and the new creation. Amen.*

# AA AND THE BODY OF CHRIST

## Frederick Buechner

I do not do the good I want, but the evil I do not want is what I do.

ROMANS 7:19 NRSV

A lcoholics Anonymous, or AA, is the name of a group of men and women who acknowledge that addiction to alcohol is ruining their lives. Their purpose in coming together is to give it up and help others do the same. They realize they can't pull this off by themselves. They believe they need each other, and they believe they need God. The ones who aren't so sure about God speak instead of their Higher Power.

You can't help thinking that something like this is what the church is meant to be and maybe once was before it got to be big business: Sinners Anonymous. "I can will what is right but I cannot do it," is the way Saint Paul put it, speaking for all of us.

No matter what far place alcoholics end up in, they know that there will be an AA meeting nearby to go to and that at that meeting they will find strangers who are not strangers to help and to heal, to listen to the truth and to tell it. That is what the body of Christ is all about.

May the church find in AA a model for what it means to be Christ's body.

*Lord, show me where I can help people do what is right and ignite the power of their Christian walk. Amen.*

# REFLECTING GOD'S PERFECT LOVE

## Henri J. M. Nouwen

The Lord appeared to him from afar, saying,
"I have loved you with an everlasting love;
Therefore I have drawn you with lovingkindness."

JEREMIAH 31:3 NASB

God's love for us is everlasting. That means that God's love for us existed before we were born and will exist after we have died. It is an eternal love in which we are embraced. Living a spiritual life calls us to claim that eternal love for ourselves so we can live our temporal loves—for parents, brothers, sisters, teachers, friends, spouses, and all people who become part of our lives—as reflections or refractions of God's eternal love. No fathers or mothers can love their children perfectly. No husbands or wives can love each other with unlimited love. There is no human love that is not broken somewhere.

When our broken love is the only love we can have, we are easily thrown into despair, but when we can live our broken love as a partial reflection of God's perfect, unconditional love, we can forgive one another our limitations and enjoy together the love we have to offer.

What does it mean to you that God has loved you with a love that has drawn you to himself by his lovingkindness? How might it look to love those around you by reflecting this same perfect love of God?

*Lord, show me how to live my broken love in a
way that reflects your perfect version. Amen.*

# A PRIMER IN THE PRIESTHOOD OF BELIEVERS

## Eugene Peterson

You are a chosen people, a royal priesthood,
a holy nation, God's special possession.

1 PETER 2:9

David's life is the premier biblical instance of what's sometimes called "the priesthood of all believers." Martin Luther made a lot of it during the Reformation, but he didn't make it up. There are a variety of offices in the community of faith—prophet, priest, wise person, elder, apostle, deacon, bishop, and so on—but throughout the church, the primary emphasis is on the *people*. All the offices/jobs are servant positions for assisting and encouraging men and women to be the people of God and not merely a crowd of religious consumers. These servants are set among the people to counter the downward-slipping inertia by which people tend to congeal into a sodden, undifferentiated mush. When Christian communities are healthy, the "little ones" aren't demeaned and dispirited into being followers and consumers but find themselves acquiring initiative and originality as their priests and pastors, deacons and bishops, friends and neighbors serve *them*.

―∞∞―

What's your role in the priesthood of all believers?

*Jesus, give me initiative and originality to
live as a priest among your people. Amen.*

# GOD'S FUTURE HAS BROKEN IN

## N. T. Wright

> "Repent, for the kingdom of heaven is at hand!"
>
> MATTHEW 3:2 NKJV

This announcement was the center of Jesus' public proclamation. He was addressing the world in which the Jewish people were anxious for their God to rescue them from pagan oppression and put the world to rights—in other words, to become king fully and finally. The Gospels tell the story in such a way as to hold together the ancient promises and the urgent current context, with Jesus in the middle of it all. There is no good reason to doubt that this was how Jesus himself saw his own work.

But what did he mean? The prophet Isaiah, in line with several psalms and other biblical passages, had spoken of God's coming kingdom as the time when (a) God's promises and purposes would be fulfilled, (b) Israel would be rescued from pagan oppression, (c) evil (particularly the evil of oppressive empires) would be judged, and (d) God would usher in a new reign of justice and peace. The world was to be turned the right way up at last. To speak of God's kingdom arriving in the present was to summon up that entire narrative and to declare that it was reaching its climax.

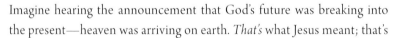

Imagine hearing the announcement that God's future was breaking into the present—heaven was arriving on earth. *That's* what Jesus meant; that's what we all long for.

*Jesus, thank you for announcing the good news of God's kingdom; through your church may that kingdom fully manifest itself. Amen.*

# March

# PROOF OF GOD'S LOVE

## James Bryan Smith

> God demonstrates His own love toward us, in that
> while we were still sinners, Christ died for us.
> ROMANS 5:8 NKJV

O ut of love Jesus was conceived, and out of love he chose to die. There is something in us that God finds lovable. It is certainly not our sanctity, nor is it our fidelity. When I look at my own baseness, my incredible ability to sin at a moment's notice, I wonder what God sees in me.

But if we doubt God's love, all we have to do is consider the birth, life, death, and resurrection of Christ. For centuries that has been the clearest sign of God's radical acceptance. In Jesus we hear God saying to us, "What you cannot do for yourself, I myself will do. Your sin stands between us, and you cannot remove it, so I will do it for you. My blood will cleanse your sins, and I will remember them no more. Nothing will stand between us. I will rise from the dead so you can live. My love is too strong for death to conquer. Once alive, I will invite you to die and rise with me. Eternal life is now available. It is in my Son."

---

If you ever doubt God's radical love for you, remember the truth we recognize via Christmas and Easter: God became one of us in order to die for us.

*Jesus, thank you for your birth and death, both signs*
*of your love for the Father and the world. Amen.*

# GIVING UP AND TAKING UP

## N. T. Wright

For everything there is a season, and a
time for every matter under heaven.

ECCLESIASTES 3:1 NRSV

Christian holiness was never meant to be merely negative. Of course you have to weed the garden from time to time; sometimes the ground ivy may need serious digging before you can get it out. That's Lent for you. But you don't want simply to turn the garden back into a neat bed of blank earth. Easter is the time to sow new seeds and to plant a few cuttings. If Calvary means putting to death things in your life that need killing off if you are to flourish as a Christian and as a truly human being, then Easter should mean planting, watering, and training up things in your life (personal and corporate) that ought to be blossoming, filling the garden with color and perfume, and in due course bearing fruit. The forty days of the Easter season, until the ascension, ought to be a time to balance out Lent by taking something up, some new task or venture, something wholesome and fruitful and outgoing and self-giving.

For everything there is a season. During Lent, what can you give up in order to flourish? On the other side of Easter, what fruitful venture can you take up for the glory of God?

*Lord, what things in my life do I need to weed out?*
*What things do I need to plant? Amen.*

# A CHRISTIAN VISION OF SPIRITUALITY

## Dallas Willard

*In Christ Jesus you are all children of God through faith.*

GALATIANS 3:26

In the Christian version of personalized spirit and spirituality, the spiritual life takes on the character of a personal relationship between individuals, with the attendant features of reciprocal attention, care, provision, assistance or service, emotional interaction, expectations, comfort, joy, and development or growth. The entire book of Psalms is a record, an enactment, a celebration of spirituality, of spiritual life, understood as an interactive relationship between persons in a personal as well as "natural" order.

This vision of life on a personal, spiritual basis in the kingdom of God is extended, for the Christian, in the person and teachings of Jesus (the Good Shepherd) in such a way as to include all of humanity, at their choice, without regard to any kind of personal, social, or cultural status, ethnic or otherwise, and to allow the individual participant to have the dignity and power to achieve a good life and become a good person.

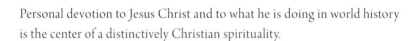

Personal devotion to Jesus Christ and to what he is doing in world history is the center of a distinctively Christian spirituality.

*Jesus, I praise you for the spiritual life you have invited me to share with you and the Father and the Spirit—a relational life of familial love, mutual comfort, and friendship. Amen.*

# GAZE UPON THE WONDER OF GOD'S BEING

## A. W. Tozer

God said to Moses, "I AM WHO I AM. This is what you are
to say to the Israelites: 'I AM has sent me to you.'"

EXODUS 3:14

It is not a cheerful thought that millions of us who live in a land of Bibles, who belong to churches and labor to promote the Christian religion, may yet pass our whole life on this earth without once having thought or tried to think seriously about the being of God. Few of us have let our hearts gaze in wonder at the I AM. And for this we are now paying a too heavy price in the secularization of our religion and the decay of our inner lives.

Perhaps some sincere but puzzled Christian may at this juncture wish to inquire about the practicality of such concepts as I am trying to set forth here. "What bearing does this have on *my* life?" he may ask.

To this I reply that, because we are the handiwork of God, it follows that *all our problems and their solutions are theological*. Some knowledge of what kind of God it is that operates the universe is indispensable to a sound philosophy of life and a sane outlook on the world scene.

How often do you reflect upon the nature of the great I AM? Do that now, jotting down what comes to mind.

> *Enable me to grasp the greatness of your being, O God,
> so I may rightly understand you and your will. Amen.*

# EASTER REVEALS WHAT'S POSSIBLE

## N. T. Wright

> Finally the other disciple, who had reached the tomb first, also
> went inside. He saw and believed. (They still did not understand
> from Scripture that Jesus had to rise from the dead.)
>
> JOHN 20:8–9

What the Easter stories do—and what, I argue, the whole existence of the church does, from the very first days onward—is to pose a huge question. We need to set our asking of that question, ultimately, in dialogue at least with the life of the community that believes the gospel and seeks by its life to live out its truth. We need to set it within the reading of the Scriptures, which by their whole narrative lay out the worldview within which it makes sense. We need to think it through within a context of personal openness to the God of whom the Bible speaks—the Creator of the world, not simply a divine presence within it, the God of justice and truth. These are not substitutes for historical inquiry or lame supplements to it. They are ways of opening the windows of mind and heart to see what really, after all, might be possible in God's world, the world not only of creation as it is but also of new creation.

---

While many people today assume that faith is merely a private matter, the Christian faith has said otherwise: we need both history and community to answer our questions.

*Lord, thank you for giving me history and community*
*to strengthen and develop my faith. Amen.*

# GOD'S INCARNATE WORD TO YOU

## Frederick Buechner

I will listen to what God the LORD says;
he promises peace to his people, his faithful servants.

PSALM 85:8

Because the word that God speaks to us is always an incarnate word—a word spelled out to us not alphabetically, in syllables, but enigmatically, in events, even in the books we read and the movies we see—the chances are we will never get it just right. We are so used to hearing what we want to hear and remaining deaf to what it would be well for us to hear that it is hard to break the habit. But if we keep our hearts and minds open as well as our ears, if we listen with patience and hope, if we remember at all deeply and honestly, then I think we come to recognize, beyond all doubt, that, however faintly we may hear him, he is indeed speaking to us, and that, however little we may understand of it, his word to each of us is both recoverable and precious beyond telling.

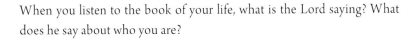

When you listen to the book of your life, what is the Lord saying? What does he say about who you are?

*Lord, tune my heart to listen to your voice, to all of what you're telling me about who you are and who I am. Amen.*

# SKIP PRAYERS, FORFEIT INFLUENCE

## Eugene Peterson

> The kings of the earth set themselves,
>
> and the rulers take counsel together,
>
> against the LORD and his anointed.
>
> PSALM 2:1-2 NRSV

Psalm 2 shows people plotting against the word of God, devising schemes for getting rid of it so they can be free of all God-interference in their lives. These people see God's words not as javelins penetrating their lives with truth, but as chains that restrict their freedom. They put their minds together to rid themselves of this word so that their words can rule.

The people who do this appear impressive: they are both numerous (nations and people) and prominent (kings and rulers). A lot of people reject the Word of God; they not only reject it, they turn their attention into a world power. If these people are in active conspiracy against the rule of God, what difference can prayer make?

Intimidation is as fatal to prayer as distractions. If we are intimidated, we will forfeit the entire world of culture and politics, of business and science to those "who set themselves . . . against the LORD."

May no one intimidate us into forfeiting our influence by making us forego our prayer.

*Lord, I pray for discernment and courage. Amen.*

# WHAT THE CROSS MEANS

## N. T. Wright

*When they had come to the place called Calvary, there they crucified Him, and the criminals, one on the right hand and the other on the left.*

LUKE 23:33 NKJV

The meaning of the story is found in every detail, as well as in the broad narrative. The pain and tears of all the years were met together on Calvary. The sorrow of heaven joined with the anguish of earth; the forgiving love stored up in God's future was poured out into the present; the voices that echo in a million human hearts, crying for justice, longing for spirituality, eager for relationship, yearning for beauty, drew themselves together into a final scream of desolation.

Nothing in all the history of paganism comes anywhere near this combination of event, intention, and meaning. Nothing in Judaism had prepared for it, except in puzzling, shadowy prophecy. The death of Jesus of Nazareth as the king of the Jews, the bearer of Israel's destiny, the fulfillment of God's promises to his people of old, is either the most stupid, senseless waste and misunderstanding the world has ever seen, or it is the fulcrum around which world history turns.

Christianity is based on the belief that it was and is the latter.

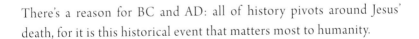

There's a reason for BC and AD: all of history pivots around Jesus' death, for it is this historical event that matters most to humanity.

*Lord Jesus Christ, Son of God, thank you for what your death means for history, for humanity, for me. Amen.*

# MY SPIRITUAL POVERTY

## Brennan Manning

> This poor soul cried, and was heard by the LORD,
> and was saved from every trouble.
>
> PSALM 34:6 NRSV

The Lord hears the cry of the poor. When the armistice with self-hatred is signed and we embrace what we really are, the process of liberation begins. But so often we are afraid to initiate the process for fear of rejection. Feeling like Quasimodo (the hunchback of Notre Dame), we daub cosmetics and spiritual makeup on our misery and supposed ugliness to make ourselves appear presentable to God. This is not our true self. Authentic prayer calls us to rigorous honesty, to come out of hiding, to quit trying to seem impressive, to acknowledge our total dependence on God and the reality of our sinful situation. It is a moment of truth when defenses fall and the masks drop in an instinctive act of humility.

How difficult it is to be honest—to accept that I am unacceptable, to renounce self-justification, to give up my preposterous pretending that my paltry prayers, spiritual insights, knowledge of Scripture, and blustering successes in ministry have made me pleasing to God.

The first step to finding liberation from self-hatred is to move from the dark delusion of self-sufficiency and into the marvelous light of our souls' poverty.

*Lord, wake me up to my true reality: reveal the poverty of my soul and the wealth of your love. Amen.*

# SHAMELESS LOVE, AUTHENTIC FAITH

## Dallas Willard

*"Her sins—and they are many—are forgiven, for she loved me much; but one who is forgiven little, shows little love."*

LUKE 7:47 TLB

Loved me much!" Simply that, and not the customary proprieties, was now the key of entry into the rule of God. Jesus went on to say to the woman, "Your sins are forgiven. Your faith has saved you. Go with peace in your heart." Here is God's rule in action.

We must not overlook the connection between faith and love. The woman *saw* Jesus and recognized who he was and who dwelt in him. That vision was her faith. She knew he was forgiving and accepting her before he ever said, "Your sins are forgiven." She knew because she had seen a goodness in him that could only be God, and it broke her heart with gratitude and love.

Speaking in the language of today, we would say she went "nuts" about Jesus. Her behavior obviously was the behavior of a "nutty" person. When we see Jesus as he is, we must turn away or else shamelessly adore him. That must be kept in mind for any authentic understanding of the power of Christian faith.

Jesus reminds us that radical love and faith are intimately connected. It's only in shamelessly adoring the Lord our God that we have authentic faith in him.

*Lord, deepen my love for you so my faith in you grows all the more authentic. Amen.*

# WHO YOU ARE IS BECAUSE OF WHO GOD IS

## A. W. Tozer

> God created humankind in his image.
>
> GENESIS 1:27 NRSV

We can never know who or what we are till we know at least something of what God is. For this reason the self-existence of God is not a wisp of dry doctrine, academic and remote. For reasons known only to himself, God honored man above all other beings by creating him in his own image. And let it be understood that the divine image in man is not a poetic fancy, not an idea born of religious longing. It is a solid theological fact, taught plainly throughout the sacred Scriptures and recognized by the church as a truth necessary to a right understanding of the Christian faith.

Man is a creative being, a derived and contingent self, who of himself possesses nothing but is dependent each moment for his existence upon the one who created him after his own likeness. The fact of God is necessary to the fact of man. Think God away and man has no ground of existence.

God is everything and humans are nothing: it is a basic tenet of Christian faith. This means that all of who you are is only because of all of who God is.

*Heavenly Father, deepen my understanding of you*
*so I may understand myself more rightly. Amen.*

# WHAT DOES RESURRECTION PROVE?

## N. T. Wright

With great power the apostles continued to testify
to the resurrection of the Lord Jesus.

Acts 4:33

Faced with an increasingly secular world all around, and with denials that there is any life at all beyond the grave, many Christians have seized upon Jesus' resurrection as the sign that there really is "life after death." This tends to confuse things. Resurrection isn't a fancy way of saying "going to heaven when you die." It is not about "life after death" as such. Rather, it's a way of talking about being bodily alive again after a period of being bodily dead. If Jesus' resurrection "proves" anything about what happens to people after they die, it is that.

But interestingly, none of the resurrection stories in the Gospels or in the book titled Acts speaks of the event proving that some kind of afterlife exists. They all say, instead: "If Jesus has been raised, that means that God's new world, God's kingdom, has indeed arrived; and that means we have a job to do. The world must hear what the God of Israel, the creator God, has achieved through his Messiah."

Jesus' resurrection matters not only for the hope of life after death; it matters for life *before* life after death.

> Jesus, thank you for the arrival of your kingdom on
> earth; show me how to help establish it. Amen.

# HOLY MIRTH

## Frederick Buechner

> "I will make my covenant between me and you
> and will greatly increase your numbers."
>
> GENESIS 17:2

When God told Abraham, who was a hundred at the time, that at the age of ninety his wife, Sarah, was finally going to have a baby, Abraham came close to knocking himself out—"fell on his face and laughed," as Genesis puts it (17:17). In another version of the story (Genesis 18:8ff), Sarah is hiding behind the door eavesdropping, and here it's Sarah herself who nearly splits a gut.

Why did the two old crocks laugh? They laughed because they knew only a fool would believe that a woman with one foot in the grave was soon going to have her other foot in the maternity ward. They laughed because God expected them to believe it anyway. They laughed because God seemed to believe it. They laughed because they half believed it themselves. They laughed because laughing felt better than crying. They laughed because if by some crazy chance it just happened to come true, they would really have something to laugh about, and in the meanwhile it helped keep them going.

Faith is "the assurance of things hoped for, the conviction of things not seen," says the Letter to the Hebrews (11:1). Faith is laughter at the promise of a child called Laughter.

———✺———

Has the revelation of God's will ever made you laugh? Why or why not?

*Father, help me to find humor in unexpected places. Amen.*

# THE VOICE OF LOVING FAVOR

## Henri J. M. Nouwen

*In love he predestined us for adoption to sonship through*
*Jesus Christ, in accordance with his pleasure and will.*

EPHESIANS 1:4–5

Many voices ask for our attention. There is a voice that says, "Prove that you are a good person." Another voice says, "You'd better be ashamed of yourself." There also is a voice that says, "Nobody really cares about you," and one that says, "Be sure to become successful, popular, and powerful." But underneath all these often very noisy voices is a still, small voice that says, "You are my Beloved, my favor rests on you." That's the voice we need most of all to hear. To hear that voice, however, requires special effort; it requires solitude, silence, and a strong determination to listen.

That's what prayer is. It is listening to the voice that calls us "my Beloved."

---

May we make room for this voice of loving favor, the voice that reminds us of our true identity as sons and daughters of the King of kings.

*Lord, I come to you seeking the still, small*
*voice that reminds me I'm yours. Amen.*

# YOU'RE A PRIEST

## Eugene Peterson

> "You shall be to Me a kingdom of priests and a holy nation."
>
> EXODUS 19:6 NKJV

A priest makes the God-connection verbal or visible. A priest represents human needs before God, sets God's word before men and women. God and humans have something to do with one another, *everything* to do with one another. A priest says and acts that reality.

The Hebrews became an entire community of people doing that for one another. Each was being trained in the rigors of a life of faith that consisted of listening to God, receiving his grace, obeying his commands, receiving his promises. Simply by being out of Egypt they were in a position to realize that nothing in them or about them could ever again be understood apart from the presence and action of God. That, and that alone, whether they carried through on it or not, *qualified* them to be priests.

Embarrassingly forgetful of the God who saves us, and easily distracted from the God who is with us, we need priests to remind us of God, to confront us with God. And we need a lot of them.

---

God put us in a kingdom of priests, made up of simple Christians like you and me. We present people to God and God to people.

*Lord, how can I speak and act your reality to those I know, presenting them to you and you to them? Amen.*

# WHAT EASTER OFFERS

## N. T. Wright

*In accordance with his promise, we wait for new heavens
and a new earth, where righteousness is at home.*

2 Peter 3:13 NRSV

A good many Easter hymns start by assuming that the point of Easter is that it proves the existence of life after death and encourages us to hope for it. This is then regularly, but ironically, combined with a view of that life after death in which the specific element of resurrection has been quietly removed. "May we go where he is gone," we sing at the end of one well-known hymn, "rest and reign with him in heaven!" But this time of rest is the prelude to something very different, which will emphatically involve earth as well. Earth—the renewed earth—is where the reign will take place, which is why the New Testament regularly speaks not of our going to be where Jesus is but of his coming to where we are.

Precisely because the resurrection has happened as an event within our own world, its implications and effects are to be felt within our own world, here and now.

———⊰⊱———

Easter's great hopeful promise is both a future and present renewal of reality through Christ's resurrection, where righteousness makes its home right here.

*Jesus, may your resurrection's effects fully
manifest themselves within my world, so heaven's
righteousness makes its home on earth. Amen.*

# HOPE TO SET THE STARS REELING

## Frederick Buechner

> "He will send out the angels, and gather his elect from the four
> winds, from the ends of the earth to the ends of heaven."
>
> MARK 13:27 NRSV

If Jesus died as dead as anybody, what hope did the rest of them have who woke every morning to the taste of their own death in their mouths? Why did he die? He died because the Jews had it in for him, Mark says, because he is hard on the Jews, himself very likely a Gentile and writing for Gentiles. He died because that's the way he wanted it—that "ransom for many" again, a wonderful thing to be bought at a terrible price. He died because that's the way God wanted it. Marvelous things would come of his death, and the one long speech Mark gives has to do with those marvelous things.

"The stars will be falling from heaven," Jesus says, "and the powers in the heavens will be shaken. Then they will see the 'Son of Man coming in clouds' with great power and glory" (13:25–26). Of course there was hope—hope that would set the stars reeling.

How does Jesus' resurrection spark your hope? When viewed through that event, how does your life look different?

> *Father, thank you for such a rich and robust hope.*
> *Inspire me to share it. Amen.*

# SKIP THE STATUS QUO

## Brennan Manning

*We do not want you to become lazy, but to imitate those who through faith and patience inherit what has been promised.*

Hebrews 6:12

From years of clinical practice, psychiatrist M. Scott Peck has not only come to believe in original sin, he has given it a precise definition—*laziness*.[7] Prayer becomes a chore rather than a joy. We drag ourselves out of bed for morning praise, shuffle off to Sunday worship with the sacramental slump of the terminally ill, get a reprieve when the pastor dismisses us with "Go in peace," and endure the tedium of night prayer with stoic resignation, knowing that "this too shall pass." The Enemy, who specializes in treacherous disguise, is the lazy part of self, resisting the effort, asceticism, and discipline that a serious life of prayer demands. The faulty logic of a darkened intellect permits dubious rationalizations such as "My work is my prayer," "I am too busy," and "I pray only when I feel a prompting of the Spirit." These lame excuses allow us lazily to maintain the status quo and indefinitely postpone the tryst with unconditional love.

From the beginning, God's desire was that we would exist in an everlasting relationship with him. Sin gets in the way of that relationship, especially laziness that sidelines praise and prayer. May we never be too busy for both.

*Lord, restore in me the joy of intentional praise and prayer so that I can fully lean into your unconditional love. Amen.*

# THE LANGUAGE OF TROUBLE

## Eugene Peterson

O Lord, how many are my foes!

PSALM 3:1 NRSV

Brief, urgent, frightened words—a person in trouble, crying out to God for help. The language is personal, direct, desperate. This is the language of prayer: men and women calling out their trouble—pain, guilt, doubt, despair—to God. Their lives are threatened. If they don't get help they will be dead, or diminished to some critical degree. The language of prayer is forged in the crucible of trouble.

Language gets its start under the pressure of pain. Our first sound is the wail. All our early speech is an inarticulate eloquence that gets us what we need to survive: food, warmth, comfort, love. We need help. We need another. We are unfinished creatures requiring complex and extensive assistance in every part of our being, and a language is the means for getting it.

Prayer, a human being conversing with a holy God, is a great mystery and defies probabilities. But it is a mystery embedded in something common and very close to us. The nature of language provides insights into the learning and practice of prayer.

---

The primal language of trouble forges our prayers.

*Lord, I come to you with my pain and my words tangled together. Hear me, O God, and help. Amen.*

# SCIENCE AND HISTORY TRANSCENDED

## N. T. Wright

What I received I passed on to you as of first importance: that Christ
died for our sins according to the Scriptures, that he was buried,
that he was raised on the third day according to the Scriptures,
and that he appeared to Cephas, and then to the Twelve.

1 CORINTHIANS 15:3-5

Faith in Jesus risen from the dead *transcends but includes* what we call history and what we call science. Faith of this sort is not blind belief, which rejects all history and science. Rather this kind of faith, which like all modes of knowledge is defined by the nature of its object, is faith in the creator God, the God who promised to put all things to rights at the last, the God who (as the sharp point where those two come together) raised Jesus from the dead within history, leaving evidence that demands an explanation from the scientist as well as anybody else.

Hope, for the Christian, is not wishful thinking or mere blind optimism. It is a mode of knowing, a mode within which new things are possible, options are not shut down, new creation can happen.

Paul confirmed Jesus' resurrection was historically witnessed, yet super-natural. Which means our faith isn't merely blind belief; it's compatible with science and history. Yet it transcends both, for it fits within God's new-creation paradigm—where even resurrection is possible.

*Lord, thank you for a faith so full of hope and possibility. Amen.*

# SALVATION AVAILABLE FOR ALL

## Dallas Willard

> If you declare with your mouth, "Jesus is Lord," and believe in your
> heart that God raised him from the dead, you will be saved.
>
> ROMANS 10:9

The kingdom of God is . . . indeed the Kingdom Among Us. You can reach it from your heart with your mouth—through even a shaky and stumbling confidence and confession that Jesus is the death-conquering Master of All.

To be sure, that kingdom has been here as long as we humans have been here, and longer. But it has been available to us through simple confidence in Jesus, the Anointed, only from the time he became a public figure. It is a kingdom that, in the person of Jesus, welcomes us just as we are, just where we are, and makes it possible for us to translate our "ordinary" life into an eternal one. It is so available that everyone who from the center of his or her being calls upon Jesus as Master of the Universe and Prince of Life will be heard and will be delivered into the eternal kind of life.

───────

The power that can make our lives far better is right near us—anyone can utilize it. Some will not accept it, some will not want to change for it, some will think they can't afford to. But the promise of salvation and an extraordinary life are just waiting to be had.

*Lord, thank you for making salvation so accessible. I accept your promise for anyone who confesses and believes! Amen.*

# EASTER: ALL IS WELL

## Frederick Buechner

"Do not be afraid, little flock, for it is your Father's
good pleasure to give you the kingdom."

LUKE 12:32 NRSV

Anxiety and fear are what we know best in this fantastic century of ours. Wars and rumors of wars. From civilization itself to what seemed the most unalterable values of the past, everything is threatened or already in ruins. We have heard so much tragic news that when the news is good we cannot hear it.

But the proclamation of Easter Day is that all is well. And as a Christian, I say this not with the easy optimism of one who has never known a time when all was not well but as one who has faced the cross in all its obscenity as well as in all its glory, who has known one way or another what it is like to live separated from God. In the end, his will, not ours, is done. Love is the victor. Death is not the end. The end is life. His life and our lives through him, in him. Existence has greater depth of beauty, mystery, and benediction than the wildest visionary has ever dared to dream. Christ our Lord has risen.

What do you fear the most? Remind yourself that your experience of God's love is victorious, death isn't the end, and all is well in Christ.

*Lord, help me trust Christ's words, to immerse
myself in the beauty of this life I live in him. Amen.*

# THE THRONING OF SELF

## A. W. Tozer

> The serpent said to the woman, "You will not die; for God
> knows that when you eat of it your eyes will be opened,
> and you will be like God, knowing good and evil."
>
> GENESIS 3:4-5 NRSV

The natural man is a sinner because and only because he challenges God's selfhood in relation to his own. In all else he may willingly accept the sovereignty of God; in his own life he rejects it. For him, God's dominion ends where his begins. For him, self becomes Self.

Yet so subtle is self that scarcely anyone is conscious of its presence. Because man is born a rebel, he is unaware that he is one. His constant assertion of self, as far as he thinks of it at all, appears to him a perfectly normal thing. He is willing to share himself, sometimes even to sacrifice himself for a desired end, but never to dethrone himself.

That is sin in its concentrated essence; yet because it is natural it appears to be good. It is only when in the gospel the soul is brought before the face of the Most Holy One without the protective shield of ignorance that the frightful moral incongruity is brought home to the conscience.

———— ∞ ————

At its core, sin is when we, who were created to worship before God's throne, sit on the thrones of our own hearts and declare, "I AM."

> *Lord, I repent of my sin and willingly*
> *dethrone the Self; you reign instead. Amen.*

# ACCEPT GOD'S LOVE IN CHRIST

## Brennan Manning

*This is how God showed his love among us: He sent his one and only Son into the world that we might live through him.*

1 JOHN 4:9

I'd like to share an exercise I learned from an old evangelical pastor who seemed to have the gift for mediating the experience of Jesus Christ, the risen Lord, to people who asked to come in touch with Christ.

Recall the presence of the risen Lord with you. Tell him you believe he is present to you.

Reflect on the fact that he loves and accepts you just as you are now. Take time out to sense his unconditional love for you as he looks at you lovingly and humbly.

Speak to Jesus—or just lovingly stay in silence and communicate with him beyond words.

A soul-deep emphasis on the love of Christ (what the ancients called "devotion to the heart of Jesus"), so vigorous in the past, so much on the decline today, would flourish once again if people would understand that it consists essentially in accepting Jesus Christ as love incarnate, as the manifestation of the unconditional love of God for us.

Anyone who accepts the truth of God's unconditional love is bound to experience joy beyond all expectation!

*Lord, thank you for your astounding love that is as close as a moment of meditation. Amen.*

87

# PRAYER: A CONVERSATION

## Dallas Willard

> I cry aloud to the LORD;
> I lift up my voice to the LORD for mercy.
>
> PSALM 142:1

What prayer as asking presupposes is simply a personal—that is, an experientially interactive—relationship between us and God, just as with a request of child to parent or friend to friend. It assumes that our natural concerns will be naturally expressed, and that God will hear our prayers for ourselves as well as for others. This is clear from the biblical practice of prayer. It is seen at its best in that greatest of all prayer books, Psalms.

Accordingly, I believe the most adequate description of prayer is simply *talking to God about what we are doing together.* That immediately focuses the activity where we are but at the same time drives the egotism out of it. Requests will naturally be made in the course of this conversational walk. Prayer is a matter of explicitly sharing with God my concerns about what he too is concerned about in my life. And of course he is concerned about my concerns and, in particular, that my concerns should coincide with his. This is our walk together. Out of it I pray.

May our prayers be as vibrant as our conversations with friends!

> *Lord, I come to you to talk about the things we're doing together. Thanks for meeting me! Amen.*

# WHAT THE WORLD IS WAITING FOR

## N. T. Wright

*I saw a new heaven and a new earth, for the first*
*heaven and the first earth had passed away.*

REVELATION 21:1 NKJV

The early Christians did not believe in progress. They did not think the world was getting better and better under its own steam—or even under the steady influence of God. They knew God had to do something fresh to put it to rights.

But neither did they believe that the world was getting worse and worse and that their task was to escape it altogether. They were not dualists.

Since most people who think about these things today tend toward one or the other of those two points of view, it comes as something of a surprise to discover that the early Christians held a quite different view. They believed that God was going to do for the whole cosmos what he had done for Jesus at Easter. This is such a surprising belief, and so little reflected on even in Christian circles, still less outside the church, that we must show how the different early writers developed different images that together add up to a stunning picture of a future for which, so they insisted, the whole world was waiting on tiptoe.

For what part of the stunning new future, the one God himself promised, are you waiting?

*Lord, I wait with eager expectation for*
*the new heavens and new earth. Amen.*

# UNHOLY ACTS OF TWO BROTHERS

## Frederick Buechner

> Esau said . . . "Bless me too, my father!"
> GENESIS 27:38

Esau was so hungry he could hardly see straight when his younger twin, Jacob, bought his birthright for a bowl of chili. He was off hunting rabbits when Jacob conned their old father, Isaac, into giving him the blessing that should have been Esau's. Eventually it dawned on Esau what his brother was up to, and he went slogging after him with a blunt instrument; but the slowness of his wits was compensated for by the generosity of his disposition, and in time the two were reconciled.

Jacob stole Esau blind, in other words, got away with it, and went on to become the father of the twelve tribes of Israel. It was not all gravy, however. He knew famine and loss. He grieved for years over the supposed death of his favorite child. He was as hoodwinked by his own sons in this as both his father and Esau had been hoodwinked by him.

Esau, on the other hand, settled down in the hill country, raised a large if comparatively undistinguished family, and died in peace. Thus it seems hard to know which of the two brothers came out ahead.

It seems plain enough, however, that the reason God bypassed Esau and made Jacob heir to the great promise is that it is easier to make a silk purse out of a sow's ear than out of a dim bulb.

———— ∞ ————

Have you ever been "hoodwinked" by a brother or sister in the Lord? How did you handle it?

*Father, give me the grace to forgive those who hurt me. Amen.*

# YEARNING FOR PERFECT LOVE

## Henri J. M. Nouwen

People of Athens! I see that in every way you are very religious. For as I walked around and looked carefully at your objects of worship, I even found an altar with this inscription: TO AN UNKNOWN GOD. So you are ignorant of the very thing you worship.

ACTS 17:22–23

When we act out of loneliness our actions easily become violent. The tragedy is that much violence comes from a demand for love. When loneliness drives our search for love, kissing easily leads to biting, caressing to hitting, looking tenderly to looking suspiciously, listening to overhearing, and surrender to rape. The human heart yearns for love: love without conditions, limitations, or restrictions. But no human being is capable of offering such love, and each time we demand it we set ourselves on the road to violence.

How then can we live nonviolent lives? We must start by realizing that our restless hearts, yearning for perfect love, can only find that love through communion with the One who created them.

Until our hearts commune with the one who created us, they will remain restless. May we lead others to that perfect love as much as we ourselves find it.

*Lord, I yearn for perfect love; give me the will to connect with you whenever I can. Amen.*

# PERSONAL AND GLOBAL HOLINESS

## N. T. Wright

> "I am the LORD your God. . . . Be holy, for I am holy."
>
> LEVITICUS 11:44 NASB

The message of Easter is neither that God once did a spectacular miracle but then decided not to do many others, nor that there is a blissful life after death to look forward to. The message of Easter is that God's new world has been unveiled in Jesus Christ and that you're now invited to belong to it. And precisely because the resurrection was and is bodily, albeit with a transformed body, the power of Easter to transform and heal the present world must be put into effect both at the macro level, in applying the gospel to the major problems of the world, and to the intimate details of our daily lives.

Christian holiness consists not of trying as hard as we can to be good but of learning to live in the new world created by Easter, the new world we publicly entered in our baptism. There are many parts of the world we can't do anything about except pray. But there is one part of the world, one part of physical reality, that we can do something about, and that is the creature each of us calls "myself."

———— ∞ ————

How do you live in the world created by Easter?

*Lord, help me heed both my own holiness*
*as well as that of the world. Amen.*

# DO YOU DO WHAT JESUS SAID IS BEST?

## Dallas Willard

"Why do you call me 'Lord, Lord,' and do not do what I tell you?"
LUKE 6:46 NRSV

Plainly, in the eyes of Jesus there is no good reason for not doing what he said to do, for he only tells us to do what is best. Just try picturing yourself standing before him and explaining why you did not do what he said was best. Now it may be that there are cases in which this would be appropriate. And certainly we can count on his understanding. But it will not do as a general posture in a life of confidence in him. He has made a way for us into easy and happy obedience—really, into personal fulfillment. And that way is apprenticeship to him. It is Christian "discipleship." His gospel is a gospel for life and Christian discipleship.

In other words, his basic message, *Rethink your life in the light of the fact that the kingdom of the heavens is now open to all* (Matthew 4:17), presents the resources needed to live human life as we all automatically sense it should be and naturally leads one to become his student or apprentice in kingdom living.

---

How would you respond if Jesus asked you the question he asked his disciples in Luke's gospel—do you see your life in Christ as an apprenticeship of doing what Jesus said is best?

*Jesus, help me take seriously what you have taught,
seeking the best by obeying you. Amen.*

# JUST AS I AM, WEAKNESS AND ALL

## James Bryan Smith

> Here is a trustworthy saying that deserves full acceptance: Christ Jesus came into the world to save sinners—of whom I am the worst.
>
> 1 TIMOTHY 1:15

One of the hardest steps for me was to admit my weaknesses and failures. I had tried to cover them up, excuse them, and rationalize them. But each time I found myself baring my soul to God, I received not judgment but mercy.

God's love for me has radically reshaped my identity. I no longer need to defend myself, make resolutions to do better, or show God that I have atoned for my sins. God is slowly making me bold.

During the period in which I felt so alienated from God, I prayed, "Lord, why did you call me into ministry? I am not worthy." God's voice seemed to remind me, "Jim, I have never used anyone *but* sinners to share my good news. The message is not about you, it is about me."

God loves me just as I am, not as I should be. I know that I am not as I should be. I know there is a lot of sin that still needs to be rooted out of me. But I know that God is not finished with me yet. I know that I am loved.

From Abraham to David, Peter to Paul, it is a remarkable truth that God accepts and uses us—weakness and all.

> *Lord, thank you for granting pardon in place of judgment.*
> *I receive your mercy. Let me extend the same to others. Amen.*

April

✓APRIL 1

# TREMBLE BEFORE THE CROSS

## Brennan Manning

> Carrying the cross by himself, he went out to
> what is called The Place of the Skull.
>
> JOHN 19:17 NRSV

Two twenty-minute periods of prime time in solitary prayer, morning and evening, before a symbol of the crucified Christ, is the most effective discipline I have found for making conscious contact with the living God and his liberating love.

Why the symbol of the crucified Christ? Because it is an icon of the greatest act of love in human history. Lamentably, Christian piety has prettified the passionate God of Golgotha; Christian art has banalized unspeakable outrage into dignified jewelry; Christian worship has sentimentalized monstrous scandal into sacred pageant. We have corrupted our sense of reality by sentimentalizing it. Pious imagination, romantic preaching, and lifeless or raucous worship overshadow the real Jesus. The Christian should tremble and the whole community quake when contemplating the cross on the Friday we call Good. But organized religion has domesticated the crucified Lord of glory into a tame theological symbol.

Would you consider making meditation part of your regular spiritual rhythm so that your comfortable piety is regularly disturbed?

*Jesus, thank you for the cross—those boards soaking with sweat, dripping with blood, the ones that bought my redemption. Amen.*

# WHAT DOES *CHURCH* MEAN TO YOU?

## N. T. Wright

They devoted themselves to the apostles' teaching and to fellowship,
to the breaking of bread and to prayer. Everyone was filled with
awe at the many wonders and signs performed by the apostles.

Acts 2:42–43

I know that for many that very word *church* carries the overtones of large, dark buildings, pompous religious pronouncements, false solemnity, and rank hypocrisy. But there is no easy alternative. I too feel the weight of that negative image. I battle with it professionally all the time.

But there is another side to it. For many, *church* means just the opposite of that negative image. It's a place of welcome and laughter, of healing and hope, of friends and family and justice and new life. It's where one group is working to help drug addicts and another is campaigning for global justice. It's where you'll find people learning to pray, coming to faith, struggling with temptation, finding new purpose, and getting in touch with a new power to carry that purpose out. It's where people bring their own small faith and discover, in getting together with others to worship the one true God, that the whole becomes greater than the sum of its parts.

Has your experience of church been negative or positive? How can you help renew the vision of Christ's community, the hope of the world?

*Jesus, use me to contribute to a positive image of your church in the world, where people find rescue and restoration. Amen.*

# TUNE YOUR MIND TO COMMUNITY

## N. T. Wright

Be transformed by the renewing of your mind.

ROMANS 12:2 NASB

For Paul, holiness is never a matter of simply finding out the way you seem to be made and trusting that that's the way God intends you to remain. Neither is it a matter of blind obedience to arbitrary and out-of-date rules. It's a matter of transformation, starting with the mind.

Of course, if you try to live a Christian lifestyle outside God's framework, you will find it as difficult, indeed nonsensical, as it would be for an orchestral performer to play his or her part separated from the rest of the players amid the crashes and metallic screeching of an automobile factory. Not that we aren't called, of course, to practice our discipleship in the hard, outside world, which rumbles on as though Easter had never happened. But if we are to be true to our risen Lord, we will need, again and again, to retune our instruments and practice once more alongside our fellow musicians.

Living a life of Christian holiness makes perfect sense within God's new world, the world into which faith brings us. Let's not forget the community we need so intensely.

*Lord, renew my mind in community so I may be fully transformed into the holy likeness of your Son. Amen.*

# THE VOICE IN THE GARDEN OF SOLITUDE

## Henri J. M. Nouwen

*In the morning, having risen a long while before daylight, He went out and departed to a solitary place; and there He prayed.*

MARK 1:35 NKJV

Solitude is the garden for our hearts, which yearn for love. It is the place where our aloneness can bear fruit. It is the home for our restless bodies and anxious minds. Solitude, whether it is connected with a physical space or not, is essential for our spiritual lives. It is not an easy place to be, since we are so insecure and fearful that we are easily distracted by whatever promises immediate satisfaction. Solitude is not immediately satisfying, because in solitude we meet our demons, our addictions, our feelings of lust and anger, and our immense need for recognition and approval. But if we do not run away, we will meet there also the One who says, "Do not be afraid. I am with you, and I will guide you through the valley of darkness."

Let's keep returning to our solitude.

What is your strategy for seeking the voice of the Lord in your own solitary place? How can you make enjoying silent periods a habit?

*Lord, help me seek your voice in the garden of solitude to obtain companionship, security, release, and guidance. Amen.*

# THE CEMENT OF COMMUNITY LIFE

## Henri J. M. Nouwen

Peter came and said to him, "Lord, if another member of the church sins against me, how often should I forgive? As many as seven times?" Jesus said to him, "Not seven times, but, I tell you, seventy-seven times."

MATTHEW 18:21–22 NRSV

Community is not possible without the willingness to forgive one another "seventy-seven times." Forgiveness is the cement of community life. Forgiveness holds us together through good and bad times, and it allows us to grow in mutual love.

But what is there to forgive or to ask forgiveness for? As people who have hearts that long for perfect love, we have to forgive one another for not being able to give or receive that perfect love in our everyday lives. Our many needs constantly interfere with our desire to be there for the other unconditionally. Our love is always limited by spoken or unspoken conditions. What needs to be forgiven? We need to forgive one another for not being God!

───※───

Forgiveness is what binds the communal life of God's people. May we heed the words of our Savior, offering forgiveness just as he provided for us.

*Lord Jesus Christ, Son of God, may I hear these words of yours and put them into practice, forgiving members of my community limitless times. Amen.*

# CRY FOR HELP, SHOUT THANKS

## Eugene Peterson

I cry aloud to the LORD,
and he answers me from his holy hill.

PSALM 3:4 NRSV

In trouble, we pray; in the course of the praying our experience of wrong becomes an experience of right, which is even more elemental than wrong, but to which our unprayed experience does not give us as immediate access. Gratitude and well-being get expressed with the same spontaneous accuracy in which we cry out pain, anger, guilt, and terror.

There is not an abstract word in this prayer. The nouns are specific; the verbs are direct. Everything is personal: God is personal, the pray-er is personal, experience is immediate, relationship is central, the emotions of terror and trust are expressed with force. This is the elemental language we always use when our life, our well-being, and deepest interests—identity, health, love, guilt, trust—are at stake. There is no mere information about God here. There is no program implemented for God here. This is a cry for survival that develops into the shout of the saved.

Elemental prayer gets its start in the time of trouble and eventually finds a way to gratitude. The genesis is always in the elemental monosyllables of "Help!" and "Thanks!"—for deliverance, for salvation, for blessing.

*Lord my God, on whom I rely for my help:
I cry for survival, I thank you for salvation. Amen.*

# HEAVENLY CITIZENSHIP, COSMIC CHANGE

## N. T. Wright

> Our citizenship is in heaven. And we eagerly await a Savior from there, the Lord Jesus Christ, who, by the power that enables him to bring everything under his control, will transform our lowly bodies so that they will be like his glorious body.
>
> PHILIPPIANS 3:20–21

When Paul says, "We are citizens of heaven," he doesn't at all mean that when we're done with this life we'll be going off to live in heaven. What he means is that the Savior, the Lord, Jesus the King—all of those were of course imperial titles—will come from heaven to earth, to change the present situation and state of his people. The key word here is *transform*. Jesus will not declare that present physicality is redundant and can be scrapped. Nor will he simply improve it, perhaps by speeding up its evolutionary cycle. In a great act of power he will *change* the present body into the one that corresponds in kind to his own as part of his work of bringing all things into subjection to himself. Philippians 3, though it is primarily speaking of human resurrection, indicates that this will take place within the context of God's victorious transformation of the whole cosmos.

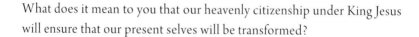

What does it mean to you that our heavenly citizenship under King Jesus will ensure that our present selves will be transformed?

*Lord, thank you for my coming resurrection, where my life, in all its fullness, will be transformed in victory. Amen.*

# DEAD TO SIN, ALIVE TO GOD

## N. T. Wright

Count yourselves dead to sin but alive to God in Christ Jesus.

ROMANS 6:11

Are we just spectators in God's great drama, sitting on the sidelines, unaffected by the big picture? If God delights to bring his grace to sinners, as Christian evangelists have always rightly insisted, should we go on being sinners in order to get more grace?

Paul's answer is clear: certainly not! We were planted with the Messiah in his death, with the result that our old identity, the old self, was crucified with him. And if that's true, it means that sin has no rights over you, no official hold over you. Instead, if the Messiah has been raised from the dead, and if you are in the Messiah—by baptism a member of his people—then it means that you too, in him, have been raised from the dead. Many have supposed that Paul meant this in a purely future sense, but the point of Romans 6:11 is that it is also a present experience: you must now calculate, do the sum, reckon it up, "consider yourself" to be dead to sin and alive to God in the Messiah, Jesus.

———✇———

In between Jesus' resurrection and the world's renewal is our personal renewal in our day-to-day lives of obedience.

*Jesus, help me ignite the genesis of the revolutionary new world launched with your resurrection within my life. Amen.*

# THE LESS-TRAVELED ROAD TO FREEDOM

## Brennan Manning

> Those who belong to Christ Jesus have crucified the flesh.
>
> GALATIANS 5:24 NASB

The gradual transformation from an attitude of self-hatred to a spirit of self-acceptance is what occurs in the process of trying to be honest. Paradoxically, the human spirit soars in the daily endeavor to make choices and decisions that are expressive of the truth of who we are in Christ Jesus, not who we think we should be or who somebody else wants us to be. Self-mastery over every form of sin, selfishness, emotional dishonesty, and degraded love is the less-traveled road to Christian freedom.

Thus the attitude of self-acceptance is not essentially self-centered. It is radically relational. It is not self-regarding but Christ-oriented. The spurious self-contentment that evolves from scrupulous self-examination, rigorous mortification, and the anxious endeavor to achieve purity of heart is bogus spirituality, the counterfeit coin of Christian integrity. As Jesus' unparalleled authenticity and inner serenity were rooted in his Father's good pleasure, so Christian self-acceptance is rooted in the conscious and experiential affirmation of Jesus in our struggle to be faithful.

In Christ, Christians are called to daily dying to self and conscious affirmation of Christ.

*Jesus, may I find true freedom by dying to myself and living for you. Amen.*

# PAY FORWARD GOD'S COMPASSION

## Dallas Willard

Clothe yourselves with compassion, kindness,
humility, meekness, and patience.
COLOSSIANS 3:12 NRSV

A person of compassion is one who feels the needs of others and whose compassion is not something that can be turned on and off like a water faucet. It is always on. It is a constant burden of life. This is why so many reject the commandment to love others: because love and compassion require resources of personal strength and wisdom in action. Loving your neighbor as yourself is a matter of who you are, not primarily of what you decide to do.

We can "afford" to be compassionate only if we know there is abundant compassion for us, toward us, by persons who have appropriate means. This is primarily God: "We love because he first loved us" (1 John 4:19). The perfect love of God toward us casts out fear (v. 18). Think of the role of fear in the good Samaritan story! So our experience of God's love is what allows us, empowers us, to set aside anger, selfishness, lusting, and so on in our relationships to others.

In light of the kindness you've received from God, how can you pay it forward to those you know?

*Lord, lead me to a deeper experience of your love, that I may pour that same mercy and compassion on others. Amen.*

# ALL THE WISDOM WE NEED

## N. T. Wright

> We speak God's wisdom, secret and hidden, which
> God decreed before the ages for our glory.
>
> 1 CORINTHIANS 2:7 NRSV

Wisdom (personified) was already thought of within Judaism as God's agent in creation, the one through whom the world was made. John, Paul, and the Letter to the Hebrews all draw on this idea to speak of Jesus himself as the one through whom God made the world. But it doesn't stop there. Paul, like the book of Proverbs, goes on to speak of this wisdom (no longer personified) being accessible to humans through the power of God's Spirit. As in Proverbs, part of the point about wisdom is that it's what you need in order to live a fully, genuinely human life. It is not, he says, a wisdom "of this age." God has given us access to a new kind of wisdom, through the Spirit.

All God's treasures of wisdom and knowledge are hidden in the Messiah himself. This means that those who belong to the Messiah have this wisdom accessible to them, and hence the chance to grow toward mature human and Christian living.

---

All we need is available in Christ. Maturity, humanity, and godly living are within our grasp.

*Jesus, you who bear all the secret and hidden wisdom of God, I seek understanding in order that I might live a radiant, productive life. Amen.*

# A VITAL PART OF OUR CHRISTIAN LIFE

## Dallas Willard

About noon the following day as they were on their journey and
approaching the city, Peter went up on the roof to pray.

ACTS 10:9

Frank Laubach wrote of how, in his personal experiment of moment-by-moment submission to the will of God, the fine texture of his work and life experience was transformed. In January of 1930 he began to cultivate the habit of turning his mind to Christ for one second out of every minute.[8]

After only four weeks he reported, "I feel simply carried along each hour, doing my part in a plan which is far beyond myself. This sense of cooperation with God in little things is what so astonishes me, for I never have felt it this way before. I need something, and turn round to find it waiting for me. I must work, to be sure, but there is God working along with me."[9]

God raised Frank Laubach from a lonely missionary post in the Philippines to the status of Christian world statesman and spokesman for Christ. But he was forever and foremost Christ's man and always knew that his brilliant ideas and incredible energy and effectiveness derived from his practice of constant conscious interface with God.

---

Conscious communion with God through intentional prayer is vital for our Christian life. Only through regular conversations with God will we experience his vision for life and be effective for his glory.

*Lord, grant me the vision and effectiveness*
*you desire to see in my life. Amen.*

# FIND YOUR WAY AGAIN

## A. W. Tozer

> All of us like sheep have gone astray,
> Each of us has turned to his own way.
>
> ISAIAH 53:6 NASB

The struggle of the Christian man to be good while the bent toward self-assertion still lives within him as a kind of unconscious moral reflex is vividly described by the apostle Paul, and his testimony is in full accord with the teaching of the prophets. Eight hundred years before the advent of Christ the prophet Isaiah identified sin as rebellion against the will of God and the assertion of the right of each man to choose for himself the way he should go.

The witness of the saints has been in full harmony with prophet and apostle that an inward principle of self lies at the source of human conduct, turning everything men do into evil. To save us completely Christ must reverse the bent of our nature; he must plant a new principle within us so that our subsequent conduct will spring out of a desire to promote the honor of God and the good of our fellow men. The old self-sins must die, and the only instrument by which they can be slain is the cross.

Jesus said that if anyone wants to follow him he must die a cross-shaped death, losing his or her life in order to gain his new one. How can you die, denying your way?

*Jesus, help me to promote the Father's honor, not my own. Amen.*

# EAT THIS BREAD, DRINK THIS CUP

## N. T. Wright

*As often as you eat this bread and drink this cup,*
*you proclaim the Lord's death till He comes.*

1 CORINTHIANS 11:26 NKJV

In the Eucharist, the bread and the wine come to us as part of God's new creation, the creation in whose reality Jesus already participates through the resurrection. They speak powerfully, as only encoded actions can speak (whether a handshake, a kiss, the tearing up of a contract, or whatever), both of the death he suffered, through which idolatry and sin have been defeated, and of his future arrival in which creation is to be renewed. We feed on that reality even though we may find it difficult to conceptualize what sort of reality it is. Knowing that we are thereby renewed as the people of Jesus who live and work in the tension between Easter and the final renewal enables us at least to relax and enjoy all that the sacrament has to offer.

Jesus said, "This is my body that is for you. Do this in remembrance of me." Likewise, he said, "This cup is the new covenant in my blood. Do this, as often as you drink it, in remembrance of me" (1 Corinthians 11:24–25 NRSV). What do the bread and cup proclaim to you about the heart of God? What does this sacrament have to offer you and your experience of that heart?

*Jesus, thank you for your body and blood, for the new*
*covenant you have established with them. Amen.*

# LIVE LIKE A CHILD

## Frederick Buechner

> He called a little child to him, and placed the child among them.
> And he said: "Truly I tell you, unless you change and become like
> little children, you will never enter the kingdom of heaven."
>
> MATTHEW 18:2–3

When the disciples, overearnest as ever, asked Jesus who was the greatest in the kingdom of heaven, Jesus pulled a child out of the crowd and said the greatest in the kingdom of heaven were people like this. Two thousand years of homiletic sentimentalizing to the contrary notwithstanding, Jesus was not being sentimental. He was saying that the people who get into heaven are people who, like children, don't worry about it too much. They are people who, like children, live with their hands open more than with their fists clenched. They are people who, like children, are so relatively unburdened by preconceptions that if somebody says there's a pot of gold at the end of the rainbow, they are perfectly willing to go take a look for themselves.

Children aren't necessarily better than other people. Like the child in "The Emperor's New Clothes," they are just apt to be better at telling the difference between a phony and the real thing.

Are you living your Christian life more like a child or an adult? If it's the latter, how might you need to change to become like the former?

> *Jesus, transform me from an adult into a*
> *child so I can enter your kingdom. Amen.*

# FORGIVING IN THE NAME OF GOD

## Henri J. M. Nouwen

> Be kind and compassionate to one another, forgiving
> each other, just as in Christ God forgave you.
>
> EPHESIANS 4:32

We are all wounded people. Who wounds us? Often those whom we love and those who love us. When we feel rejected, abandoned, abused, manipulated, or violated, it is mostly by people very close to us: our parents, our friends, our spouses, our lovers, our children, our neighbors, our teachers, our pastors. Those who love us wound us too. That's the tragedy of our lives. This is what makes forgiveness from the heart so difficult. It is precisely our hearts that are wounded. We cry out, "You, who I expected to be there for me, you have abandoned me. How can I ever forgive you for that?"

Forgiveness often seems impossible, but nothing is impossible for God. The God who lives within us will give us the grace to go beyond our wounded selves and say, "In the name of God you are forgiven." Let's pray for that grace.

Consider the incomprehensible reality that the God of the universe has forgiven every unloving, hurtful, wounding act we have perpetuated against him. Why should we treat any differently those who've unloved, hurt, and wounded us?

*Lord, please give me the grace to do what seems overwhelming: forgiving others the same way you have forgiven me. Amen.*

# WHERE ARE YOUR FEET TAKING YOU?

## Frederick Buechner

> How lovely on the mountains
> Are the feet of him who brings good news.
>
> ISAIAH 52:7 NASB

Not how beautiful are the herald's lips, which proclaim the good tidings, or his eyes as he proclaims them, or even the good tidings themselves, but how beautiful are the feet—the feet without which he could never have made it up into the mountains, without which the good tidings would never have been proclaimed at all.

When the disciples first came upon the risen Christ that Sunday morning of their confusion and terror, it wasn't his healing hands they touched or his teaching lips or his holy heart. Instead, it was those same ruined, tired dogs that had carried him to them three years earlier, when they were at their accounts and their nets, that had dragged him all the way from Galilee to Jerusalem, that had stumbled up the hill where what was to happen happened. "They took hold of His *feet* and worshiped Him," Matthew says (28:9, italics mine).

Generally speaking, if you want to know who you really are, as distinct from who you like to think you are, keep an eye on where your feet take you.

The herald had to decide to employ his body to spread that news. Where are your feet taking you?

> *Jesus, may my feet follow you in bearing*
> *a message of good news. Amen.*

# LORD, FLOOD CREATION WITH YOURSELF!

## N. T. Wright

When all things are subjected to him, then the Son himself
will also be subjected to the one who put all things in
subjection under him, so that God may be all in all.

1 Corinthians 15:28 nrsv

The answer to the pantheism of the evolutionary or progressive opti-
mist, on the one hand, and to the dualism of the Gnostic or Manichee,
on the other, begins to come into full view in the form of the cosmic
eschatology offered in the New Testament. The world is created good but
incomplete. One day, when all forces of rebellion have been defeated and
the creation responds freely and gladly to the love of its Creator, God will
fill it with himself so that it will both remain an independent being, other
than God, and also be flooded with God's own life.

This is part of the paradox of love, in which love freely given creates a
context for love to be freely returned, and so on in a cycle where complete
freedom and complete union do not cancel each other out but rather celebrate each other and make one another whole.

God will be all in all in the future. Until the final victory over evil and death
this moment has not yet arrived. When it does, God will fill creation with
his very own presence and love.

*Lord, every day I feel the incompleteness and brokenness of
creation; I long for the day you remake it in all your beauty. Amen.*

# LIVE GLADLY

## James Bryan Smith

> "You will seek Me and find Me, when you
> search for Me with all your heart."
>
> JEREMIAH 29:13 NKJV

How do we come to know such love? We must ask for it. We must pray that we will come to know and feel this love. We must plead to God before we will hear this gentle voice. God will not delay in reply. But he is so gracious that he will never intrude. God has promised that if we seek him with all of our heart, we will find him.

Frederick Buechner writes, "If you have never known the power of God's love, then maybe it is because you have never asked to know it—I mean really asked, expecting an answer."[10] Are you ready to ask? God is ready to give. Nothing gives God more pleasure than filling his children with love and hearing them exclaim, "Abba, Daddy!"

Julian of Norwich once wrote, "The greatest honor we can give to Almighty God is to live gladly because of the knowledge of his love." Ask God to give you this knowledge, not in your head but in your heart.

Consider your regular rhythm when it comes to searching after the heart of God. Do you have a regular plan or intervals of time for pursuing him? When you do, he promises you will find him.

> *Lord, I long to know the power of your love.*
> *Would you help me recognize and feel it? Amen.*

# THE CHURCH'S URGENT PRIORITIES

## Brennan Manning

"You will receive power when the Holy Spirit has come upon you; and you will be my witnesses in Jerusalem, in all Judea and Samaria, and to the ends of the earth."

ACTS 1:8 NRSV

With time slipping away like sand in an hourglass, the church has no more urgent priority than proclaiming the values of Jesus, preparing the way for him, and restraining panic when he appears on the scene. It is neither bogged down in heresy-hunting nor mired in the ecclesiastical morass of theological controversies. Ignoring every issue that is petty and irrelevant, the body of Christ must come together in fraternal love, forgive one another for centuries of malfeasance, let people hear and respond to the Master's life-giving question to Peter, "Do you love me?" and allow Jesus' sovereignty to become a reality in the realm of Christian freedom.

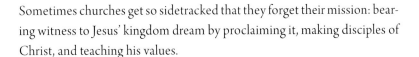

Sometimes churches get so sidetracked that they forget their mission: bearing witness to Jesus' kingdom dream by proclaiming it, making disciples of Christ, and teaching his values.

*Jesus, help me ignore petty, irrelevant issues and instead help people respond to your love through my witness. Amen.*

# COUNTING THE COST

## Dallas Willard

> "The kingdom of heaven is like a merchant seeking fine
> pearls, and upon finding one pearl of great value, he
> went and sold all that he had and bought it."
>
> MATTHEW 13:45–46 NASB

Only with such images before us can we correctly assess the famous "cost of discipleship" of which so much is made. Do you think the businessman who found the pearl was sweating over its cost? An obviously ridiculous question! What about the one who found the treasure in the field—perhaps crude oil or gold? No. Of course not. The only thing these people were sweating about was whether they would "get the deal." Now that is the soul of the disciple.

No one goes sadly, reluctantly into discipleship with Jesus. No one goes in bemoaning the cost. They understand the opportunity. And one of the things that has most obstructed the path of discipleship in our Christian culture today is this idea that it will be a terribly difficult thing that will certainly ruin your life.

So this counting of the cost is not a moaning and groaning session. The counting of the cost is to bring us to the point of clarity and decisiveness. It is to help us to see.

---

The man who discovered the pearl counted the cost of pursuing it. When he did, he was ecstatic and determined to get it.

*Lord, forgive me for sometimes finding the cost of discipleship burdensome. Help me instead to rejoice in this glorious gift! Amen.*

# GOD DOESN'T NEED OUR HELP

## A. W. Tozer

The God who made the world and everything in it, he who is Lord
of heaven and earth, does not live in shrines made by human hands,
nor is he served by human hands, as though he needed anything,
since he himself gives to all mortals life and breath and all things.

ACTS 17:24–25 NRSV

Almighty God, just because he is almighty, needs no support. The picture of a nervous, ingratiating God fawning over men to win their favor is not a pleasant one; yet if we look at the popular conception of God that is precisely what we see. Twentieth-century Christianity has put God on charity. So lofty is our opinion of ourselves that we find it quite easy, not to say enjoyable, to believe that we are necessary to God. But the truth is that God is not greater for our being, nor would he be less if we did not exist. That we do exist is altogether of God's free determination, not by our desert nor by divine necessity.

Probably the hardest thought of all for our natural egotism to entertain is that God does not need our help.

While we often represent God as a busy, eager, and somewhat frustrated heavenly Father who seeks help to carry out his plan to bring peace and salvation to the world, God needs no help and no helpers.

*Lord, I acknowledge your all-sufficiency,
and I ask only to serve you. Amen.*

# NEW CREATION'S BIRTH PANGS

## N. T. Wright

> We know that the whole creation groans and suffers
> the pains of childbirth together until now.
>
> ROMANS 8:22 NASB

Paul uses the image of birth pangs—a well-known Jewish metaphor for the emergence of God's new age—not only of the church in Romans 8:23 and of the Spirit a couple of verses later but also here in verse 22 of creation itself. Once again this highlights both continuity and discontinuity. This is no smooth evolutionary transition, in which creation simply moves up another gear into a higher mode of life. This is traumatic, involving convulsions and contractions and the radical discontinuity in which mother and child are parted and become not one being but two.

But neither is this a dualistic rejection of physicality as though, because the present creation is transient and full of decay and death, God must throw it away and start again from scratch. The very metaphor Paul chooses for this decisive moment in his argument shows that what he has in mind is not the unmaking of creation or simply its steady development but the drastic and dramatic birth of new creation from the womb of the old.

Although creation is not the way it's supposed to be, God isn't finished with it. The Father, Son, and Holy Spirit are birthing something new in our midst—a new creation. What do you long to see made new?

> God, I praise you for the creation work you are
> birthing; I look forward to its full arrival. Amen.

# WHAT IS A CHRISTIAN?

## Frederick Buechner

"I am the way, and the truth, and the life. No one
comes to the Father except through me."

JOHN 14:6 NRSV

Some think of a Christian as one who necessarily *believes* certain things. That Jesus was the Son of God, say. Or that Mary was a virgin. Or that the pope is infallible. Or that all other religions are wrong.

Some think of a Christian as one who necessarily *does* certain things. Such as going to church. Getting baptized. Giving up liquor and tobacco. Reading the Bible. Doing a good deed today.

Some think of a Christian as just a Nice Guy.

Jesus didn't say that any particular ethic, doctrine, or religion was the way, the truth, and the life. He said that he was. He didn't say that it was by believing or doing anything in particular that you would "come to the Father." He said that it was only by him—by living, participating in, being caught up by the way of life that he embodied, that was his way.

A Christian is one who is on the way, though not necessarily very far along it, and has at least some dim and half-baked idea of whom to thank. A Christian isn't necessarily any nicer than anybody else. Just better informed.

───ᘓᘈᘍ───

What do you think when you hear the word *Christian*? Does it reflect Jesus' definition?

> *Father, I want to be caught up in Jesus' way of life.*
> *Will you help me accomplish that? Amen.*

# SOMETHING UNIMAGINABLE

## Frederick Buechner

> He is not here; for He is risen, as He said.
>
> MATTHEW 28:6 NKJV

The Gospels are far from clear as to just what happened. It began in the dark. The stone had been rolled aside. Matthew alone speaks of an earthquake. There were two white-clad figures or possibly just one. Mary Magdalen seems to have gotten there first. One account says Peter came with another disciple. There was the sound of people running, of voices. Matthew speaks of "fear and great joy." Confusion was everywhere. There is no agreement even as to the role of Jesus himself. Did he appear at the tomb or only later? Where? To whom?

It is not a major production at all, and it's not really even much of a story, and that is of course the power of it. It doesn't have the ring of great drama. It has the ring of truth. When it comes to just what happened, there can be no certainty. That something unimaginable happened, there can be no doubt.

He rose. A few saw him briefly and talked to him. If it is true, there is nothing left to say. If it is not true, there is nothing left to say. For believers and unbelievers both, life has never been the same again. For some, neither has death. What is left now is the emptiness. There are those who, like Magdalen, will never stop searching it till they find his face.

What "unimaginable" things have happened in your life because of Easter?

*Lord Jesus, thank you for the promise and life shining
in the world because of your resurrection. Amen.*

# THE DNA OF PRAYER

## Eugene Peterson

A Psalm of David the servant of the Lord, who spoke to the Lord
the words of this song on the day that the Lord delivered him
from the hand of all his enemies and from the hand of Saul.

NOTE PREFACING PSALM 18 NKJV

Spiritualized prayer is denatured prayer, prayer in which all the dirt and noise of ordinary life is boiled out. It is a prayer that cultivates exalted feelings and sublime thoughts. It is prayer that is embarrassed by the coarse subject matter that intrudes itself into most twenty-four-hour periods but takes great pleasure in grand aphorisms. It is escapist prayer, with scheduled flights to the empyrean.

The psalm titles tug at our attention, saying, "Remember, this is a *story* you are in. By praying you do not get out of the difficult work of sin and enemy and family, you get further into it. Instead of finding it easier, you will find it more demanding. You will not become spiritualized and above it all. You are no longer exterior; you are an insider to yourself, to others, and to God."

The editors of Psalms, knowing our weakness for spiritualizing prayer, offered details to connect prayer to peoples' stories. The details form the DNA of prayer.

*Lord, help me to pray about the nitty-gritty*
*as well as the sublime in my story. Amen.*

# WHEN YOU SUFFER, EXPECT THE SPIRIT

## N. T. Wright

> We are more than conquerors through him who loved us.
>
> ROMANS 8:37 NRSV

Christian spirituality normally involves a measure of suffering. Both Paul and John lay great stress on this. Those who follow Jesus are called to live by the rules of the new world rather than the old one, and the old one won't like it.

Suffering may, then, take the form of actual persecution. Even in the liberal modern Western world—perhaps precisely in that world!—people can suffer discrimination because of their commitment to Jesus Christ. But suffering comes in many other forms, too: illness, depression, bereavement, moral dilemmas, poverty, tragedy, accidents, and death. Nobody reading the New Testament or any of the other Christian literature from the first two or three centuries could have accused the early Christians of painting too rosy a picture of what life would be like for those who follow Jesus.

But the point is this: it is precisely when we are suffering that we can most confidently expect the Spirit to be with us.

Just before the cross Jesus asked his Father if he really had to experience the horrible suffering that lay ahead. The answer was yes. Quite often, so do we. Yet the Spirit is with us.

*Lord, when suffering for your name befalls me, may I trust your Spirit to strengthen and help me. Amen.*

# A JUDGE WITH JUSTICE AND MERCY

## Frederick Buechner

According to my gospel, God, through Jesus Christ,
will judge the secret thoughts of all.

Romans 2:16 nrsv

We are all of us judged every day. We are judged by the face that looks back at us from the bathroom mirror. We are judged by the faces of the people we love and by the faces and lives of our children and by our dreams. Each day finds us at the junction of many roads, and we are judged as much by the roads we have not taken as by the roads we have.

There will come a Day on which all our days and all the judgments upon us and all our judgments upon each other will themselves be judged. The judge will be Christ. In other words, the one who judges us most finally will be the one who loves us most fully.

Romantic love is blind to everything except what is lovable and lovely, but Christ's love sees us with terrible clarity and sees us whole. Christ's love so wishes our joy that it is ruthless against everything in us that diminishes our joy. The worst sentence Love can pass is that we behold the suffering which Love has endured for our sake, and that is also our acquittal. The justice and mercy of the Judge are ultimately one.

───◈───

One day the one who will stand as your Judge will also be the one who loves you beyond imagining.

*Jesus, thank you that your justice and loving mercy are one. Amen.*

# OFFER FORGIVENESS BEFORE WORSHIP

## Dallas Willard

> "If you are offering your gift at the altar and there remember that
> your brother or sister has something against you, leave your gift
> there in front of the altar. First go and be reconciled to them."
>
> MATTHEW 5:23–24

To get the full impact of this illustration we have to imagine ourselves being married or baptized or ordained to some special role, such as pastor. In the midst of the proceedings, we walk out to seek reconciliation with someone who is not even there. That pictures the kingdom love that is kingdom rightness. Jesus' selection of this scene to illustrate the quality of the kingdom heart continues the long-established prophetic emphasis in Israel, which always weighted the moral over the ritual.

Now just think of what the quality of life and character must be in a person who would routinely interrupt sacred rituals to pursue reconciliation with a fellow human being. What kind of thought life, what feeling tones and moods, what habits of body and mind, what kinds of deliberations and choices would you find in such a person? When you answer these questions, you will have a vision of the true "rightness beyond" that is at home in God's kingdom of power and love.

---

Do you have any strained relationships? As Jesus instructs, make peace, then bring your gift. The Lord desires mercy.

> *Lord, help me keep my relationships in good*
> *order that I may freely worship you. Amen.*

# THROUGH JESUS WE KNOW GOD

## N. T. Wright

Long ago God spoke to our ancestors in many and various ways by the prophets, but in these last days he has spoken to us by a Son, whom he appointed heir of all things, through whom he also created the worlds.

HEBREWS 1:1–2 NRSV

Jesus exploded into the life of ancient Israel—the life of the whole world, in fact—not as a teacher of timeless truths, nor as a great moral example, but as the one through whose life, death, and resurrection God's rescue operation was put into effect, and the cosmos turned its great corner at last. It is because of Jesus that Christians claim they know who the Creator God of the world really is. It is because he, a human being, is now with the Father in the dimension we call "heaven" that Christians came so quickly to speak of God as both Father and Son. It is because he remains as yet in heaven while we are on earth (though the Spirit makes him present to us) that Christians came to speak of the Spirit too as a distinct member of the divine Trinity. It is all because of Jesus that we speak of God the way we do.

---

Through Jesus, God has revealed more of himself than through any other means. Let's sit with Jesus to discover who God is and what he is like.

*Jesus, reveal to me the depths of the character of God so I can know him more fully. Amen.*

May

# BE HONEST ABOUT WHO YOU ARE

## James Bryan Smith

> Most gladly I will . . . boast in my infirmities, that
> the power of Christ may rest upon me.
>
> 2 Corinthians 12:9 nkjv

In order for us to begin the process of self-acceptance we will have to acknowledge our true selves. We do not need to beat ourselves up or call ourselves names or excessively confess our sinfulness. All we have to do is be realistic.

We are imperfect. We are highly dependent. We have no claims and no rights. We are sinners. Pretending that we are righteous simply keeps God at bay and delays our healing.

Saint Paul knew who he was, and therefore he relied all the more on God's grace. He even went so far as to say that he would boast of his weaknesses. The truth that we must accept if we are to be healed is the truth that we are weak and broken and imperfect, for that is who we are.

The inability to be weak before God is the nemesis of the spiritual life. Paul would often boast, but not of his own abilities, his wisdom, or his accomplishments. God's love and acceptance rested on him, a man who did not deserve it. Consequently he made his life a gift back to God.

Paul was proud not in himself but in God, for he understood who he was and the truth of God's undeserved acceptance.

*Jesus, show me how to be weak before you that I
may experience even more of your grace. Amen.*

# LIVE JESUS' DREAM

## Brennan Manning

"I will give you the keys of the kingdom of heaven."

MATTHEW 16:19

Even when preoccupied, distracted, or salivating, we each have a dream, a vision of life that corresponds to our convictions, embodies our uniqueness, and expresses what is life-giving within us. Whether altruistic or ignoble, the dream gives definition to our lives.

If security represents our highest aspiration, we may be owned and indentured by Aetna Life and Casualty; if pleasure is our priority, we will distribute our time and money in hedonistic pursuits; if scholarship rules, we will be properly pedigreed and securely settled in an academic environment. Even if the dream is unrealistic or temporarily on hold due to uncontrollable circumstances, it prods our consciousness, nurtures our fantasies, and inchoately sustains our will-to-meaning in the world.

The dream of Jesus Christ is the kingdom of God, and the committed Christian buys into his dream.

⁕

Jesus' kingdom dream is not an abstraction but a concrete, visible reality, forged by the personal commitment to act on his teachings. A commitment to Jesus that doesn't result in humble service, suffering discipleship, and creative love is an illusion.

*Jesus, may I build every moment of my
life upon your kingdom dream. Amen.*

# TINY GESTURES LEAD TO GREAT LIGHT

## Henri J. M. Nouwen

> Let the message of Christ dwell among you richly as
> you teach and admonish one another with all wisdom
> through psalms, hymns, and songs from the Spirit,
> singing to God with gratitude in your hearts.
>
> COLOSSIANS 3:16

How can we choose love when we have experienced so little of it? We choose love by taking small steps of love every time there is an opportunity. A smile, a handshake, a word of encouragement, a phone call, a card, an embrace, a kind greeting, a gesture of support, a moment of attention, a helping hand, a present, a financial contribution, a visit—all these are little steps of love.

Each step is like a candle burning in the night. It does not take the darkness away, but it guides us through the darkness. When we look back after many small steps of love, we will discover that we have made a long and beautiful journey.

———

What candles can you light today? Watch for opportunities. They'll come.

> *Jesus, teach me how to destroy darkness*
> *wherever I can, whenever I can. Amen.*

# SMALL YET TALL

## Henri J. M. Nouwen

> When I consider your heavens,
> the work of your fingers . . .
> what is mankind that you are mindful of them,
> human beings that you care for them?
>
> PSALM 8:3–4

As we look at the stars and let our minds wander into the many galaxies, we come to feel so small and insignificant that anything we do, say, or think seems completely useless. But if we look into our souls and let our minds wander into the endless galaxies of our interior lives, we become so tall and significant that everything we do, say, or think appears to be of great importance.

We have to keep looking both ways to remain humble *and* confident, humorous *and* serious, playful *and* responsible. Yes, the human being is very small and very tall. It is the tension between the two that keeps us spiritually awake.

———⛬———

Do you more often feel tall or small? How can you find a balance so that you don't become too great or too insignificant in your own or others' eyes?

*Lord, show me the way to a right balance between being great and small, since I am both. Amen.*

# OUR TRUE FUTURE CHRISTIAN HOPE

## N. T. Wright

> "Behold, the tabernacle of God is among men, and He will
> dwell among them, and they shall be His people, and God
> Himself . . . will wipe away every tear from their eyes; and there
> will no longer be any death; there will no longer be any mourning,
> or crying, or pain; the first things have passed away."
>
> REVELATION 21:3–4 NASB

All our language about the future is like a set of signposts pointing into a bright mist. The signpost doesn't provide a photograph of what we will find when we arrive but offers instead a true indication of the direction we should be traveling in. The New Testament image of the future hope of the whole cosmos, grounded in the resurrection of Jesus, gives as coherent a picture as we need or could have of the future that is promised to the whole world, a future in which, under the sovereign and wise rule of the creator God, decay and death will be done away with and a new creation born, to which the present one will stand as mother to child. What creation needs is neither abandonment nor evolution but rather redemption and renewal; and this is both promised and guaranteed by the resurrection of Jesus from the dead. This is what the whole world's waiting for.

---

Two extremes characterize our world's future hope: a secular humanistic progress and a divine abandonment. Both are hopeless. In Christ we await our full re-creation—that's our Christian hope.

> *Jesus, because of your resurrection I look forward
> to your coming to put all things to rights. Amen.*

# A HOLY EARTH

## Frederick Buechner

Let the heavens be glad, and let the earth rejoice;
And let them say among the nations, "The Lord reigns."

1 Chronicles 16:31 NASB

For thousands upon thousands of years people couldn't see the earth whole—only as much of it at a time as there was between wherever they happened to be and the horizon. Whatever wild ideas they had about how it came into being or who made it, they knew it had been around more or less forever.

Then suddenly pictures were taken from miles away, and we saw it at last for what it truly is. It is about the size of a dime. It is blue with swirls of silver. It shines. The blackness it floats in is so immense, it seems almost miraculously not to have swallowed it up long since. Seeing it like that for the first time, you think of Jesus seeing Jerusalem for the last time. His eyes fill with tears, as Luke describes it. "Would that even today you knew the things that make for peace!" he says. "For the days shall come . . ." (Luke 19:42–43). The holy city.

The holy earth. We must take such care of it. It must take such care of us. This side of paradise, we are each of us so nearly all the other has. There is darkness beyond our wildest imagining all around us. Among us there is just about enough light to get by.

———— ⟞⟡⟝ ————

How do you care for our one hand-made earth?

*Lord Jesus, remind me to appreciate*
*the beautiful world you made. Amen.*

# WORDS THAT CREATE AND DESTROY

## Henri J. M. Nouwen

> God said, "Let there be light"; and there
> was light. God saw that the light was good.
>
> GENESIS 1:3–4 NASB

Words, words, words. Our society is full of words: on billboards, on television screens, in newspapers and books. Words whispered, shouted, and sung. Words that move, dance, and change in size and color. Words that say, "Taste me, smell me, eat me, drink me, sleep with me," but most of all, "Buy me." With so many words around us, we quickly say, "Well, they're just words." Thus words have lost much of their power.

Still, the word has the power to create. When God speaks, God creates. When God says, "Let there be light" (Genesis 1:3), light is. God speaks light. For God, speaking and creating are the same. It is this creative power of the word we need to reclaim. What we say is very important. When we say, "I love you" and say it from the heart, we can give another person new life, new hope, new courage. When we say, "I hate you," we can destroy another person. Let's watch our words.

---

When God speaks, he creates—from light to our very own lives. Let's join him in using words to create goodness, being quick to breathe words of love in the lives of those we know and meet.

*Lord, stop me when I'm about to use words to destroy. Amen.*

# LOVE AS AN ACT OF THE WILL

## Frederick Buechner

My little children, let us not love in word
or in tongue, but in deed and in truth.

1 JOHN 3:18 NKJV

In the Christian sense, love is not primarily an emotion, but an act of the will. When Jesus tells us to love our neighbors, he is not telling us to love them in the sense of responding to them with a cozy emotional feeling. You can as easily produce a cozy emotional feeling on demand as you can a yawn or a sneeze. On the contrary, he is telling us to love our neighbors in the sense of being willing to work for their well-being even if it means sacrificing our own well-being to that end, even if it means sometimes just leaving them alone. Thus in Jesus' terms, we can love our neighbors without necessarily liking them. In fact liking them may stand in the way of loving them by making us overprotective sentimentalists instead of reasonably honest friends.

This does not mean that liking may not be a part of loving, only that it doesn't have to be. Sometimes liking follows on the heels of loving. It is hard to work for people's well-being very long without coming in the end to rather like them too.

---

Have you ever prayed regularly for an enemy? What happened? Did the enemy change? Did you?

*Father, show me how to contribute to my neighbor's*
*life, whether it's by contact or peace. Amen.*

# THE PRICE OF IDOLATRY

## N. T. Wright

They exchanged the truth about God for a lie, and worshiped and served created things rather than the Creator—who is forever praised. Amen.

ROMANS 1:25

You become like what you worship. When you gaze in awe, admiration, and wonder at something or someone, you begin to take on something of the character of the object of your worship. Those who worship money become, eventually, human calculating machines. Those who worship sex become obsessed with their own attractiveness or prowess. Those who worship power become more and more ruthless.

So what happens when you worship the creator God whose plan to rescue the world and put it to rights has been accomplished by the Lamb who was slain? The answer comes in the second golden rule: because you were made in God's image, worship makes you more truly human. When you gaze in love and gratitude at the God in whose image you were made, you do indeed grow. You discover more of what it means to be fully alive.

The opportunity, the invitation, the summons is there before us: to come and worship the true God, the Creator, the Redeemer, and to become more truly human by doing so.

---

When you worship an aspect of creation as though it were the Creator, you do so at a cost: you become less of a human. That's the price of idolatry.

*Creator, may I never exchange my worship of you for anything in creation; may I serve you alone. Amen.*

# LAUGH AND WEEP AT SUFFERING

## Frederick Buechner

"Blessed are you who weep now,
for you will laugh."

Luke 6:21 NRSV

This verse means not just that you shall laugh when the time comes, but that you can laugh a little even now in the midst of the weeping because you know that the time is coming. All appearances to the contrary notwithstanding, the ending will be a happy ending. That is what the laughter is about. It is the laughter of faith. It is the divine comedy.

In the meantime you weep, because if you have a heart to see it with, the world you see is in a thousand ways heartbreaking. Only the heartless can look at it unmoved, and that is presumably why Jesus says, "Woe to you that laugh now, for you shall mourn and weep" (Luke 6:25), meaning a different sort of laughter altogether—the laughter of callousness, mockery, indifference.

The happiness of the happy ending—what makes the comedy so rich—is the suggestion that ultimately even the callous and indifferent will take part in it. The fact that Jesus says they too will weep and mourn before they're done seems to mean that they too will grow hearts at last, the hard way, and once that happens, the sky is the limit.

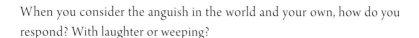

When you consider the anguish in the world and your own, how do you respond? With laughter or weeping?

*Jesus, may I weep when the world suffers and laugh when I suffer—all with faith in happy endings. Amen.*

# RESPONDING TO GOD'S SPEECH

## Eugene Peterson

> Day to day pours forth speech,
> and night to night declares knowledge.
>
> PSALM 19:2 NRSV

Prayer is everywhere and always answering speech. It is never initiating speech, and to suppose that it is is presumptuous. *Miqra*, the Hebrew word for Bible, properly means "calling out"—the calling out of God to us. "God must become a person,"[11] but in order for us to speak in answer to him he must make us into persons. We become ourselves as we answer, sometimes angrily disputing with him about how he rules the world, sometimes humbling ourselves before him in grateful trust. Prayer is language used to respond to the most that has been said to us, with the potential for saying all that is in us. Prayer is the development of speech into maturity, the language that is adequate to answering the one who has spoken comprehensively to us. Prayer is not a narrow use of language for specialty occasions, but language catholic, embracing the totality of everything and everyone everywhere. This conversation is both bold and devout—the utterly inferior responding to the utterly superior. In this exchange we become persons.

---

What would you like to discuss with God?

*Lord, I want to respond to your day-by-day speech,
talking with you about my life. Amen.*

# THE MEANING OF JESUS' ASCENSION

## N. T. Wright

"Do not hold on to me, because I have not yet ascended to the Father. But go to my brothers and say to them, 'I am ascending to my Father and your Father, to my God and your God.'"

JOHN 20:17 NRSV

What happens when you downplay or ignore the ascension? The answer is that the church expands to fill the vacuum. If Jesus is more or less identical with the church—if, that is, talk about Jesus can be reduced to talk about his presence within his people rather than his standing over against them and addressing them from elsewhere as their Lord, then we have created a high road to the worst kind of triumphalism.

Only when we grasp firmly that the church is not Jesus and Jesus is not the church—when we grasp, in other words, the truth of the ascension, that the one who is indeed present with us by the Spirit is also the Lord who is strangely absent, strangely other, strangely different from us and over against us, the one who tells Mary Magdalene not to cling to him—only then are we rescued from both hollow triumphalism and shallow despair.

The real time-space event of Jesus' ascension into heaven to the right hand of the Father means that he is Lord, over the church as much as the world. How should we respond to this reality?

*Jesus, you stand over me as Lord from heaven;*
*help me submit to your lordship on earth. Amen.*

# CHRIST'S DREAM

## Brennan Manning

> Just as a body, though one, has many parts, but all its
> many parts form one body, so it is with Christ.
>
> 1 CORINTHIANS 12:12

The dream of Jesus Christ is the kingdom of God, and the committed Christian buys into his dream. A life of integrity is born of fidelity to the dream. Daily we make choices that are either consistent with or contrary to the gospel vision. The mature Christian harmoniously integrates his or her faith, intellect, and feelings in consistent and fairly predictable behavior patterns. The sense of serenity that springs from this internal continuity is self-acceptance. The need for approval and the hunger for human respect diminish in proportion to our integrity. (The Scriptures call it *righteousness*, but the word has a pejorative tone in our times, as does *piety*, and both ought to be scrapped until such time as words are restored to their original meaning. They conjure up notions of legalism, spiritual superiority, and sanctimonious moralism that would make Jesus shudder.)

Each Christian gives flesh and bone to the dream with his or her unique, mysterious, and irreplaceable personality. The Word of God calls into being a faith community characterized by unity without uniformity. Jesus is the way, but his light is refracted in myriad ways by multiple personalities.

Christians show forth the light of Jesus' personality in countless ways. How can you refract his light?

*Lord, show me how to flesh out your kingdom. Amen.*

# WHO IS WELL-OFF IN GOD'S KINGDOM?

## Dallas Willard

> "Blessed are you who are poor,
> for yours is the kingdom of God."
>
> LUKE 6:20 NRSV

The financially poor addressed in the Beatitudes have available to them now and forever all of the resources of God's reign. Of course the rich too can be blessed. But if they are, their blessedness will not consist in their possessions, any more than that of the poor consists in their lack of possessions. Blessedness is in either case entirely a matter of provision enjoyed at the ever-present hand of God.

The Beatitudes are not a list that one must be on in order to be blessed, nor is the blessing they announce caused by the condition of those said to be blessed. Poverty, for example, is not the cause or reason for blessedness. Only entry into the kingdom of God provides such blessing. Instead, in the Beatitudes we have a list of those commonly regarded among humanity as being unblessable. In these teachings Jesus lays his ax to the root of the merely human value system and proclaims irrelevant those factors that humanity invokes in deciding who is and who is not well-off.

How do the Beatitudes redefine the blessed? Whom have you freshly realized is truly drenched with God's favor?

*Jesus, teach me what it means to be blessed in your kingdom. Amen.*

# MAKE WAY

## A. W. Tozer

> It is good for me to draw near to God;
> I have put my trust in the Lord GOD,
> That I may declare all Your works.
>
> PSALM 73:28 NKJV

The world is evil, the times are waxing late, and the glory of God has departed from the church as the fiery cloud once lifted from the door of the temple in the sight of Ezekiel the prophet.

The God of Abraham has withdrawn his conscious presence from us, and another god whom our fathers knew not is making himself at home among us. This god we have made and because we have made him we can understand him; because we have created him he can never surprise us, never overwhelm us, nor astonish us, nor transcend us.

The God of glory sometimes revealed himself like a sun to warm and bless indeed, but often to astonish, overwhelm, and blind before he healed and bestowed permanent sight. This God of our fathers wills to be the God of their succeeding race. We have only to prepare him a habitation in love and faith and humility. We have only to want him badly enough, and he will come and manifest himself to us.

Let us prepare room in our life habitations for the true God of glory. May we burn for his reappearance, believing we will find him when we seek him.

> *Lord, I seek your true self this day, beseech*
> *you to manifest yourself, believing you will. Amen.*

# TWO KINDS OF SPACE BROUGHT NEAR

## N. T. Wright

You alone are God over all the kingdoms of the
earth. You have made heaven and earth.

2 KINGS 19:15

When the Bible speaks of heaven and earth it is not talking about two localities related to each other within the same space-time continuum or about a nonphysical world contrasted with a physical one, but about two different kinds of what we call space, two different kinds of what we call matter, and also quite possibly (though this does not necessarily follow from the other two) two different kinds of what we call time. Although New Age thinkers, and indeed quite a lot of contemporary novelists are quite capable of taking us into other parallel worlds, spaces, and times, we retreat into our rationalistic closed-system universe as soon as we think about Jesus. C. S. Lewis of course did a great job in the Narnia stories and elsewhere of imagining how two worlds could relate and interlock. But the generation that grew up knowing its way around Narnia does not usually know how to make the transition from a children's story to the real world of grown-up Christian devotion and theology.

What the New Testament encourages us to grasp is that God's space and ours—heaven and earth—are very different yet not far away from one another.

*Lord, may your will be done in my*
*space as it is in your space. Amen.*

# JESUS DRAWS NEAR

## James Bryan Smith

> The centurion said, "Lord, I am not worthy
> for You to come under my roof."
>
> MATTHEW 8:8 NASB

The path of our healing is not one of self-improvement, but rather of self-surrender. Trying to improve our existing selves is precisely our problem. When we cease from the battle of trying to think well of ourselves and turn to God in complete nakedness, we will find nothing but acceptance.

We may fear that God will draw away from us, but in fact the opposite movement occurs. God is able to draw near to us the moment we surrender our need to control how he feels about us through our behavior. "Here I am, God. You know I am broken and wayward and foolish." These words dismantle our pride and allow God to penetrate our hearts.

All that really matters is being sincere about who we are. This is liberating in that we can now concentrate on the relationship that God has established with us through Christ. We can take our eyes off of ourselves and our vain notions of perfection and simply accept our failures and faults, not excusing them but seeing them as a part of who we are. We can then walk with Christ.

Like the centurion, we are invited to be honest about who we are. When we are, Jesus will draw near and answer us.

*Lord, I lay myself bare before you,*
*acknowledging all my poverty and need. Amen.*

# SEE THE WITHIN-YOU KINGDOM

## Brennan Manning

"The kingdom of God does not come with observation; nor will they say, 'See here!' or 'See there!' For indeed, the kingdom of God is within you."

LUKE 17:20–21 NKJV

The gospel portrait of Jesus is that of a man exquisitely attuned to his emotions and uninhibited in expressing them. One finds in Christ no attitude of scorn, contempt, fear, ridicule, or rejection of feelings as being fickle, flaky, and unreliable. They were sensitive emotional antennae to which he listened carefully and through which he perceived the will of his Father for congruent speech and action. There's an untapped mine of spiritual wisdom in the soporific slogan, "If it feels good, do it." Good feelings, consonant with our faith-commitment and intellectual perception, are signals for creative Christian conduct fruitful for ourselves, others, and the building of the kingdom.

The light we are seeking is inside. So often we search for God willy-nilly and do not find him until we return to ourselves. In active listening to our feelings we encounter the Holy, not in the earthquake and fire outside but, like Elijah, "in the sound of a gentle breeze" (1 Kings 19:12). The kingdom of God is in our midst.

How can you tune the ear of your heart to perceive the kingdom-will of God?

*Lord, give me a heart attuned to my feelings, seeking the within-me kingdom, in order to express your will. Amen.*

# TRANSCEND RELIGIOUS ACTS

## Dallas Willard

> "I tell you, unless your righteousness exceeds that of the scribes
> and Pharisees, you will never enter the kingdom of heaven."
>
> MATTHEW 5:20 NRSV

True blessedness is of course founded upon true righteousness. The poor and others can possess the kingdom that is their blessedness only by contacting it at the level of the heart or innermost personality. But in his fallen condition man identifies being right and good with the externals of behavior rather than with the aims and attitudes of his heart, the source of his life and personality.

But Jesus pointed out that entry into the rule of heaven, the experiential reign of God over our existence, comes to us only when we seek our righteousness beyond the field of specific action, where the scribe and the Pharisee play, at the level of fundamental aims and attitudes. It is at this point that the law and prophets see their intent realized. Here they can be fulfilled and not abolished. Attitudes of heart inspired by faith's vision of good in God's living rule over us, a vision brought to stunning focus in the death and resurrection of his Son on our behalf, reshape all of human relationships.

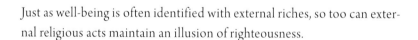

Just as well-being is often identified with external riches, so too can external religious acts maintain an illusion of righteousness.

*Jesus, show me how to pursue true righteousness*
*via the attitudes of my heart. Amen.*

# WHERE MOURNING AND DANCING TOUCH

## Henri J. M. Nouwen

> For everything there is a season. . . .
> a time to mourn, and a time to dance.
> ECCLESIASTES 3:1, 4 NRSV

Mourning and dancing are never fully separated. Their times do not necessarily follow each other. In fact, their times may become one time. Mourning may turn into dancing and dancing into mourning without showing a clear point where one ends and the other starts.

Often our grief allows us to choreograph our dance while our dance creates the space for our grief. We lose a beloved friend, and in the midst of our tears we discover an unknown joy. We celebrate a success, and in the midst of the party we feel deep sadness. Mourning and dancing, grief and laughter, sadness and gladness—they belong together as the sad-faced clown and the happy-faced clown, who make us both cry and laugh. Let's trust that the beauty of our lives becomes visible where mourning and dancing touch each other.

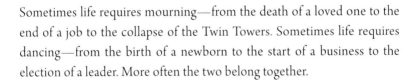

Sometimes life requires mourning—from the death of a loved one to the end of a job to the collapse of the Twin Towers. Sometimes life requires dancing—from the birth of a newborn to the start of a business to the election of a leader. More often the two belong together.

*Lord, thank you for the truth of Ecclesiastes and the joining of mourning and dancing. Amen.*

# WHAT LIFE IS ABOUT

## Dallas Willard

> "Therefore I tell you, do not worry about your life, what you
> will eat or drink; or about your body, what you will wear. Is not
> life more than food, and the body more than clothes?"
>
> MATTHEW 6:25

If we do value "mammon" as normal people seem to think we should, our fate is fixed. Our fate is anxiety. It is worry. It is frustration. The words *anxious* and *worry* both have reference to strangling or being choked. Certainly that is how we feel when we are anxious. Things and events have us by the throat and seem to be cutting off our life. We are being harmed, or we fear what will come upon us, and all our efforts are insufficient to do anything about it. Perhaps more energy has gone into dealing with this human situation than into anything else—from songs about "Don't Worry! Be Happy!" to $250-an-hour sessions with a therapist.

Because we have the option, in reliance upon Jesus, of having abundant treasures in the realm of the heavens, Jesus gives us another of his "therefores." Life is not about food, he continues to say, or the body about clothes. It is about a place in God's immortal kingdom now. Eternity is, in part, what we are now living.

———⚬⚬⚬———

Life isn't about stuff—food or clothes. It also isn't about worrying over such things. It's about God and life in his kingdom.

> *Lord, show me where I've made my life about
> anything less than you and kingdom living. Amen.*

# WHAT DOES JESUS WANT US TO DO?

## Dallas Willard

> When Jesus spoke again to the people, he said, "I am
> the light of the world. Whoever follows me will never
> walk in darkness, but will have the light of life."
>
> JOHN 8:12

A disciple, or apprentice, is simply someone who has decided to be with another person, under appropriate conditions, in order to become capable of doing what that person does or to become what that person is.

How does this apply to discipleship to Jesus? What is it, exactly, that he, the incarnate Lord, does? What, if you wish, is he "good at"? The answer is found in the Gospels: he lives in the kingdom of God, and he applies that kingdom for the good of others and even makes it possible for them to enter it for themselves. It is what he calls us to by saying, "Follow me."

Another important way of putting this is to say that I am learning from Jesus to live my life as he would live my life if he were I. I am not necessarily learning to do everything he did, but I am learning how to do everything I do in the manner that he did all that he did.

The life we were meant to live is found in the light of Jesus' life. May we follow him to be with him, in order to learn how to live in God's kingdom and show forth that light.

> *Jesus, shine your light through me as
> I follow you out of darkness. Amen.*

149

# THOU CHANGEST NOT

## A. W. Tozer

> "I am the Lord, I do not change."
>
> MALACHI 3:6 NKJV

In this world where men forget us, change their attitude toward us as their private interests dictate, and revise their opinion of us for the slightest cause, is it not a source of wondrous strength to know that God with whom we have to do changes not?

What peace it brings to the Christian's heart to realize that our heavenly Father never differs from himself. He is always receptive to misery and need, as well as to love and faith. He does not keep office hours nor set aside periods when he will see no one. Neither does he change his mind about anything. Today, at this moment, he feels toward his creatures, toward babies, toward the sick, the fallen, the sinful, exactly as he did when he sent his only begotten Son into the world to die for mankind.

In all our efforts to find God, to please Him, to commune with Him, we should remember that all change must be on our part. We have but to meet his clearly stated terms, bring our lives into accord with his revealed will, and his infinite power will become instantly operative toward us.

As the hope-filled hymn exclaims, "Thou changest not, thy compassions they fail not; as thou hast been, thou forever will be."[12]

*Lord, I'm thankful and awed that your attitude toward me now is the same as it was in eternity past and will be in eternity future. Amen.*

# THE LORD'S PRAYER SAYS "I'M IN"

## N. T. Wright

One day Jesus was praying in a certain place. When he
finished, one of his disciples said to him, "Lord, teach
us to pray, just as John taught his disciples."

Luke 11:1

The Lord's Prayer is a prayer about God's honor and glory. It's a prayer about God's kingdom coming on earth as in heaven—which pretty much sums up what a lot of Christianity is all about. It's a prayer for bread, for meeting the needs of every day. And it's a prayer for rescue from evil.

The prayer says: I want to be part of his kingdom-movement. I find myself drawn into his heaven-on-earth way of living. I want to be part of his bread-for-the-world agenda, for myself and for others. I need forgiveness for myself—from sin, from debt, from every weight around my neck—and I intend to live with forgiveness in my heart in my own dealings with others. And because I live in the real world, where evil is still powerful, I need protecting and rescuing. And in and through it all, I acknowledge and celebrate the Father's kingdom, power, and glory.

───⊶⊷───

Learn the Lord's Prayer (see Matthew 6:9–13). It is a way of saying to God that Jesus has caught you in the net of his good news.

*Jesus, thank you for prayer, and for allowing
me to join in your kingdom-movement. Amen.*

# GOD IS GREATER

## James Bryan Smith

> God is greater than our hearts, and he knows everything.
>
> 1 JOHN 3:20 NRSV

God has chosen to accept what we deem unacceptable. The parts of us that cause us shame do not shame God. Here is the good news: even if we feel condemned by our own hearts, God is greater than our hearts.

We may feel deep shame, and we may condemn ourselves unmercifully, but God does not. And if God does not condemn us, then who are we to condemn ourselves? Are we greater than God? Is our insight greater than God's?

God's acceptance should lead us to self-acceptance. Grace heals our shame not by trying to find something good and lovely within us that is worth loving but by looking at us as we are, the good and the bad, the lovely and the unlovely, and simply accepting us. God accepts us with the promise that we will never be unacceptable to him. It is ours to do the same for ourselves.

---

Do you accept that you're accepted—by the God of the universe, the one who made and saved you? Receive this truth this day, rest in it, and live in it.

> *Lord, if my heart condemns me, remind me that I am accepted—by you. Amen.*

# BRINGING THE KINGDOM INTO REAL LIFE

## Dallas Willard

"Your kingdom come.
Your will be done,
on earth as it is in heaven."

MATTHEW 6:10 NRSV

When Jesus directs us to pray, "Thy kingdom come," he does not mean we should pray for it to come into existence. Rather we pray for it to take over at all points in the personal, social, and political order where it is now excluded: "on earth as it is in heaven." With this prayer we are invoking it, as in faith we are acting it, into the real world of our daily existence.

Within his overarching dominion God has created us and has given each of us, like him, a range of will—beginning from our minds and bodies and extending outward, ultimately to a point not wholly predetermined but open to the measure of our faith. His intent is for us to learn to mesh our kingdom with the kingdoms of others. Love of neighbor, rightly understood, will make this happen. But we can only love adequately by taking as our primary aim the integration of our rule with God's. That is why love of neighbor is the second, not the first, commandment and why we are told to seek first the kingdom, or rule, of God.

※

It is only as we discover God's kingdom, settle into it, and live its love that we can properly walk with God as he intended—on earth as in heaven.

*Lord, may I love adequately and seek first your rule. Amen.*

# FACE-TO-FACE WITH JESUS

## N. T. Wright

*Now we see only a reflection as in a mirror; then we shall see face to face.
Now I know in part; then I shall know fully, even as I am fully known.*

1 CORINTHIANS 13:12

The presence we know at the moment—the presence of Jesus with his people in word and sacrament, by the Spirit, through prayer, in the faces of the poor—is of course related to that future presence, but the distinction between them is important and striking. Jesus' appearing will be, for those of us who have known and loved him here, like meeting face-to-face someone we have only known by letter, telephone, or perhaps email. Communication theorists insist that for full human communication you need not only words on a page but also a tone of voice. For full communication between human beings you need not only a tone of voice but also body language, facial language, and the thousand small ways in which, without realizing it, we relate to one another. At the moment, by the Spirit, the Word, the sacraments and prayer, and in those in need whom we are called to serve for his sake, the absent Jesus is present to us; but one day he will be there with us, face-to-face.

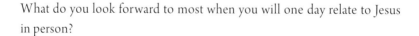

What do you look forward to most when you will one day relate to Jesus in person?

*Lord Jesus, I long for the day when we can talk as friends do on a day-to-day basis. Come quickly. Amen.*

# THE GOD WHO CREATES FROM NOTHING

## Frederick Buechner

In the beginning God created the heavens and the earth.

GENESIS 1:1 NASB

To *make* suggests making something out of something else the way a carpenter makes wooden boxes out of wood. To *create* suggests making something out of nothing the way an artist makes paintings or poems. It is true that artists, like carpenters, have to use something else—paint, words—but the beauty or meaning they make is different from the material they make it out of. To create is to make something essentially new.

When God created the creation, God made something where before there had been nothing. Using the same old materials of earth, air, fire, and water, every twenty-four hours God creates something new out of them. If you think you're seeing the same show all over again seven times a week, you're crazy. Every morning you wake up to something that in all eternity never was before and never will be again. And the you that wakes up was never the same before and will never be the same again either.

The ancient Christian creeds remind us that God the Father is the Maker of heaven and earth. What does it mean to you and your experience of the heart of God that he *makes*, that he *creates*—the universe, the world, even you and your life?

> *Lord, I praise you as you make my life*
> *into something with meaning. Amen.*

# MAKE YOUR CHOICE THIS DAY

## A. W. Tozer

> Choose for yourselves this day whom you will serve.
>
> JOSHUA 24:15

Within the broad field of God's sovereign, permissive will the deadly conflict of good and evil continues with increasing fury. God will yet have his way in the whirlwind and the storm, but the storm and the whirlwind are here, and as responsible beings we must make our choice in the present moral situation.

The whole matter of moral choice centers around Jesus Christ. The gospel message embodies three distinct elements: an announcement, a command, and a call. It announces the good news of redemption accomplished in mercy, it commands all men everywhere to repent, and it calls all men to surrender to the terms of grace by believing on Jesus Christ as Lord and Savior.

We must all choose whether we will obey the gospel or turn away in unbelief and reject its authority. Our choice is our own, but the consequences of that choice have already been determined by the sovereign will of God, and from this there is no appeal.

———— ∞∞∞ ————

Jesus said plainly if we are not with him, we are against him (Matthew 12:30). What choice have you made? Whom will you serve?

> *Jesus, I choose this day to serve you and*
> *you alone, fully and wholeheartedly. Amen.*

# HOLY ORDERS, HOLY WORK

## Eugene Peterson

*You made [humankind] rulers over the works of your hands;*
*you put everything under their feet.*

PSALM 8:6

Work derives from and represents the sovereign God, who expresses his sovereignty as a worker: kingwork. Sovereigns work to bring order out of chaos; guard and fight for the sanctity of things and people; deliver victims from injustice and misfortune and wretchedness; grant pardon to the condemned and damned; heal sickness; and by their very presence bring dignity and honor to people and land. God's sovereignty isn't abstract—it's a *working* sovereignty and is expressed in work. All of our work is intended as an extension of and participation in that sovereignty.

When the psalmist reflects on the unique place of humans in God's creation, it's our work that's singled out for attention. God works and we work; in the workplace we become aware of the continuities.

Dignity is inherent in work. Royalty is inherent in work. A major and essential task of the Christian is to recover work as vocation—as holy work. Every Christian takes holy orders.

---

Let us recapture the essence of vocation, for we are kingworkers.

*Lord, reveal to me the specific orders you have*
*for me to help complete your holy work. Amen.*

# DO YOU *BELIEVE* OR *BELIEVE IN*?

## Frederick Buechner

> Yes, Lord, I believe that You are the Christ, the Son
> of God, who is to come into the world.
>
> JOHN 11:27 NKJV

Believing in God is an intellectual position. It need have no more effect on your life than believing in Freud's method of interpreting dreams or the theory that Sir Francis Bacon wrote *Romeo and Juliet*. Believing God is something else again. It is less a position than a journey, less a realization than a relationship. It doesn't leave you cold like believing the world is round. It stirs your blood like believing the world is a miracle. It affects who you are and what you do with your life like believing your house is on fire or somebody loves you.

We believe in God when for one reason or another we choose to do so. We believe God when somehow we run into God in a way that by and large leaves us no choice to do otherwise.

When Jesus says that whoever believes "into" him shall never die, he does not mean that to be willing to sign your name to the Nicene Creed guarantees eternal life. Eternal life is not the result of *believing in*. It is the experience of *believing*.

In regard to your faith, have you taken a position, or are you on a journey?

*Father, thank you for the option to believe. I do. Amen.*

June

# BELOVED, ADOPTED CHILD

## James Bryan Smith

> You did not receive a spirit of slavery to fall back into
> fear, but you have received a spirit of adoption.
>
> ROMANS 8:15 NRSV

We are able to accept ourselves only on God's terms. His acceptance of us is not based on any qualities we possess. Trying to build a proper self-image on those grounds would surely collapse. But his acceptance is a promise, and therefore it is received through an act of faith.

Perhaps *trust* is the better word. Just as a child trusts in his or her parents' acceptance, not based on performance but on the basis of being a child, so too we are being called to become children again. We are learning to trust. We are urged to make peace with our flawed existence and, even more, to risk that the mystery of our being is trustworthy.

May we have the courage not to run when the voice of our condemning heart would tear us from the place where we can hear the voice of God saying to us, "You are my beloved child, in whom I am well pleased."

God's acceptance of me as I am allows me to accept myself as I am. In fact, not to accept myself would be to reject God's voice, the voice that tells me I am his "Beloved"—his fully adopted child.

> *Lord, thank you for adopting me as your own child;*
> *help me to accept that acceptance. Amen.*

# OTHER CHRISTS

## Brennan Manning

As many of you as were baptized into Christ have put on Christ.

GALATIANS 3:27 NKJV

When we "put on Christ" and fully accept who we are, a healthy independence from peer pressure, people-pleasing, and human respect develops. Christ's preferences and values become our own. The kingdom of God is built on earth when we do the will of our Father in heaven. We become "other Christs" through a life of Christian integrity. The same openness to feelings, simplicity of speech, intimacy with the Father, spirit of humble service, compassionate healing, suffering disciple-ship, and obedient love is wrought in us by the Paraclete, accomplishing what Paul means by "new creation."

We ought to humbly underline the title "other Christs," for nothing less describes the reality. In days of yore, this dignity was reserved for an elite, a select few of the "holy nation" on the basis of ordination through the laying on of hands. Nothing is further from the gospel truth. This is a serious injustice to the "royal priesthood," which includes all the holy people of God. Every Christian who walks in the way of integrity and fidelity to the dream of the kingdom is "another Christ."

Have you ever noticed the qualities of Christ—simple speech, intimate acquaintance with the Father, love shown in obedience—in yourself?

*Jesus, build in me the qualities of integrity and fidelity. Amen.*

# PLANK-EYE SYNDROME

## Dallas Willard

> "How can you say to your neighbor, 'Let me take the speck out
> of your eye,' while the log is in your own eye? You hypocrite."
>
> MATTHEW 7:4–5 NRSV

How does Jesus know that those who "judge," in the sense of condemning others, are hypocrites? Is it merely that there must be something wrong with us, because there is something wrong with everyone, and that we should not condemn others until we are perfect? Is it just the let-him-who-is-without-sin-cast-the-first-stone routine? No, that's not it. Rather it is because he understands what condemnation is and involves.

Condemnation is the board in our eye. He knows that the mere fact that we are condemning someone shows our heart does not have the kingdom rightness he has been talking about. Condemnation, especially with its usual accompaniments of anger and contempt and self-righteousness, blinds us to the reality of the other person. We cannot "see clearly" how to assist our brother, because we cannot see our brother. And we will never know how to truly help him until we have grown into the kind of person who does not condemn. Period.

We all suffer from plank-eye syndrome. But the reason we cure it isn't so we can justifiably correct or condemn our brother. It's because we want to be the kind of persons Jesus calls us to be.

> *Jesus, cure me of plank-eye syndrome, growing
> me into a person free from condemnation. Amen.*

# NO ESCAPING GOD'S GAZE

## A. W. Tozer

You have set our iniquities before you,
our secret sins in the light of your presence.
PSALM 90:8

In the divine omniscience we see set forth against each other the terror and fascination of the Godhead. That God knows each person through and through can be a cause of shaking fear to the man who has something to hide. The unblessed soul may well tremble that God knows the flimsiest of every pretext and never accepts the poor excuses given for simple conduct, since he knows perfectly the real reason for it.

And to us who have fled for refuge to lay hold upon the hope that is set before us in the gospel, how unutterably sweet it is that our heavenly Father knows us completely. No talebearer can inform on us, no forgotten skeleton can come tumbling out of some hidden closet to abash us and expose our past; and no unsuspected weakness in our characters can come to light to turn God away from us, since he knew us utterly before we knew him and called us to himself in the full knowledge of everything that was against us.

We don't have to hide, for in Christ we face no condemnation for our deeds done in darkness.

> Lord, I am thankful I can stand before you,
> for I am not condemned. Amen.

# GOD IS GOOD, AND JUDGE

## N. T. Wright

> The LORD will judge the ends of the earth.
>
> 1 SAMUEL 2:10 NASB

The picture of Jesus as the coming Judge is the central feature of another absolutely vital and nonnegotiable Christian belief: that there will indeed be a judgment in which the creator God will set the world right once and for all. The word *judgment* carries negative overtones for a good many people in our liberal and postliberal world. We need to remind ourselves that throughout the Bible, not least in the Psalms, God's coming judgment is a good thing, something to be celebrated, longed for, yearned over. It causes people to shout for joy and the trees of the field to clap their hands.

In a world of systematic injustice, bullying, violence, arrogance, and oppression, the thought that there might come a day when the wicked are firmly put in their place and the poor and weak are given their due is the best news there can be. Faced with a world in rebellion, a world full of exploitation and wickedness, a good God *must* be a God of judgment.

Why might God's judgment—against the bully and vile, the murderers and oppressors—be cause for celebration and a reflection of his goodness?

*Lord, your coming judgment is another praiseworthy aspect of your character. Therefore I long for it and the revelation of justice on earth. Amen.*

# ONE LOAF, ONE BODY

## Frederick Buechner

Because there is one loaf, we, who are many, are
one body, for we all share the one loaf.

1 CORINTHIANS 10:17

All the duplication of effort and waste of human resources. All the counterproductive competition. All the unnecessarily empty pews and unnecessary expense. Then add to that picture the Roman Catholic Church, still more divided from the Protestant denominations than they are from each other, and by the time you're through, you don't know whether to burst into laughter or into tears.

When Jesus took the bread and said, "This is my body, which is broken for you" (1 Corinthians 11:24), it's hard to believe that even in his wildest dreams he foresaw the tragic and ludicrous brokenness of the church as his body. There's no reason why everyone should be Christian in the same way and every reason to leave room for differences, but if all the competing factions of Christendom were to give as much of themselves to the high calling and holy hope that unite them as they do now to the relative inconsequentialities that divide them, the church would look more like the kingdom of God for a change and less like an ungodly mess.

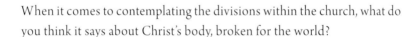

When it comes to contemplating the divisions within the church, what do you think it says about Christ's body, broken for the world?

*Lord, make me aware of the ways in which I focus on
petty differences rather than the reasons for unity among
the different branches of your church. Amen.*

# HOW ARE YOU GOING TO LIVE?

## Eugene Peterson

> Saul clothed David with his armor; he put a bronze helmet on his head and clothed him with a coat of mail. . . . Then David said to Saul, "I cannot walk with these; for I am not used to them." So David removed them.
>
> 1 Samuel 17:38–39 NRSV

The way we do our work is as important as the work we do. Means must be authentic, true, appropriate to our prayers and proclamations.

David left Saul's armor behind and walked out into the Valley of Elah clean and spare, traveling light, delivered from an immense clutter; and he kneeled at the brook.

David at that moment, kneeling at the brook, frames something that's absolutely essential for each of us. Are we going to live this life from our knees, imaginatively and personally? Or are we going to live it conventionally and secondhand? Are we going to live out of our God-created, Spirit-anointed, Jesus-saved being? Or are we going to toady and defer to eunuch professionals? Are we going to be shaped by our fears of Goliath or by God? Are we going to live by our admiration of Saul or by God?

David rejected the suggestion that he live inauthentically by using Saul's armor; instead he lived out of the fullness of who he truly was. And then he killed the giant.

*Lord, show me how to travel light, unburdened by others' expectations and demands, so I can fulfill your will for me. Amen.*

# WORK FOR THE "DAY"

## N. T. Wright

Each one's work will become clear; for the Day will
declare it, because it will be revealed by fire; and the
fire will test each one's work, of what sort it is.

1 CORINTHIANS 3:13 NKJV

The task of the church between ascension and Parousia is set free both from the self-driven energy that imagines it has to build God's kingdom all by itself and from the despair that supposes it can't do anything until Jesus comes again. We do not "build the kingdom" all by ourselves, but we do build for the kingdom. All that we do in faith, hope, and love in the present, in obedience to our ascended Lord and in the power of his Spirit, will be enhanced and transformed at his appearing. This too brings a note of judgment, of course, as Paul makes clear in 1 Corinthians 3:10–17. The "day" will disclose what sort of work each builder has done.

People who believe that Jesus is already Lord and that he will appear again as Judge of the world are called and equipped (to put it mildly) to think and act quite differently in the world from those who don't.

How do you think the fruits of your labor, when Jesus evaluates them, will fare? Any changes you need to make?

*Lord, remind me of my responsibility to build for the kingdom;*
*I want your Day to disclose my work as sound. Amen.*

# RICH OR POOR, GOD MADE THEM BOTH

## Dallas Willard

> Rich and poor have this in common:
> The LORD is the Maker of them all.
>
> PROVERBS 22:2

The indispensable first step in right love and care for the poor and needy is to be conscious of them, to see them as God's creatures of equal significance with anyone else in the divine purpose. As we are to honor all human beings (1 Peter 2:17), so we are to honor the poor. We are to respect them and show them our respect. The distinction between rich and poor is permanently affixed to human life. It is the natural and inevitable consequence of differentiation within peoples' histories and family contexts, as well as of differences in genetic endowment that are an arrangement instituted by God, which explains why Scripture never suggests that poverty is to be abolished. On the other hand, it always insists that the needy are to be cared for, that the poor are not to be taken advantage of but defended, and that they are to be taken into consideration in all aspects of life.

The overarching command is to love, and the first act of love is always attention. Therefore, the poor are not to be avoided and forgotten.

———— ✺ ————

What steps can you take to remember the commonality shared between rich and poor, in order to notice and consider them?

> *Heavenly Father, help me heed the poor in my path, and make sure I provide whatever care for them I can. Amen.*

# BE HONEST IN PRAYER

## Eugene Peterson

Do not remember the sins of my youth
and my rebellious ways.

PSALM 25:7

Sin is not what is wrong with our minds; it is the catastrophic disorder in which we find ourselves at odds with God. This is the human condition. The facts of this disorder are all around and within us, but we would prefer to forget them. To remember them is also to remember God, and to remember God is to have to live strenuously, vigorously, and in love. We have moments when we desire to do this, but the moments don't last long. We would rather play golf. We would rather take another battery of tests at the hospital. We would rather take another course at the university. We keep looking for ways to improve our lives without dealing with God. But we can't do it.

When we pray, we immerse ourselves in the living presence of God. When we pray the Psalms we pray through all the parts of our lives and our history and cover the ground of our intricate implication in sin.

When we confront sins in prayer, the Lord promises to forgive them, forget them, and cleanse us.

*Lord, I confront my sins, praying you will forgive them, cleanse me of them, and remember them no longer. Amen.*

# WHAT IS COMPASSION?

## Brennan Manning

> Jesus called His disciples to Him, and said,
> "I feel compassion for the people."
>
> MATTHEW 15:32 NASB

The church, the visible extension of Jesus Christ in time and space, is the image of the Compassionate One. Compassion is not sloppy sentimentality, nor does it compromise the truth. Clearly, the teaching of first-century Rabbi Hillel, which sanctioned a husband divorcing his wife because she was not a good cook, is lunatic liberalism. Any spirituality that tampers with the Word of God from naive humanitarian motives is bankrupt. Saint Augustine observed long ago that, where there is any scent of a lie, the authority of the truth is immediately weakened. Biblical compassion, combining heartfelt emotion with active relief for the suffering, transcends psychological personalism and privatized pity to enter into the very heart and mystery of God. Clear-minded, hardheaded, and softhearted, Jesus revealed in his ministry of mercy the face of the compassionate God.

As the continuing presence of Christ, we should ask, *How would Jesus show empathy in this situation?* and then act as he would.

*Jesus, show me how to follow you
by being compassionate. Amen.*

# THE ESSENCE OF ETERNAL LIFE

## Dallas Willard

"Very truly I tell you, whoever hears my word and
believes him who sent me has eternal life and will not be
judged but has crossed over from death to life."

JOHN 5:24

The invitation to come out of the darkness and live right-side up in the light makes no sense to many. Thus we need to restate and further explain some of the essential points about the eternal kind of life now available to us within the ever-present governance of God.

Jesus came among us to show and teach the life for which we were made. He came very gently, opened access to the governance of God with him, and set afoot a conspiracy of freedom in truth among human beings. Having overcome death he remains among us. By relying on his word and presence we are enabled to reintegrate the little realm that makes up our life into the infinite rule of God. And that is the eternal kind of life. Caught up in his active rule, our deeds become an element in God's eternal history. They are what God and we do together, making us part of his life and him a part of ours.

Jesus invites us to cross over from death to life right now, so that our every day is enmeshed with God's activity, rule, life. He promises that when we listen to him and believe him, we've got that kind of life.

*Jesus, may I experience the essence
of your eternal life right now. Amen.*

# OUR FAITH'S "TODAY" PROMISE

## N. T. Wright

> Jesus answered him, "Truly I tell you, today
> you will be with me in paradise."
>
> LUKE 23:43

Paradise is here: not a final destination but the blissful garden, the parkland of rest and tranquility, where the dead are refreshed as they await the dawn of the new day. The main point of the sentence lies in the apparent contrast between the brigand's request and Jesus' reply: "Remember me," he says, "when you come in your kingdom." Jesus' answer brings this future hope into the present, implying of course that with his death the kingdom is indeed coming even though it doesn't look like what anyone had imagined. There will still, of course, be a future completion involving ultimate resurrection; Luke's overall theological understanding leaves no doubt on that score. Jesus, after all, didn't rise again "today," that is, on Good Friday. Luke must have understood him to be referring to a state of being-in-paradise, which would be true, for him and for the man dying beside him, at once, that very day—in other words, prior to the resurrection. With Jesus, the future hope has come forward into the present.

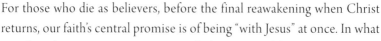

For those who die as believers, before the final reawakening when Christ returns, our faith's central promise is of being "with Jesus" at once. In what way does this promise matter to your faith—now and later?

*Jesus, thank you for the promise I have that when I die*
*I will be with you "today"—at once, forever. Amen.*

# THE IRONIES OF MONEY

## Frederick Buechner

Whoever loves money never has enough;
whoever loves wealth is never satisfied with their income.

ECCLESIASTES 5:10

The more you think about money, the less you understand it. The paper it's printed on isn't worth a red cent. There was a time you could take it to the bank and get gold or silver for it, but all you'd get now would be a blank stare.

If the government declared that the leaves of the trees were money so there would be enough for everybody, money would be worthless. It has worth only if there is not enough for everybody. It has worth only because the government declares that it has worth and because people trust the government in that one particular although in every other particular they wouldn't trust it around the corner. There are people who use up their entire lives making money so they can enjoy the lives they have entirely used up.

Jesus says that it's easier for a camel to go through the eye of a needle than for a rich man to enter the kingdom of God. Maybe the reason is not that the rich are so wicked they're kept out of the place, but that they're so out of touch with reality they can't see it's a place worth getting into.

When has money—too much or too little—skewed your reality? What happened to correct you? What is a healthy view of money?

*Lord, balance my perspective on wealth so I can walk in truth. Amen.*

# ALL EXISTS BY DESIGN

## Eugene Peterson

> He spoke, and it came to be;
> he commanded, and it stood firm.
>
> PSALM 33:9

Everything is created. Everything carries within its form and texture the signature of its Creator. No part of this material world is unconnected with God. Biblical religion cannot be lived apart from matter—the seen, felt, tasted, smelled, and listened to creation.

Nothing merely happened along. Chokecherries and tundra and weasels are not random accidents. Since everything is by design, no part of creation can be bypassed if we intend to live in the fullest possible relation to our Creator in his creation. None of it is an inconvenience we are forced to put up with. None of it is a stumbling block introduced by the devil to trip the feet of those whose eyes are piously lifted in praise to God. Creation is our place for meeting God and conversing with him. The voice that spoke Behemoth and Leviathan into being is the same voice that says, "Your sins are forgiven you" and invites us to call upon him in the day of trouble. External and internal are the same reality. Heaven and earth are formed by a single will of God.

———— ∞ ————

What does it mean to you that you carry the "form and texture" of your Creator? If all is by design, can any of God's creations—including you—be a mistake?

> *Father, thank you for speaking the wild beauty*
> *of all created things, including me. Amen.*

# CHRIST THE EMPATHIC SHEPHERD

## Brennan Manning

*When he saw the crowds, he had compassion on them, because they were harassed and helpless, like sheep without a shepherd.*

MATTHEW 9:36

The Christ who weeps over godforsaken neighborhoods such as the old Times Square is a man of sorrows moved in the pit of his stomach for the lostness of the sheep who do not know him. Jesus is the incarnation of the compassion of the Father. What do all the exalted names—Son of God, Second Person of the Blessed Trinity, Kyrios, Pantocrator, and other christological titles bestowed on Jesus by a later age—signify but that God was present in the Compassionate One in a unique, extravagant, and definitive way? Through meal-sharing, storytelling, miraculous healing, preaching, teaching, and a life of compassion that knew no frontiers, boundaries, or sectarian divisions, Jesus inaugurated in his person the reign of God. In Jesus' own conduct the new age dawned: the messianic era erupted into history. His present-day disciples' loving concern, nonjudgmental attitude, and compassionate care for their brothers and sisters is the visible form in which the reign of God is manifested today. What makes the kingdom come is heartfelt compassion. It is the way that God's lordship takes.

The heart of our crucified Lord Jesus Christ does not turn away in disgust at the wretchedness of our human condition. Instead he turns toward it, desiring to shepherd us in compassion.

*Jesus, thank you for your heart of concern.*
*Develop that same heart in me, to your glory. Amen.*

# DO WE FAVOR "OUR KIND OF PEOPLE"?

## Dallas Willard

Believers in our glorious Lord Jesus Christ must not show favoritism. Suppose a man comes into your meeting wearing a gold ring and fine clothes, and a poor man in filthy old clothes also comes in. If you show special attention to the man wearing fine clothes . . . have you not discriminated among yourselves and become judges with evil thoughts?

JAMES 2:1-4

What an indictment! And yet one hardly ever finds a church or a Christian free from knee-jerk favoritism toward those who are impressive in the world's scale of values. It is heartbreaking to behold. Our most biblical of churches are permeated with favoritism toward the rich and comfortable, the beautiful and famous—or at least toward "our kind of people." Yet many will insist that this is necessary for the advancement of the cause of Christ. We cannot sustain our programs, we are told, unless we can attract and hold the right kinds of people. It seems forgotten that the church's business is to make the right kind of people out of the wrong kind—who more often than not are precisely the "right" kind by the world's standards.

Two people: one rich and one poor. James goes on to say that if we give special attention to the man wearing fine clothes but shove the poor "over there," we discriminate and judge with evil thinking. May we never favor "our kind of people."

*Lord, identify the ways I practice knee-jerk favoritism so I can correct it. Amen.*

# COWORKERS OF THE CREATOR

## Dallas Willard

"Let Us make man . . . and let them rule over the fish of the sea and over the birds of the sky and over the cattle and over all the earth, and over every creeping thing that creeps on the earth."

GENESIS 1:26 NASB

We will not be surprised at the Bible's simple, consistent picture of human beings in relation to God. The human job description (the "creation covenant," we might call it) found in chapter 1 of Genesis indicates that God assigned to us collectively the rule over all living things on earth, animal and plant. We are responsible before God for life on the earth.

However unlikely it may seem from our current viewpoint, God equipped us for this task by framing our nature to function in a conscious, personal relationship of interactive responsibility with him. We are meant to exercise our "rule" only in union with God, as he acts with us. He intended to be our constant companion or coworker in the creative enterprise of life on earth. That is what his love for us means in practical terms.

Our divine vocation to rule over life on earth isn't a license for selfishness; it's a calling to stewardship, care, and love—in cooperation with God. How can you join God in the creative enterprise of life on earth?

*Lord, show me how I can better cooperate*
*with you in the rule of life on earth. Amen.*

# FRIENDSHIP AND SPIRITUALITY

## Eugene Peterson

> Jonathan said to David, "Go in peace, for we have sworn
> friendship with each other in the name of the Lord."
>
> 1 Samuel 20:42

Friendship is a much-underestimated aspect of spirituality. It's every bit as significant as prayer and fasting. Like the sacramental use of water and bread and wine, friendship takes what's common in human experience and turns it into something holy. Friendship with David complicated Jonathan's life enormously. He risked losing his father's favor and willingly sacrificed his own royal future. But neither the risk nor the loss deterred him; he became and stayed David's friend.

Jonathan's friendship was essential to David's life. It's highly unlikely that David could have persisted in serving Saul without the friendship of Jonathan. Jonathan, in striking contrast to his father, discerned God in David, comprehended the danger and difficulty of his anointing, and made a covenant of friendship with him. Jonathan's friendship entered David's soul in a way that Saul's hatred never did.

When we lack the confirming presence of a trusted friend, promising beginnings fizzle and brave ventures unravel. Let's find and be friends for the sake of our and others' spiritual journeys.

> Lord, give me a Jonathan to help me continue and
> persevere; may I be such a friend to others. Amen.

# THE RESTING CHRIST

## Frederick Buechner

It is the Lord Christ you are serving.

<small>COLOSSIANS 3:24</small>

Something of who Christ was and what he was like and what it was like to be with him filters through each meeting as it comes along, but for some reason it's the moment in the boat that says most. The way he lay down, bone tired, and fell asleep with the sound of the lapping waves in his ears. The way, when they woke him, he opened his eyes to the howling storm and to all the other howling things that he must have known were in the cards for him and that his nap had been a few moments of vacation from. The helplessness of the disciples and the way he spoke to them. The things he said to the wind and to the sea.

Lamb of God, Rose of Sharon, Prince of Peace—none of the things people have found to call him has ever managed to say it quite right. You can see why when he told people to follow him, they often did, even if they backed out later when they started to catch on to what lay ahead. If you're religiously inclined, you can see why they went even so far as to call him Messiah, the Lord's Anointed, the Son of God. And even if you're not religiously inclined, you can see why it is you might give your immortal soul to have been the one to raise that head a little from the hard deck and slip a pillow under it.

When have you experienced a tender moment looking at the Savior? What inspired it?

*Father, I wish I'd been in the boat with Jesus and had indeed put something soft beneath his head. Jesus, thank you for everything.*

# SALVATION OF THE "REAL YOU"

## N. T. Wright

> Though you have not seen him, you love him; and even though
> you do not see him now, you believe in him and are filled
> with an inexpressible and glorious joy, for you are receiving
> the end result of your faith, the salvation of your souls.
>
> 1 PETER 1:8–9

The word *soul* is rare in this sense in the early Christian writings. The Greek word *psyche* was very common in the ancient world and carried a variety of meanings. Despite its frequency both in later Christianity and (for instance) in Buddhism, the New Testament doesn't use it to describe, so to speak, the bit of you that will ultimately be saved. The word *psyche* seems here to refer, like the Hebrew *nephesh*, not to a disembodied inner part of the human being but to what we might call the person or even the personality. And the point in 1 Peter 1 is that this person, the "real you," is *already* being saved and will one day receive that salvation in full bodily form. That is why Peter quite rightly plants the hope for salvation firmly in the resurrection of Jesus.

———— ∞ ————

Remember: because God "has given us new birth into a living hope" (1 Peter 1:3) through Christ's resurrection, the "real you" experiences salvation now as much as you will when he returns.

*Jesus, thank you for valuing and saving*
*the real me. I love you too. Amen.*

# BE THE HELP YOU WANT TO SEE

## Dallas Willard

*Live in harmony with one another. Do not be proud, but be willing
to associate with people of low position. Do not be conceited.*
ROMANS 12:16

It will prove very useful for us to experience the life of the poor in some further measure. No adequate elaboration of practical strategies can be undertaken here. But, depending upon our family and other circumstances, we might do some of our ordinary business in the poorer districts of our community. Shopping, banking, even living in the poorer districts of our area will do much to lend substance to our grasp of how the economically deprived experience their world—and ours. This will add a great substance to one's understanding, prayers, and caring that can never be gained by an occasional "charity run" or by sending money to organizations that work with the poor.

Remember, Jesus did not send help. He came among us. He was victorious under our conditions of existence (Romans 8:3). That makes all the difference. We continue in the incarnational model when we follow the apostle's command to "associate with people of low position" by in some measure walking with them in the path of their daily affairs, not just on special occasions created because of their need.

Don't just send help; be help. Walk with the poor in daily life, showing and sharing Christ's love.

*Lord, illustrate ways I can walk with the poor,
doing life with them each day. Amen.*

# BROKEN BY THE FALL, AWAITING DELIVERANCE

## A. W. Tozer

> The creation was subjected to futility . . . the creation itself
> also will be delivered from the bondage of corruption
> into the glorious liberty of the children of God.
>
> ROMANS 8:20–21 NKJV

Many through the centuries have declared themselves unable to believe in the basic wisdom of a world wherein so much appears to be so wrong. But the Christian view of life is altogether more realistic: this is *not* at the present moment the best of all possible worlds, but one lying under the shadow of a huge calamity, the fall of man. The inspired writers insist that a whole creation now groans and travails under the mighty shock of the fall.

But there is hope in all our tears. When the hour of Christ's triumph arrives, the suffering world will be brought out into the glorious liberty of the sons of God. For men of the new creation the golden age is not past but future, and when it is ushered in, a wondering universe will see that God has indeed abounded toward us in all wisdom and prudence. In the meantime we rest our hope in the only wise God, our Savior, and wait with patience the slow development of his benign purposes.

How have you personally experienced the reality of creation's brokenness? What does it mean to you that one day it will be put back together again?

*Lord, I can hardly wait for your abundance to be revealed! Amen.*

# GOD IS COMMITTED TO JUDGMENT

## N. T. Wright

For God will bring every work into judgment,

Including every secret thing,

Whether good or evil.

ECCLESIASTES 12:14 NKJV

Judgment—the sovereign declaration that *this* is good and to be upheld and vindicated, and *that* is evil and to be condemned—is the only alternative to chaos. Judgment is necessary—unless we were to conclude, absurdly, that nothing much is wrong or, blasphemously, that God doesn't mind very much.

God is utterly committed to set the world right in the end. This doctrine, like that of resurrection itself, is held firmly in place by the belief in God as Creator, on the one side, and the belief in his goodness, on the other. And that setting right must necessarily involve the elimination of all that distorts God's good and lovely creation and in particular of all that defaces his image-bearing human creatures.

God is as committed to ensuring justice in his kingdom as he is in his offer to save unjust people from it.

> Lord, thanks for being as committed to judgment and
> justice as you are to redemption and rescue. Amen.

# TWO KINDS OF DOUBT

## Frederick Buechner

> Be merciful to those who doubt.
>
> JUDE v. 22

There are two principal kinds of doubt, one of the head and the other of the stomach. In my head there is almost nothing I can't doubt when the fit is upon me—the divinity of Christ, the efficacy of the sacraments, the significance of the church, the existence of God.

I have never experienced stomach doubt, but I think Jesus did. When he cried out, "My God, my God, why hast thou forsaken me?" I don't think he was raising a theological issue any more than he was quoting Psalm 22. I think he had looked into the abyss itself and found there a darkness that spiritually, viscerally, totally engulfed him. I think God allows that kind of darkness to happen only to God's saints. The rest of us aren't up to doubting that way—or maybe believing that way either.

If you say you don't have any doubts about faith, you are either kidding yourself or asleep. Doubts are the ants in the pants of faith, for they keep it awake and moving. And when our faith is strongest, we believe both with our hearts as well as with our heads.

When do doubts assail you? How can you use them as springboards to belief?

> Lord Jesus Christ, show me how doubt
> implies faith, and strengthen my belief. Amen.

# LIFE IN THE WILDERNESS

## Eugene Peterson

At once the Spirit sent him out into the wilderness, and he
was in the wilderness forty days, being tempted by Satan.
He was with the wild animals, and angels attended him.

MARK 1:12–13

There are times, no matter how thoroughly we're civilized, when we're plunged into the wilderness—not a geographical wilderness but what I'm going to call a *circumstantial wilderness*. Everything is going along fine—and then suddenly we're beside ourselves. We don't know what's going on within us or in another who is important to us; feelings erupt in us that call into question what we've never questioned before. There's a radical change in our bodies, or our emotions, or our thinking, or our friends, or our job. We're out of control. We're in the wilderness.

What I want to say is this: I readily acknowledge that this circumstantial wilderness is a terrible, frightening, and dangerous place; but I also believe that it's a place of beauty. In the wilderness we're plunged into an awareness of danger and death; at the very same time we're plunged, if we let ourselves be, into an awareness of the great mystery of God and the extraordinary preciousness of life.

In the wilderness we find things that can't be found anywhere else. What would happen if we leaned into it rather than ran away?

*Lord, when your Spirit sends me into the wilderness,
please be near me, teach me, change me. Amen.*

# GOD SPEAKS TO ALL, GENEROUSLY

## Dallas Willard

> There is no distinction between Jew and Greek; the same
> Lord is Lord of all and is generous to all who call on him.
>
> ROMANS 10:12 NRSV

Do Jesus and his Father hear Buddhists when they call upon them? They hear *anyone* who calls upon them. "The LORD is near to the brokenhearted and saves those who are crushed in spirit" (Psalm 34:18). You cannot call upon Jesus Christ or upon God and not be heard. You live in their house, their *ecos* (Hebrews 3:4). We usually call it simply "the universe." But they fully occupy it. It is their place, their "kingdom," where through their kindness and sacrificial love we can make our present life an eternal life. Only as we understand this is the way open for a true ecology of human existence, for only then are we dealing with what the human habitation truly is.

The God who hears is also one who speaks. He has spoken and is still speaking. Humanity remains his project, not its own, and his initiatives are always at work among us. He certainly "gives us space," as we say, and this is essential. But he continues to speak in ways that serious inquirers can hear if they will.

We need not stagger through darkness concerning what is good and of God. There is light, and everyone can find it. God speaks to all, generously.

> *Lord, I call upon you for help and guidance,*
> *anticipating a generous response. Amen.*

# WHAT YOU DO MATTERS

## N. T. Wright

My beloved, be steadfast, immovable.

1 CORINTHIANS 15:58 NRSV

How does believing in the future resurrection lead to getting on with the work in the present? Quite straightforwardly. The point of the resurrection, as Paul has been arguing throughout the 1 Corinthians letter, is that the present bodily life is not valueless just because it will die. God will raise it to new life. What you do with your body in the present matters because God has a great future in store for it.

What you *do* in the present—by painting, preaching, singing, sewing, praying, teaching, building hospitals, digging wells, campaigning for justice, writing poems, caring for the needy, loving your neighbor as yourself—will last into God's future. These activities are not simply ways of making the present life a little less beastly, a little more bearable, until the day when we leave it behind altogether. They are part of what we may call *building for God's kingdom*.

---

What valuable things does God want you to do in your present body to build his future kingdom?

*Lord, I offer you my life's activities for your glory as much as its content, trusting that both will last into your future kingdom. Amen.*

# LOVE YOURSELF TO LOVE OTHERS

## James Bryan Smith

"Love your neighbor as yourself."

MARK 12:31 NASB

The way I love others is a direct reflection of how I love myself. If I am ruthless with myself, exact with my judgment, and prone to condemn myself, I will be the same toward others. When Jesus said we are to love our neighbors as ourselves he was not so much stating a proposition as a fact. We do love our neighbors as ourselves.

When God graciously revealed himself to me as a God of acceptance, it took me several years to begin to internalize and appropriate it. I still have moments of doubt. But once I began to trust in God's acceptance of me I noticed that it immediately influenced the way I dealt with others. As I began to feel loved, I began reaching out to others in love; as I learned to believe that I was chosen, I found myself wanting to tell everyone that they too were chosen.

Everywhere I go I meet people who feel alienated from God, and it is a special privilege to tell them about God's acceptance. Ministry became easier when I realized that I do not have a ministry, but rather I am simply an extension of Christ's ministry to the world.

Our ability to tell others about God's acceptance is related to the degree to which we accept ourselves. Love yourself to help others find Christ's love.

*Lord, help me experience and express the unfathomable truth of your acceptance. Amen.*

# UP-AND-IN OR DOWN-AND-OUT?

## Dallas Willard

I can do all things through him who strengthens me.

PHILIPPIANS 4:13 NRSV

The usual Christian quotes Philippians 4:13 only when facing hard times. But that is not Paul's meaning. In the previous verses he said, "I have learned to be content whatever the circumstances. I know what it is to be in need, and I know what it is to have plenty. I have learned the secret of being content in any and every situation." Thus, when he adds that Christ gives him strength for everything, he is saying also that Christ enables him to abound, be full, and prosper.

He succeeded in abundance because of his relation to Christ just as much as he succeeded by grace in his times of need. Few people understand that they need help to abound. The gospel is for the up-and-in as well as the down-and-out, equally so, and equally needed, from God's point of view. The church's solidarity with the poor cannot be realized until spirituality has a place in the boardrooms and factories, the universities and government offices, equal to what it has in the church house, the religious retreat, or the rescue mission.

---

Where are you today, up or down? Where is God in your circumstance?

*Jesus, I fully acknowledge that whether I struggle or abound, you are my strength! Amen.*

July

# HOPE LIKE ISRAEL

## Frederick Buechner

> O Lord, my heart is not lifted up,
> my eyes are not raised too high;
> I do not occupy myself with things
> too great and too marvelous for me.
>
> PSALM 131:1 NRSV

To be in a state of depression is like what Psalm 131:1 describes. It is to be unable to occupy yourself with anything much except your state of depression. You do not raise either your heart or your eyes to the heights, because to do so only reminds you that you are yourself in the depths.

"But I have calmed and quieted my soul," he continues then, and you can't help thinking that, although maybe that's better than nothing, it's not much better. Depression is itself a kind of calm, as in becalmed, and a kind of quiet, as in a quiet despair.

Finally he tells us that hope is what his mouth is milky with, which is to the hopelessness of depression what love is to the lovesick and lovelorn. "O Israel, hope in the Lord," he says, "from this time forth and forevermore." Hope like Israel. Hope for deliverance the way Israel hoped and you are already half delivered.

---

Though you may not raise either your heart or your eyes to the heights, raise your head to the Lord in hope. Like Israel.

*Lord, teach me how to hold on when hope seems elusive, because you always deliver me. Amen.*

# BE ANGRY, DON'T SIN

## Eugene Peterson

Be angry, and do not sin.
Meditate within your heart on your bed, and be still.
PSALM 4:4 NKJV

*B*e angry." No day is perfect. Things go wrong. Some things always go wrong, many of them out of spite, malice, blasphemy. Face squarely the worst of the day, and be angry. Don't make excuses for yourself or others. Don't paper over any flaws. You do well to be angry. *"But sin not."* Your anger is not a work agenda for you to plan a vengeance that will fix the wrong. What is wrong with the world is God's business. Meanwhile God is giving help at a far deeper level than any of your meddling will ever reach.

*"Commune with your own hearts on your beds."* Speak to yourself. Listen to yourself. Get acquainted again with the being that God created, not just the passport version that you have used to get more or less successfully through the day. *"And be silent."* Nothing more need be said. No explanation, no boasts, no apologies. This is who you are. There is something more important than liking or not liking yourself, more significant than the day's accomplishments and failures; there is *you*.

———∞———

Follow honest emotion with silent meditation. And in the silence, simply be the person God is gathering into salvation.

> *Lord, as I face the challenges of the day, empower me not to sin; as I meditate in silence, restore me. Amen.*

# A LIVING SIGN

## Henri J. M. Nouwen

> [Bear] fruit in every good work.
>
> Colossians 1:10

How does the Spirit of God manifest through us? Often we think that to witness means to speak up in defense of God. This idea can make us very self-conscious. We wonder where and how we can make God the topic of our conversations and how to convince our families, friends, neighbors, and colleagues of God's presence in their lives. But this explicit missionary endeavor often comes from an insecure heart and therefore easily creates divisions.

The way God's Spirit manifests most convincingly is through fruit. It is always better to raise the question "How can I grow in the Spirit?" than the question "How can I make others believe in the Spirit?"

To be a witness for God is to be a living sign of God's presence in the world. What we live is more important than what we say, because the right way of living always leads to the right way of speaking. When we forgive our neighbors from our hearts, our hearts will speak forgiving words. When we are grateful, we will speak grateful words, and when we are hopeful and joyful, we will speak hopeful and joyful words.

How has God made his presence known to you through other people?

*Lord, help me become a living sign of your presence. Amen.*

# KINGDOM, COME

## Frederick Buechner

> "To you it has been given to know the
> secrets of the kingdom of heaven."
>
> MATTHEW 13:11 NRSV

The kingdom of God is not a place, of course, but a condition. *Kingship* might be a better word. "Thy kingdom come, thy will be done," Jesus prayed. The two are in apposition.

Insofar as here and there, and now and then, God's kingly will is being done in various odd ways among us even at this moment, the kingdom has come already. Insofar as all the odd ways we do God's will at this moment are at best half-baked and halfhearted, the kingdom is still a long way off.

As a poet, Jesus is maybe at his best in describing the feeling you get when you glimpse the Thing Itself—the kingship of the king official at last and all the world his coronation. It's like finding a million dollars in a field, he says, or a jewel worth a king's ransom. It's like finding something you hated to lose and thought you'd never find again—an old keepsake, a stray sheep, a missing child. When the kingdom really comes, it's as if the thing you lost and thought you'd never find again is yourself.

At what moments now do you witness the coming of God's kingdom even in small ways?

*Lord, draw near to your kingdom. Let me
spread its light everywhere I can. Amen.*

# GOD RESPONDS TO OUR CRIES

## Eugene Peterson

> The LORD is my rock, my fortress, and my deliverer,
> my God, my rock in whom I take refuge,
> my shield, and the horn of my salvation, my stronghold.
>
> PSALM 18:2 NRSV

At the outset God is addressed as *strength*, *rock*, *fortress*, *deliverer*, *shield*, *horn*, and *stronghold*. This is followed by a description of extensive personal trouble: cords of death, torrents of perdition, cords of Sheol, snares of death. God responds to the cry for help. His response is fierce: smoke streams from his mouth, he descends from the heavens mantled in darkness under a canopy of rain clouds, and mounted on a cherub. Out of this soaring darkness/brightness, coals-of-fire hailstones rain destruction, and arrow-lightnings impale evildoers, while an enormous blast of breath from God's nostrils parts the sea and lays bare the world's foundations. And then, abruptly, the metaphors of ferocity give way to one of immense gentleness—God reaches down with his own hand, pulls the one who is praying from the clutch of waters and enemies, and places him on a dry and spacious land, saved.

---

When we pray, our task isn't to dilute our language in an abstract spirituality. Instead we should thicken it into a spirituality of actual experience— it's in our honesty that God responds.

*Lord, help me. I need your ferocity and*
*tenderness here in my despair. Amen.*

# THE HOLY SPIRIT AND THE CHURCH, WORKING HAND IN HAND

## N. T. Wright

*All of them were filled with the Holy Spirit and began to speak in other tongues as the Spirit enabled them.*

Acts 2:4

The Holy Spirit and the task of the church: the two walk together, hand in hand. We can't talk about them apart. Despite what you might think from some excitement in the previous generation about new spiritual experiences, God doesn't give people the Holy Spirit in order to let them enjoy the spiritual equivalent of a day at Disneyland. The point of the Spirit is to enable those who follow Jesus to take into all the world the news that he is Lord, that he has won the victory over the forces of evil, that a new world has opened up, and that we are to help make it happen.

Equally, the task of the church can't be attempted without the Spirit. I have sometimes heard Christian people talk as though God, having done what he's done in Jesus, now wants us to do our part by getting on with things under our own steam. But that is a tragic misunderstanding. Without God's Spirit, there is nothing we can do that will count for God's kingdom. Without God's Spirit, the church simply can't be the church.

How closely are you walking with the Holy Spirit? When you walk hand in hand, you can be the church and live God's mission.

*Holy Spirit, may we walk and work together for God's glory. Amen.*

# A USEFUL TYPE OF LONELINESS

## Henri J. M. Nouwen

> With You is the fountain of life;
> In Your light we see light.
>
> PSALM 36:9 NKJV

In the spiritual life we have to make a distinction between two kinds of loneliness. In the first loneliness, we are out of touch with God and experience ourselves as anxiously looking for someone or something that can give us a sense of belonging, intimacy, and home. The second loneliness comes from an intimacy with God that is deeper and greater than our feelings and thoughts can capture.

We might think of these two kinds of loneliness as two forms of blindness. The first blindness comes from the absence of light, the second from too much light. The first loneliness we must try to outgrow with faith and hope. The second we must be willing to embrace in love.

When have you experienced each type of loneliness? How can you outgrow the first so you can more fully embrace the second?

*Jesus, flood me with light! Amen.*

# HISTORY—HUMANKIND'S AND YOURS

## Frederick Buechner

To him be glory and dominion forever and ever.

<small>REVELATION 1:6 NRSV</small>

Biblical faith takes history very seriously because God takes it very seriously. The biblical view is that history is not an absurdity to be endured or an illusion to be dispelled. Instead, it is for each of us a series of crucial, precious, and unrepeatable moments that are seeking to lead us somewhere.

The true history of humankind and of each individual has less to do than we tend to think with the kind of information that gets into most histories, biographies, and autobiographies. True history has to do with the saving and losing of souls, and both of these are apt to take place when most people are looking the other way. The real turning point in our lives is less likely to be the day we win the election or get married than the morning we decide not to mail the letter or the afternoon we watch the woods fill up with snow. The real turning point in human history is less apt to be the day the wheel is invented or Rome falls than the day a child is born in a stable.

———— ⟐ ————

What are the most significant events of your history so far? Were you prepared for them, or did they happen when you "were looking the other way"?

*Jesus, may your life shine forth through mine, so my personal history may affect humankind's in some small way. Amen.*

# DEALING WITH GOD-ALIVE

## Eugene Peterson

> You, God, are my God,
> earnestly I seek you;
> PSALM 63:1

In the David wilderness story we see a young man hated and hunted like an animal, his very humanity profaned, forced to decide between a life of blasphemy and a life of prayer—and choosing prayer. In choosing prayer he entered into the practice of holiness.

I'm nervous about using the words *holy* and *holiness*—nervous because the words have picked up some bad associations and I don't want to be misunderstood. Still, there's no other word strong enough to mark what emerges in David in the wilderness years. What happens is that no matter what else David is doing, he's basically dealing with God; and the more he deals with God, the more human he becomes—the more he becomes "David." *Holy* is our best word to describe that life—the most aliveness that comes from dealing with God-Alive. We're most human when we deal with God. Any other way of life leaves us less human, less ourselves.

———✺———

In the wilderness David learned to seek his God wholly and he emerged holy; he emerged more wholly himself.

> *Lord, remind me that no matter what I'm involved in, I'm dealing with you. Amen.*

# ABRAM'S EARTHY FAITH

## Dallas Willard

Abram believed the LORD, and he credited it to him as righteousness.

GENESIS 15:6

What did Abraham believe that led God to declare or "reckon" him righteous? Was it that God had arranged payment for his sins? Not at all. He trusted God, of course, but it was for things involved in his current existence.

He believed that *God* would interact with him now—just as those who later gathered around Jesus did. He even dared to ask God how he could know that the promise of a male heir would be fulfilled. In response, God directed him to prepare animals for sacrifice. Abraham did so and then waited for God to act (Genesis 15:8–11). He waited until God materialized fire "out of thin air." God acted from surrounding space, the atmosphere—that is, from the "first heaven" of the Bible. This was the answer to Abraham's question.

In the face of such faith, God declared Abraham to be righteous. Does that mean he declared he would go to heaven when he died? Not precisely that, but certainly that Abraham's sins and failures would not cut him off from God in the present moment and in their ongoing relationship in life together.

⸺

Abram's faith was profound because it was an earthy faith, for he believed God would show up in his life in tangible ways.

> *Lord, give me the faith of Abram to believe you make your presence known in my life right now. Amen.*

# CREATION LONGS FOR YOUR REVELATION

## N. T. Wright

> The creation waits in eager expectation
> for the children of God to be revealed.
>
> ROMANS 8:19

When God saves people in this life, by working through his Spirit to bring them to faith and by leading them to follow Jesus in discipleship, prayer, holiness, hope, and love, such people are designed—it isn't too strong a word—to be a sign and foretaste of what God wants to do for the entire cosmos. What's more, such people are not just to be a sign and foretaste of that ultimate salvation; they are to be part of the means by which God makes this happen in both the present and the future.

That is what Paul insists on when he says that the whole creation is waiting with eager longing not just for its own redemption, its liberation from corruption and decay, but for God's children to be revealed: in other words, for the unveiling of those redeemed humans through whose stewardship creation will at last be brought back into that wise order for which it was made.

It's true: all of creation has been eagerly awaiting your full unveiling—of all of who you are and what you are capable of—in order to experience God's re-creation. How do you see God's purpose for you in that unveiling?

> *Lord, in your time and in your way, reveal me as your child that I might reveal you as the Father. Amen.*

# WHOM DOES GOD FAVOR?

## Dallas Willard

> "It is easier for a camel to go through the eye of a needle than for someone who is rich to enter the kingdom of God." . . . They were greatly astounded and said, "Then who can be saved?"
>
> MATTHEW 19:24–25 NRSV

The common assumption of the time, as in many times since, was that the prosperity of the rich indicated God's special favor. How else could they be rich, since it is supposedly God himself who controls the wealth of the earth?

It is crucial to note here what Jesus did not say. He did not say that the rich cannot enter the kingdom. In fact he said they could—with God's help, which is the only way anyone can do it. Nor did he say that the poor have, on the whole, any advantage over the rich so far as "being saved" is concerned. By using the case at hand, he simply upset the prevailing general assumption about God and riches. For how could God favor a person, however rich, who loves him less than wealth?

So being rich does not mean that one is in God's favor—which further suggests that being poor does not automatically mean one is out of God's favor.

Jesus made it possible to think more of God's relationship with us, which has nothing to do with whether we are rich or poor.

*Lord, teach me what you favor and what brings me into relationship with you. Amen.*

# GOD'S NEAR IN YOUR EXILE

## Eugene Peterson

> By the rivers of Babylon—
> there we sat down and there we wept
> when we remembered Zion.
>
> PSALM 137:1 NRSV

Psalm 137 was first prayed out of Israel's painful exile. In the loneliness of exile, the Israelites with their far-flung reputation for robust song and hearty praise are grist for Babylonia taunts: "Sing us one of your Zion songs!" But all the music has been knocked out of them. Their lives and voices are flat as the desert plain of their exile.

Stanza two deepens the sorrow: "How shall we sing the LORD's song in a foreign land?" Silence is their only dignity. To sing in this place, among these people, would be a sacrilege. They will be loyal to their homeland and honor the memories of their grand and holy place of worship in reverberating silence.

In these two stanzas, the fine-tempered steel forged in the exile sufferings of loss, rejection, and violation is fashioned into sharp images and penetrating rhythms that cut to the center of our hearts and make us companions in their weeping prayer and silent pain. Their pathos and art bring us to our knees in prayer with and for them.

---

How has your own exile brought you to your knees, weeping and in silent pain? How has God shown himself faithful in the midst of it?

*Lord, I call out to you. Please warm me with your presence. Amen.*

# CARRY GOD'S ACCEPTANCE

## James Bryan Smith

*We have this treasure in jars of clay to show that this
all-surpassing power is from God and not from us.*

2 Corinthians 4:7

God's love for us is without limit. In the economy of divine love we will discover that the more we give, the more we have to give. I have noticed that no matter how much I try, I cannot exhaust God's love. I have never seen it run out. But I can only give as much as I have received, and the measure of love I receive is in direct proportion to how much I desire to know it, feel it, and give it away.

Paul used the metaphor of a jar made of clay that has been filled with an enormous treasure to describe the Christian life. You and I are simply jars. The jar itself is not what really matters. What is important is the treasure inside.

All we have to do is carry God's acceptance to the people around us. "Look at this treasure, this wealth, that is for you," we say to one another. In giving it away we will find that, far from diminishing the treasure within us, it has increased.

We may not feel we have the capacity to accept one another unconditionally. We are right. We don't have the ability to love as God loves. Thankfully, he has given us his own wealth of love to share.

*Lord, may I, this clay jar, generously share
your treasure of acceptance. Amen.*

# REAL LIFE IN ALL ITS FULLNESS

## Dallas Willard

> God has given us eternal life, and this life is in his Son.
>
> 1 JOHN 5:11

Certainly forgiveness and reconciliation are essential to any relationship where there has been offense, and also between us and God. But such a reconciliation involves far more than the forgiveness of our sins or a clearing of the ledger. And the faith and salvation of which Jesus speaks obviously is a much more positive reality than mere reconciliation. The stories of biblical characters beautifully illustrate this.

*The* issue, so far as the gospel in the Gospels is concerned, is whether we are alive to God or dead to him. Do we walk in an interactive relationship with him that constitutes a new kind of life, life "from above"?

What must be emphasized in all of this is the difference between trusting Christ, the real person Jesus, with all that that naturally involves, versus trusting some arrangement for sin-remission set up through him—trusting only his role as guilt remover. To trust the real person Jesus is to have confidence in him in every dimension of our real life, to believe that he is right about and adequate to everything.

---

Forgiveness and reconciliation are important, but they are not all of what we've received in and through the Son. What we've received is real life in all its fullness.

*Jesus, make me confident in all the dimensions of my life. Amen.*

# GOD GIVES HIMSELF

## Frederick Buechner

"Who is this that darkens counsel
By words without knowledge?"

JOB 38:2 NASB

The world hides God from us, or we hide ourselves from God, or for reasons of his own God hides himself from us, but however you account for it, he is often more conspicuous by his absence than by his presence, and his absence is much of what we labor under and are heavy laden by.

It is out of the whirlwind that Job first hears God say the words in Job 38:2. It is out of the absence of God that God makes himself present, and it is not just the whirlwind that stands for his absence, not just the storm and chaos of the world that knock into a cocked hat all man's attempts to find God in the world, but God is absent also from all Job's words about God, and from the words of his comforters, because they are words without knowledge that obscure the issue of God by trying to define him as present in ways and places where he is not present, to define him as moral order, as the best answer man can give to the problem of his life. God is not an answer man can give, God says. God himself does not give answers. He gives himself, and into the midst of the whirlwind of his absence gives himself.

When have you experienced God himself in the midst of the whirlwind and chaos of life, and you discovered the ignorance you'd carried about his character? How did you change as a result?

*Lord, reveal yourself to me in ways that
even words cannot convey. Amen.*

# HIDDENNESS: WHERE HOLINESS GROWS

## Henri J. M. Nouwen

> He Himself often withdrew into the wilderness and prayed.
>
> LUKE 5:16 NKJV

Hiddenness is an essential quality of the spiritual life. Solitude, silence, ordinary tasks, being with people without great agendas, sleeping, eating, working, playing . . . all of that without being different from others, that is the life Jesus lived and the life he asks us to live. It is in hiddenness that we, like Jesus, can increase "in wisdom and stature, and in favour with God and man" (Luke 2:52). It is in hiddenness that we can find a true intimacy with God and a true love for people.

Even during his active ministry, Jesus continued to return to hidden places to be alone with God. If we don't have a hidden life with God, our public life for God cannot bear fruit.

How would you describe your own hidden life? What has developed because of it?

*Father, draw me to meet with you privately.*
*I want to reflect you as accurately as Jesus did. Amen.*

# HOW DOES GOD LOVE?

## James Bryan Smith

Love never ends.

1 CORINTHIANS 13:8 NRSV

God is love, we read in the Bible. But what does that mean? What is God's love like? In 1 Corinthians 13:4–8 we have one of the most beautiful descriptions of what love is: it is patient and kind, it is not boastful or rude, keeps no record of wrongs, hopes all things, believes all things, and never ends.

This is what God's love toward us is like. God is patient—he puts up with our faults and failures without grumbling. God is kind—he does not seek to coerce or control us. God is not boastful—he does not need to impress us. God is not rude—he never needs to offend or manipulate us. God keeps no record of wrongs—he does not keep an account of our mistakes so that he may one day judge us. God hopes and believes—he sees our potential even when we doubt and despair of ourselves.

If God is this way with us, then as extensions of his life in us, we too can offer this kind of love to those around us. When we offer this kind of love to those around us we enable them to become something beautiful.

God's love toward us is unending: he has been patient with us, showered us with kindness, incinerated our record of wrongs, and believed in our potential. May we love the way he does.

*Lord, energize me to love with your patience
and kindness, forgiveness and hope. Amen.*

# CEASE DOING EVIL

## Dallas Willard

> All have turned away, all have become corrupt;
> there is no one who does good.
>
> PSALM 14:3

If I am truly concerned about moral evil in the world, I should at least worry as much about my responsibility for it as about God's. By ceasing to do evil I can make a significant impact on the moral evil that is in my world. By trusting the goodness and greatness of God, I can turn loose of the chain that drags me into moral evil, along with the chain of self-deification, which puts me in the position of the one I trust to take care of myself.

If I rely upon God, I can relinquish the realization of my aims to him. I can stop doing what I, and everyone else, knows to be wrong, and I can calmly cease cooperation with immoral behavior occurring around me. I also can stand against the evils in my world, unconcerned about what is going to happen to me if I do. We need not try to be perfect. We can concentrate on just doing a lot better. That is the surest way of vastly improving the world we live in.

---

Let us look inward, asking how we can immediately improve our world.

*Lord, show me how I am responsible for the bad things that happen to good people, and help me repent. Amen.*

# WOUNDS: A SOURCE OF HEALING

## Henri J. M. Nouwen

> Blessed be the God and Father of our Lord Jesus Christ, the Father of mercies and God of all comfort, who comforts us all in our tribulation, that we may be able to comfort those who are in any trouble.
>
> 2 CORINTHIANS 1:3–4 NKJV

Nobody escapes being wounded. We all are wounded people, whether physically, emotionally, mentally, or spiritually. The main question is not, "How can we hide our wounds?" so we don't have to be embarrassed but "How can we put our woundedness in the service of others?" When our wounds cease to be a source of shame and become a source of healing, we have become wounded healers.

Jesus is God's Wounded Healer: through his wounds we are healed. Jesus' suffering and death brought joy and life. His humiliation brought glory; his rejection brought a community of love. As followers of Jesus we can also allow our wounds to bring healing to others.

———∞———

Healing can be infectious—something to be shared, joyfully, with others. Are you weighed down by your wounds or rejoicing in your healing?

*Lord, teach me to love my neighbor as myself*
*and to share the relief of restoration. Amen.*

# COINCIDENCE OR HINT OF HEAVEN?

## Frederick Buechner

> You . . . are acquainted with all my ways.
>
> PSALM 139:3 NKJV

I think of a person I haven't seen or thought of for years, and ten minutes later I see her crossing the street. I turn on the radio to hear a voice reading the biblical story of Jael, which is the story that I have spent the morning writing about. A car passes me on the road, and its license plate consists of my wife's and my initials side by side. When you tell people stories like that, their usual reaction is to laugh. One wonders why.

I believe that people laugh at coincidence as a way of relegating it to the realm of the absurd and of therefore not having to take seriously the possibility that there is a lot more going on in our lives than we either know or care to know. Who can say what it is that's going on? But I suspect that part of it, anyway, is that every once and so often we hear a whisper from the wings that goes something like this: "You've turned up in the right place at the right time. You're doing fine. Don't ever think that you've been forgotten."

How do you view coincidences—as amusing moments or divine appearances? What if God really is fueling such experiences?

> Lord, please make me alert to all the ways
> you speak to me throughout the day. Amen.

# FOCUS ON THE NOW

## N. T. Wright

*We are God's handiwork, created in Christ Jesus to do good works, which God prepared in advance for us to do.*

EPHESIANS 2:10

Heaven and hell are not, so to speak, what the whole game is about. This is one of the central surprises in the Christian hope. The question of what happens to me after death is not the major, central, framing question that centuries of theological tradition have supposed. The New Testament, true to its Old Testament roots, regularly insists that the major, central, framing question is that of God's purpose of rescue and re-creation for the whole world, the entire cosmos. The destiny of individual human beings must be understood within that context—not simply in the sense that we are only part of a much larger picture but also in the sense that part of the whole point of being saved in the present is so that we can play a vital role within that larger picture and purpose. And that in turn makes us realize that the question of our own destiny, in terms of the alternatives of joy or woe, is probably the wrong way of looking at the whole question.

---

Rather than worry about a future heaven and hell, we ought to focus on what good works we can contribute now to the renewal of creation and to the fresh projects the creator God will launch in his new world.

> *Lord, how can I contribute my good works to your present work? Please show me. Amen.*

# EXPERIENCE BEFORE DOCTRINE

## Frederick Buechner

> There are also many other things that Jesus did; if every one
> of them were written down, I suppose that the world itself
> could not contain the books that would be written.
>
> JOHN 21:25 NRSV

No matter how fancy and metaphysical a doctrine sounds, it was a human experience first. The doctrine of the divinity of Christ, for instance. The place it began was not in the word processor of some fourth-century Greek theologian, but in the experience of basically untheological people who had known Jesus of Nazareth and found something happening to their lives that had never happened before.

Unless you can somehow participate yourself in the experience that lies behind a doctrine, simply to subscribe to it doesn't mean much. Sometimes, however, simply to subscribe to a doctrine is the first step toward experiencing the reality that lies behind it.

---

It's easy to forget that Christian truths about God, humanity, Jesus, and salvation arose out of lived experience, not stale doctrinal debates. From Jesus' divinity to the Trinity to salvation by grace through faith, we believe what we believe because people, like the apostle John, experienced it first. What truths about Christianity have you yourself participated in, ones that changed your life?

*Lord, give me experiences of your truth, ones that change
my life and testify to the reality behind belief. Amen.*

# LAMENT IS GOOD FOR THE SOUL

## Eugene Peterson

David took up this lament concerning Saul and his son Jonathan.

2 SAMUEL 1:17

If we're not taught to lament with this lamentation, we'll grow up believing that our immediate feelings determine our fate. We'll deny every rejection and thereby be controlled by rejection. We'll avoid every frustration and thereby be diminished by frustration. Year by year, as we deny and avoid the pains and losses, the rejections and frustrations, we'll become less and less, trivial and trivializing, empty shells with smiley faces painted on them.

I'm not suggesting Davidic lamentation as a cure to addiction or depression. But I'm bold to say that it's our most promising preventative. We don't become mature human beings by getting lucky or cleverly circumventing loss, and certainly not by avoidance and distraction. Learn to lament. Learn *this* lamentation. We're *mortals*, after all. We and everyone around are scheduled for death (*mortis*). Get used to it. Take up your cross. It prepares us and those around us for resurrection.

Practicing the Christian life involves learning to lament so we find and experience spiritual health and human holiness.

*Lord, show me how to deal with loss honestly by lamenting. Amen.*

# PEOPLE AS THEY ARE

## James Bryan Smith

> "A new command I give you: Love one another.
> As I have loved you, so you must love one another."
>
> JOHN 13:34

How do I show this kind of acceptance to my neighbor? The better question is, how has Jesus shown acceptance to me? The way he loves us is a reflection of how we are to love others.

A large part of acceptance is letting people be who they are, with all of their uniqueness, all of their beauty, all of their flaws. I find this easier to say than to do. I have a terrible habit of looking at a person as someone I can help, rather than as someone I can accept and love. "I wonder what he struggles with," I will say to myself. Then I reason about how I can fix him. I have learned that I can do more for others by trying not to fix them and by accepting them wholesale.

The world we live in judges people from a "human standpoint," putting them in classes and castes, revering the rich and despising the poor. Why? There is not a living soul for whom Jesus did not die.

By looking at what people are not instead of at what they are, we can't sympathize with them, struggle with them, or rejoice with them.

*Jesus, help me stop judging people so
I can love them as they are. Amen.*

# GOD LOOKS AFTER OUR EVERYTHING

## Dallas Willard

"Do not worry then, saying, 'What will we eat?' or
'What will we drink?' or 'What will we wear for clothing?' . . .
Your heavenly Father knows that you need all these things."

MATTHEW 6:31-32 NASB

This bold and slyly humorous assurance about all the basic elements of our existence—food and drink and clothing and other needs of life—can only be supported on a clear-eyed vision that a totally good and competent God is right here with us to look after us. And his presence is precisely what the word *heaven* or, more accurately, the *heavens* in plural, conveys in the biblical record as well as through much of Christian history.

The Old Testament experience of God is one of the direct presence of God's person, knowledge, and power to those who trust and serve him. Nothing—no human being or institution, no time, no space, no spiritual being, no event—stands between God and those who trust him. The "heavens" are always there with you no matter what, and the "first heaven," in biblical terms, is precisely the atmosphere or air that surrounds your body. But it is precisely from the space immediately around us that God watches and God acts.

How have you witnessed God's direct presence in your life, watching and acting to provide food, drink, clothing, and other needs of life? How would you like him to look after all of who you are?

*Lord, thank you for watching all that concerns me and providing all I need. Make me alert to your provision. Amen.*

# REPUDIATE YOUR WISDOM, TAKE GOD'S INSTEAD

## A. W. Tozer

"I will turn the darkness into light before them
and make the rough places smooth."

ISAIAH 42:16

To believe actively that our heavenly Father constantly spreads around us providential circumstances that work for our present good and our everlasting well-being brings to the soul a veritable benediction. Most of us go through life praying a little, planning a little, jockeying for position, hoping but never being quite certain of anything, and always secretly afraid that we will miss the way. This is a tragic waste of truth and never gives rest to the heart.

There is a better way. It is to repudiate our own wisdom and take instead the infinite wisdom of God. Our insistence upon seeing ahead is natural enough, but it is a real hindrance to our spiritual progress. God has charged himself with full responsibility for our eternal happiness and stands ready to take over the management of our lives the moment we turn in faith to him. Here is his promise.

How can you lay aside your own wisdom and instead take the promised wisdom of God as your only guide?

*Lord, I believe you're working for my good; help my unbelief. Amen.*

# LOOK AT YOUR ENEMIES TO LOVE THEM

## Frederick Buechner

"I tell you, love your enemies and pray for those who persecute you."

MATTHEW 5:44

Jesus says we are to love our enemies and pray for them, meaning love not in an emotional sense but in the sense of willing their good, which is the sense in which we love ourselves. It is a tall order even so. But when you see clearly who your enemies are, at least you see your enemies clearly too.

You see the lines in their faces and the way they walk when they're tired. You're still light-years away from loving them, to be sure, but at least you see how they are human even as you are human, and that is at least a step in the right direction. It's possible that you may even get to where you can pray for them a little, if only that God forgive them because you yourself can't, but any prayer for them at all is a major breakthrough.

In the long run, it may be easier to love the ones we look in the eye and hate, the enemies, than the ones whom—because we're as afraid of ourselves as we are of them—we choose not to look at, at all.

The next time enemies persecute and confront you, look them in the eyes. It's in looking that we're able to love.

*Jesus, enable me to see and pray for my enemies. Amen.*

# LORD, DO BATTLE AGAINST THE WICKED

## Eugene Peterson

> Break the arm of the wicked and the evildoer,
> Seek out his wickedness until You find none.
>
> PSALM 10:15 NASB

The psalmists are angry people. In the presence of God they have realized that the world is not a benign place where everyone is doing their best to get along with the others and that if we all just try a little harder things are going to turn out all right. Their prayers have brought them to an awareness in their souls and in society of the prophesied consequences of the "enmity between you [Satan] and the woman" (Genesis 3:15).

We are easily duped by evil. Evil almost never looks like an enemy in its presenting forms. There was nothing in the wilderness temptation of Jesus to indicate that anything evil was involved—provide bread for hunger, furnish a miracle to encourage belief, acquire power that could be used to establish a just world society. But Jesus had been in prayer for forty days and nights and saw through the polite and plausible offers. His prayers had given him discernment. He identified the options as enemies. When he emerged from the wilderness it was not to negotiate in sweet reasonableness but to do battle.

Our world is filled with the same kind of evildoers against whom the psalmists prayed. May our prayers ask God to do battle against such wickedness, until no more is found.

*Lord, the wicked and evildoers fill the world:*
*break them to pieces. Amen.*

# WHY DO WE HIDE? ✓

## James Bryan Smith

*The man and his wife heard the sound of the L*ORD *God . . . and*
*they hid from the L*ORD *God among the trees of the garden.*

GENESIS 3:8

When we feel alone in our struggle, we will find ourselves hiding not only from one another but also from God. Yet we will also be reluctant to turn to God after we commit a shameful act if we fear that we will be scolded and punished. It is better to avoid God, we reason, than to face his fury. This too is a misconception that prevents us from walking in freedom and enjoying our life with God. We end up hiding from the one who longs to heal us and, in fact, is the only one who *can* heal us.

Adam and Eve hid from God after they did what they knew they were not supposed to do. God knew where they were but went looking for them anyway, calling out, "Adam, where are you?" Yet God was so tender and gracious toward them that he even bent down and made them clothes to cover their newly discovered nakedness.

We have no need to hide from God. We should never be afraid to go to him, for he loves us no matter what. He will treat us as his beloved children.

*Lord, when I want to hide, remind me of your love. Amen.*

# OUR GOD-ARRANGED FUTURE

## Dallas Willard

> "My Father's house has many rooms; if that were not so, would I have told you that I am going there to prepare a place for you? And if I go and prepare a place for you, I will come back and take you to be with me."
>
> JOHN 14:2-3

At this present time the eternally creative Christ is preparing places for his human sisters and brothers to join him. Some are already there—no doubt busy with him in his great works. On the day he died, he covenanted with another man being killed along with him to meet that very day in a place he called Paradise.

Too many are tempted to dismiss what Jesus says as just "pretty words." But those who think it is unrealistic or impossible are more short on imagination than long on logic. They should have a close look at the universe God has already brought into being before they decide he could not arrange for the future life of which the Bible speaks.

Anyone who realizes that reality is God's and has seen a little bit of what God has already done will understand that such a "paradise" would be no problem at all.

In heaven God will preserve every one of his friends in the wholeness of their personal existence because he treasures them. That's the future he's arranged for us.

*Jesus, thank you for loving me so intensely that you created a delightful future for me. Amen.*

August

# THE WISDOM OF GOD'S WORKS

## A. W. Tozer

> O Lord, how manifold are your works!
> In wisdom you have made them all;
> the earth is full of your creatures.
>
> Psalm 104:24 nrsv

Wisdom, among other things, is the ability to devise perfect ends and to achieve those ends by the most perfect means. It sees the end from the beginning, so there can be no need to guess or conjecture. Wisdom sees everything in focus, each in proper relation to all, and is thus able to work toward predestined goals with flawless precision.

All God's acts are done in perfect wisdom, first for his own glory, then for the highest good of the greatest number for the longest time. And all his acts are as pure as they are wise, and as good as they are wise and pure. Not only could his acts not be better done: a better way to do them could not be imagined. An infinitely wise God must work in a manner not to be improved upon by finite creatures.

Without the creation, the wisdom of God would have remained forever locked in the boundless abyss of the divine nature. God brought his creatures into being that he might enjoy them and they rejoice in him.

---

Of all God's wondrous works, which do you feel reflect the manifold wisdom of our Lord the most?

*God, Maker of heaven and earth, I praise you for the wisdom embedded in your creation, recognizing it reflects the depths and grandeur of your character. Amen.*

# BUILD FOR GOD'S KINGDOM

## N. T. Wright

All things are of God, who has reconciled us to Himself through Jesus Christ, and has given us the ministry of reconciliation.

2 CORINTHIANS 5:18 NKJV

God builds God's kingdom. But God ordered his world in such a way that his own work within that world takes place not least through one of his creatures in particular, namely, the human beings who reflect his image. That, I believe, is central to the notion of being made in God's image. God intends his wise, creative, loving presence and power to be reflected into his world through his human creatures. He has enlisted us to act as his stewards in the project of creation. And, following the disaster of rebellion and corruption, he has built into the gospel message the fact that through the work of Jesus and the power of the Spirit, he equips humans to help in the work of getting the project back on track.

But what we can and must do in the present, if we are obedient to the gospel, if we are following Jesus, and if we are indwelt, energized, and directed by the Spirit, is to build *for* the kingdom.

Though it seems humble and pious to object to building God's kingdom by our own efforts, this can actually be a way of hiding from our responsibility to be vessels through which God is reconciling the world.

*Lord, use me to build your kingdom; show me
how I can help reconcile the world. Amen.*

# FORGIVE TO HEAL

## James Bryan Smith

> Bear with each other and forgive one another if any of you has a grievance against someone. Forgive as the Lord forgave you.
>
> <small>Colossians 3:13</small>

When we have been hurt—really hurt—forgiveness is very difficult. In fact, forgiving the one who hurt us is the last thing we want to do. As C. S. Lewis said, "Everyone says forgiveness is a lovely idea, until they have something to forgive."[13] We want to see our offender punished, we yearn to see justice served, and we long for the day when the person who hurt us crawls at our feet and begs us to forgive them.

Forgiving is difficult because it seems unjust. If a person has truly harmed us, it is only right that they pay for their crime. It appears to be an unjust acquittal to forgive someone before they have paid their debt for having harmed us. Forgiveness does not make sense to us; retribution seems warranted.

But it is the way to real freedom, and if we can navigate through the turbulent waters of our pain and ask God's help in forgiving those we need to forgive, we will experience an inner peace that this world does not understand.

It's difficult to forgive because we all long for justice. Yet forgiveness isn't about justice, it's about healing.

> *Lord, may I join you in forgiving those who harm me,*
> *so I can find healing and peace? Amen.*

# FULFILLING OUR MISSION OF SENT-NESS

## Henri J. M. Nouwen

"As You sent Me into the world, I also have sent them into the world."
JOHN 17:18 NASB

Each of us has a mission in life. Jesus prays to his Father for his followers. We seldom realize fully that we are sent to fulfill God-given tasks. We act as if we have to choose how, where, and with whom to live. We act as if we were simply dropped down in creation and have to decide how to entertain ourselves until we die. But we were sent into the world by God, just as Jesus was. Once we start living our lives with that conviction, we will soon know what we were sent to do.

When we live our lives as missions, we become aware that there is a home from which we are sent and to which we have to return. When the message has been delivered and the project is finished, we want to return home to give an account of our mission and to rest from our labors.

One of the most important spiritual disciplines is to develop the knowledge that the years of our lives are years "on a mission."

Just as the Father sent the Son on mission, so has the Son sent you on mission. What do you think you've been sent to do, for God's glory and the common good?

*Lord Jesus Christ, Son of God, reveal my mission and deepen my understanding of your sending me here. Amen.*

# PRAY YOUR HATE, LAY GOD'S JUSTICE

## Eugene Peterson

> O that you would kill the wicked, O God. . . .
>
> I hate them with perfect hatred;
>
> I count them my enemies.
>
> PSALM 139:19, 22 NRSV

It is easy to be honest before God with our hallelujahs; it is somewhat more difficult to be honest in our hurts; it is nearly impossible to be honest before God in the dark emotions of our hate. So we commonly suppress our negative emotions (unless, neurotically, we advertise them). Or when we do express them, we do it far from the presence, or what we think is the presence, of God, ashamed or embarrassed to be seen in these curse-stained bib overalls.

But when we pray the Psalms, these classic prayers of God's people, we find that will not do. We must pray who we actually are, not who we think we should be. In prayer, all is not sweetness and light. The way of prayer is not to cover our unlovely emotions so that they will appear respectable but expose them so that they can be enlisted in the work of the kingdom. Hate, prayed, takes our lives to bedrock where the foundations of justice are being laid.

———ᙍ———

Let's lean into our emotions when we pray so we can leverage God's justice in the world.

*Lord, I entrust to you my most precious hatreds, knowing you will take them seriously and work your justice. Amen.*

# AMBASSADORS OF A SURPRISING HOPE

## N. T. Wright

> We are therefore Christ's ambassadors, as though
> God were making his appeal through us. We implore
> you on Christ's behalf: Be reconciled to God.
>
> 2 CORINTHIANS 5:20

God's new world of justice and joy, of hope for the whole earth, was launched when Jesus came out of the tomb on Easter morning, and I know that he calls his followers to live in him and by the power of his Spirit and so to be new-creation people here and now, bringing signs and symbols of the kingdom to birth on earth as in heaven. The resurrection of Jesus and the gift of the Spirit mean that we are called to bring real and effective signs of God's renewed creation to birth even in the midst of the present age. Not to bring works and signs of renewal to birth within God's creation is ultimately to collude, as Gnosticism always does, with the forces of sin and death themselves. But don't focus on the negative. Think of the positive: of the calling, in the present, to share in the surprising hope of God's whole new creation.

How can you birth real, effective signs of God's renewed creation?

*Lord Jesus Christ, help me speak the message of your reconciliation as an instrument of your rescue. Amen.*

# PARTAKE OF THE PAIN

## Brennan Manning

> Jesus had compassion on them and touched their eyes.
> Immediately they received their sight and followed him.
>
> MATTHEW 20:34

The etymology of the word *compassion* lies in two Latin words, *cum* and *patior*, meaning "to suffer with," to endure with, to struggle with, and to partake of the hunger, nakedness, loneliness, pain, and broken dreams of our brothers and sisters in the human family. Commitment to Jesus Christ without compassion for his people is a lie.

The life of integrity born of fidelity to the dream has a precise meaning in the mind of Christ. It leaves no room for romanticized idealism, condescending pity, or sentimental piety. When a disciple's every response, word, and decision is motivated by compassion, he has "put on Christ" and walks in the way of integrity. Biblically, compassion means action. Copious Christian tears shed for the dehydrated babies in Juarez is heartfelt emotion; when combined with giving them a cup of water, it is compassion.

Every time the Gospels mention that Jesus was moved with the deepest emotions or felt sorry for people, it led to his doing something—physical or inner healing, deliverance or exorcism, feeding the hungry crowds or intercessory prayer.

———— ∞ ————

How might you share the pain of those you know?

*Lord Jesus Christ, show me how to activate compassion,*
*relieving whatever struggle I can. Amen.*

# SEEK HIM, SEE HIM

## Dallas Willard

The upright will see his face.

PSALM 11:7

No doubt God wants us to see him. That is a part of his nature as outpouring love. Love always wants to be known. Thus he seeks for those who could safely and rightly worship him. God wants to be present to our minds with all the force of objects given clearly to ordinary perception.

Seeing is no simple thing, of course. Often a great deal of knowledge, experience, imagination, patience, and receptivity are required. Some people, it seems, are never able to see bacteria or cell structure through the microscope. But seeing is all the more difficult in spiritual things, where the objects, unlike bacteria or cells, must be willing to be seen.

Persons rarely become present where they are not heartily wanted. Certainly that is true for you and me. We prefer to be wanted, warmly wanted, before we reveal our souls—or even come to a party. The ability to see and the practice of seeing God and God's world come through a process of seeking and growing in intimacy with him.

---

God is seen by those who long for him.

*Lord, shine within me the countenance of your knowledge as I seek and live for you. Amen.*

# GOD'S FUTURE SURPRISES

## N. T. Wright

> He who sits on the throne said, "Behold, I am making all things
> new." And He said, "Write, for these words are faithful and true."
>
> REVELATION 21:5 NASB

The majestic but mysterious ending of the Revelation of John leaves us with fascinating and perhaps frustrating hints of future purposes, further work of which the eventual new creation is just the beginning. The description of the New Jerusalem in chapters 21 and 22 is quite clear that some categories of people are "outside": the dogs, the fornicators, those who speak and make lies. But then, just when we have in our minds a picture of two nice, tidy categories, the insiders and the outsiders, we find that the river of the water of life flows *out of* the city; that growing on either bank is the tree of life, not a single tree but a great many; and that "the leaves of the tree are for the healing of the nations." There is a great mystery here, and all our speaking about God's eventual future must make room for it. This is not at all to cast doubt on the reality of final judgment for those who have resolutely worshiped and served the idols that dehumanize us and deface God's world. It is to say that God is always the God of surprises.

———— ⌘ ————

Although God promises to come and make everything new, that newness is still a mystery full of surprises.

> *Lord, thank you for being a God beyond*
> *my imagining or understanding. Amen.*

# COME TO CHRIST IN NEED

## Frederick Buechner

"Come to me, all you that are weary and are carrying heavy burdens, and I will give you rest. Take my yoke upon you, and learn from me; for I am gentle and humble in heart, and you will find rest for your souls. For my yoke is easy, and my burden is light."

MATTHEW 11:28–30 NRSV

In a sense we are all hungry and in need, but most of us don't recognize it. With plenty to eat in the Deepfreeze, with a roof over our heads and a car in the garage, we assume that the empty feeling inside must be just a case of the blues that can be cured by a weekend in the country or an extra martini at lunch or the purchase of a color TV.

The poor, on the other hand, are under no such delusion. The poor stand to bear a better chance than most us of knowing what he's talking about in this passage and knowing that he's talking to them. In desperation they may even be willing to consider the possibility of accepting his offer. This is perhaps why Jesus on several occasions called them peculiarly blessed.

In what ways are you hungering and in need because of weariness and burdens? How would you like Jesus to give you rest?

*Lord Jesus Christ, Son of God, I come to you in hunger and need, in weariness and with burdens—ready to accept your offer of rest. Amen.*

# LOSE YOUR LIFE TO KEEP YOUR LIFE

## Henri J. M. Nouwen

> "Whoever seeks to keep his life will lose it, and
> whoever loses his life will preserve it."
>
> LUKE 17:33 NASB

The great paradox of life is that those who lose their lives will gain them. This paradox becomes visible in very ordinary situations. If we cling to our friends, we may lose them, but if we are nonpossessive in our relationships, we will make many friends. If fame is what we seek and desire, it often vanishes as soon as we acquire it, but if we have no need to be known, we might be remembered long after our deaths. When we want to be in the center, we easily end up on the margins, but when we are free enough to be wherever we must be, we often find ourselves in the center.

Giving away our lives for others is the greatest of all human acts. This will gain us our lives.

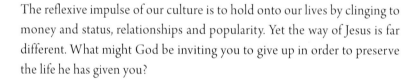

The reflexive impulse of our culture is to hold onto our lives by clinging to money and status, relationships and popularity. Yet the way of Jesus is far different. What might God be inviting you to give up in order to preserve the life he has given you?

*Lord, reveal to me the ways in which you're inviting me to gain life by giving it up to develop your kingdom life within me. Amen.*

# SEE YOUR ENEMIES

## Eugene Peterson

"Do good to those who hate you."

LUKE 6:27 NRSV

Loving enemies presupposes that we know that they are there, whether many or few, and have begun to identify them. Enemies, especially for those who live by faith, are a fact of life. If we don't know we have them or who they are, we live in a dangerous naïveté.

Our hate is used by God to bring the enemies of life and salvation to notice and then involve us in active compassion for the victims. Once involved we find that while hate provides the necessary spark for ignition, it is the wrong fuel for the engines of judgment; only love is adequate to sustain these passions.

But we must not imagine that loving and praying for our enemies in love is a strategy that will turn them into good friends. Love is the last thing that our enemies want from us and often acts as a goad to redoubled fury. Love requires vulnerability, forgiveness, and response; the enemies want power and control and dominion. The enemies that Jesus loved and prayed for killed him.

How might it look to name and love those whom the psalmists identified as the "pestilence that stalks in darkness" and "the destruction that lays waste at noon" (Psalm 91:6 NASB)?

*Lord, may I honestly identify the enemies of
the world but love them as you do. Amen.*

# LET CHRIST REWRITE YOUR SCRIPT

## Brennan Manning

> Let all who take refuge in You be glad,
>
> Let them ever sing for joy.
>
> PSALM 5:11 NASB

Who will rewrite the script for self-hatred? The Compassionate One! With a graciousness, a kindness, and an understanding of human weakness that only God could inhabit and exhibit, he liberates us from alienation and self-condemnation and offers a new possibility to each of us in our brokenness. He is the Savior who saves us from ourselves. His gospel is Good News indeed! Jesus, in effect, says, "Burn the old tapes spinning round in your head that bind you up and lock you into a self-centered stereotype. Listen to the new song of salvation written for those who know that they are poor. Let go of your fear of my Father and your dislike of yourself."

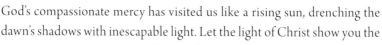

God's compassionate mercy has visited us like a rising sun, drenching the dawn's shadows with inescapable light. Let the light of Christ show you the way into a new attitude toward yourself.

*Lord Jesus, I praise you for the light of your mercy.*
*Show me the way of peace. Amen.*

# NOBLE LEADERSHIP

## Dallas Willard

The overseer is to be above reproach.

1 Timothy 3:2

Those of us who exercise leadership for Christ must constantly look to him for power to accomplish what lies far beyond human strength and ingenuity. More deeply, we must find from him his character to bear his power.

Our contemporary situation calls for Christian leaders and followers alike to plan for Christlikeness through the full though sensible use of disciplines for life from the Spirit. As with Jesus himself, periods of solitude and silence, study and worship, sacrifice and fellowship, make our lives accessible to our Father and open to us the resources of his kingdom. The great ones for Christ through the ages have known this, and with all their shortcomings have combined a high degree of inner Christlikeness with astonishing effectiveness in their missions. Today as never before, we require strength and insight to love and honor our role among Christ's people and to inspire the same in others.

———

How would Christ live within your leadership role?

*Lord, empower me to lead and serve the way you do. Amen.*

# REST IN WHAT GOD IS

## A. W. Tozer

> "Because you have seen Me, have you believed? Blessed
> are they who did not see, and yet believed."
>
> JOHN 20:29 NASB

In spite of tears and pain and death we believe that the God who made us all is infinitely wise and good. As Abraham staggered not at the promises of God through unbelief but was strong in faith, giving the glory to God, and was fully persuaded that what he had promised he was able to perform, so do we base our hope in God alone and hope against hope till the day breaks. We rest in *what God is*. I believe that this alone is true faith. Any faith that must be supported by the evidence of the senses is not real faith.

The testimony of faith is that, no matter how things look in this fallen world, all God's acts arrive in perfect wisdom. The incarnation of the Eternal Son in human flesh was one of God's mighty deeds, and we may be sure that this awesome deed was done with a perfection possible only to the Infinite.

———— ᴑᴙᴑ ————

To understand what it means to have true faith read Hebrews 11, which catalogs those who risked all by trusting in God's promises and performance. No matter how disastrous circumstances appeared, they trusted God fully.

*Lord, teach me to fully believe that you are infinitely wise and good, and able to perform your promises. Amen.*

# SAVED IN HOPE, SAVED AS A WHOLE

## N. T. Wright

In hope we were saved.

ROMANS 8:24 NRSV

The verb "we were saved" indicates a past action, something that has already taken place. But this remains "in hope" because we still look forward to the ultimate future salvation of which Paul speaks in (for instance) Romans 5:9–10.

It is fascinating to see how many passages are juxtaposed with others that speak of salvation in larger terms, seeming to go beyond present physical healing or rescue. This juxtaposition makes some Christians nervous (surely, they think, salvation ought to be a *spiritual* matter!), but it doesn't seem to have troubled the early church at all. For the first Christians, the ultimate salvation was all about God's new world, and the point of what Jesus and the apostles were doing when they were healing people or being rescued from shipwreck or whatever it was that this was a proper anticipation of that ultimate salvation, that healing transformation of space, time, and matter. The future rescue that God had planned and promised was starting to come true in the present. We are saved not as souls but as wholes.

In what way do you want to be saved as a whole—physically, emotionally, relationally—as much as you are saved spiritually?

*Lord, save me wholly in the present; may that salvation inspire my hope in the future. Amen.*

# NO MANIPULATION REQUIRED

## Frederick Buechner

> Jacob replied, "I will not let you go unless you bless me."
>
> GENESIS 32:26

God told Jacob that the land he was lying on was to belong to him and his descendants and that someday his descendants would become a great nation. God then added a personal PS by saying, "Behold, I am with you and will keep you wherever you go" (Genesis 28:15).

It wasn't holy hell that God gave him, in other words, but holy heaven, not to mention the marvelous lesson thrown in for good measure. The lesson was, needless to say, that even for a dyed-in-the-wool, double-barreled con artist like Jacob there are a few things in this world you can't get but can only be given, and one of these things is love in general, and another is the love of God in particular.

Another part of the lesson was that, luckily for Jacob, God doesn't love people because of who they are, but because of who God is. "It's on the house" is one way of saying it and "It's by grace" is another, just as it was by grace that it was Jacob of all people who became not only the father of the twelve tribes of Israel, but the many-times great-grandfather of Jesus of Nazareth, and just as it was by grace that Jesus of Nazareth was born into this world at all.

---

Because God loves you not for who you are but who he is, how reliable do you think God is?

*Father, thank you for the favor that rests upon me because of you, not me. Amen.*

# OUR ANCIENT HUMAN MANDATE

## N. T. Wright

*Always give yourselves fully to the work of the Lord, because
you know that your labor in the Lord is not in vain.*

1 CORINTHIANS 15:58

What we do in the Lord is "not in vain," and that is the mandate we need for every act of justice and mercy, every program of ecology, every effort to reflect God's wise stewardly image into his creation. In the new creation the ancient human mandate to look after the garden is dramatically reaffirmed, as John hints in his resurrection story, where Mary supposes Jesus is the gardener. The resurrection of Jesus is the reaffirmation of the goodness of creation, and the gift of the Spirit is there to make us the fully human beings we were supposed to be, precisely so that we can fulfill that mandate at last.

The work we do in the present, then, gains its full significance from the eventual design in which it is meant to belong.

We must work now to show forth signs of God's future renewal and reign. How can you live this mandate in your own life?

> *Lord, I acknowledge my calling to look after the garden
> of your creation; reveal how I can do that. Amen.*

# FORGIVENESS ISN'T LOGICAL

## James Bryan Smith

> The message of the cross is foolishness to those who are perishing,
> but to us who are being saved it is the power of God.
>
> 1 CORINTHIANS 1:18 NKJV

If a person asks me, "Jim, how do you know you are forgiven?" I can only point to the cross. I cannot rely on my own feelings, nor can I explain it logically. God's forgiveness is a promise made to us, but it takes time for us to let it sink in.

John Wesley, the eighteenth-century theologian who founded Methodism, lived as a Christian for thirty-five years before he accepted God's forgiveness for himself. He was an ordained minister for thirteen years, preaching the gospel to countless people, before he believed in the message himself. His friend, Peter Böhler, told him, "Preach faith until you have it." One evening a few months later he let the message of forgiveness penetrate his soul.

Like Wesley, it may take us years to receive the message of God's complete forgiveness. We may need to hear it over and over, to teach it and even preach it, before we can make it our own. Once we do, we can expect that our heart too will be "strangely warmed."

———— ✏ ————

Have you fully wrapped your mind around the idea that God has forgiven you? Or is it foolish, illogical, nonsensical? Let the idea sink in and penetrate your soul.

> *Lord, your forgiveness seems too good to*
> *be true, but I receive it and rest in it. Amen.*

# NEVER-CEASING BEINGS

## Dallas Willard

"Those who believe in me, even though they die, will live."

JOHN 11:25 NRSV

Jesus made a special point of saying that those who rely on him and have received the kind of life that flows in him and in God will never experience death. So as we think of our life and make plans for it, we should not be anticipating going through some terrible event called "death," to be avoided at all costs even though it can't be avoided. That is the usual attitude for human beings, no doubt. But, immersed in Christ in action, we may be sure that our life—yes, that familiar one we are each so well acquainted with—will never stop. We should be anticipating what we will be doing three hundred or a thousand or ten thousand years from now in this marvelous universe.

The hymn "Amazing Grace" accurately presents the future of redeemed humanity:

> When we've been there ten thousand years,
> Bright shining as the sun,
> We've no less days to sing God's praise,
> Than when we first begun.

We are never-ceasing spiritual beings with an eternal destiny in God's future world.

> *Jesus, through you I will never experience that*
> *most dreaded of realities, death. Thank you. Amen.*

# AMAZING FAITH

## Brennan Manning

> Jesus said to the centurion, "Go your way; and as you have believed, so let it be done for you." And his servant was healed that same hour.
>
> MATTHEW 8:13 NKJV

Remember the day that Jesus healed the centurion's servant? The military man falls down and says, "Sir, I am not worthy to have you enter under my roof. Just give an order and my boy will get better" (Matthew 8:8). But the most revealing line in that story, according to Matthew, is that "Jesus was astonished." He spun round and cried out, "I tell you solemnly, nowhere in Israel have I found faith like this" (8:10). *At last,* Jesus is saying—*finally someone who understands me and what I want to be for my people: a Savior of boundless compassion, unbearable forgiveness, infinite patience, and healing love. Will the rest of you let me be who I am and stop imposing your small, silly, and self-styled ideas of who you think I ought to be!*

Small wonder that [one] biblical scholar . . . said, "The old Baltimore catechism isn't wrong, just inadequate. When it says, 'Man is made to know, love, and serve God,' it should read, man is made to know how God longs to love and serve him." Jesus remains Lord by serving us.

---

A God who serves was a revolutionary idea in Jesus' day, and it still is today. How do you respond to the idea that the Lord longs to serve you?

*Lord, help me imitate you by serving others. Amen.*

# DEFINING NEIGHBOR, DOING MERCY

## Frederick Buechner

Wanting to justify himself, he asked Jesus, "And who is my neighbor?"

LUKE 10:29 NRSV

When Jesus said to love your neighbor a lawyer who was present asked him to clarify what he meant by *neighbor*. He wanted a legal definition he could refer to in case the question of loving one ever happened to come up. He presumably wanted something on the order of: "a neighbor (hereinafter referred to as *the party of the first part*) is to be construed as meaning a person of Jewish descent whose legal residence is within a radius of no more than three statute miles from one's own legal residence unless there is another person of Jewish descent (hereinafter to be referred to as *the party of the second part*) living closer to the party of the first part than one is oneself, in which case the party of the second part is to be construed as neighbor to the party of the first part and one is oneself relieved of all responsibility of any sort or kind whatsoever."

Instead Jesus told the story of the good Samaritan, the point of which seems to be that your neighbor is to be construed as meaning anybody who needs you. The lawyer's response is left unrecorded.

———— ∞ ————

Jesus defines neighbor-love as showing mercy to any around us who have need. May we follow Jesus' closing words: "Go and do likewise" (Luke 10:37 NRSV).

*Jesus, give me eyes to see all those around me as neighbors and compassion to respond to their needs. Amen.*

# LIKE JESUS, BE PREPARED

## Henri J. M. Nouwen

> "Remember the word that I said to you, 'A servant is not greater than his master.' If they persecuted Me, they will also persecute you."
>
> JOHN 15:20 NKJV

Jesus is the Blessed One. And the face of the Blessed One shows poverty, gentleness, grief, hunger, and thirst for uprightness, mercy, purity of heart, a desire to make peace, and the signs of persecution.

Jesus, the favorite Child of God, is persecuted. He who is poor, gentle, mourning; he who hungers and thirsts for uprightness; he who is merciful, pure of heart, and a peacemaker is not welcome in this world. The Blessed One of God is a threat to the established order and a source of constant irritation to those who consider themselves the rulers of this world. In their eyes, he cannot be tolerated and needs to be destroyed, because letting him be seems like a confession of guilt.

When we strive to become like Jesus, we cannot expect always to be liked and admired. We have to be prepared to be rejected.

The whole gospel message is this: become like Jesus. When we keep his teachings, we can expect some to disagree with us. Suffering for his sake is part of what it means to follow him.

*Lord Jesus Christ, Son of God, strengthen me to face critics and scoffers as gracefully as you did. Amen.*

# FOR LOVE OF YOU

## Brennan Manning

By this we know love, because He laid down His life for us.

1 JOHN 3:16 NKJV

My own glimpse of Jesus moved from obscurity to increasing clarity on a winter's night in the Zaragoza desert in Spain. The world was asleep, but my heart was awake to God. During prayer I heard Jesus say, "For love of you I left my Father's side. I came to you who ran from me, who fled me, who did not want to hear my name. For love of you I was covered with spit, punched and beaten, and fixed to the wood of the cross."

Although it was many years ago, this morning in an hour of quiet time, I realized that those words still burned on my life. Whether I am in a state of grace or disgrace, the words impose themselves with the stark realism of objective truth. That night in the cave I stared at a crucifix for hours, figuratively seeing the blood streaming from every wound and pore in Christ's body. The longer I looked, the more I realized that no man has ever loved me and no woman could ever love me as he does. I cried out in the darkness, "Jesus, are you crazy—are you out of your mind to have loved me so much?" I learned that night what a wise old Franciscan told me: "Once you come to know the love of Jesus Christ, nothing else in the world will seem beautiful or desirable."

Is any love more attractive than Jesus'?

*Lord, thank you for letting love move you to save me. Amen.*

# GOD'S ESTABLISHED FORGIVENESS

## James Bryan Smith

> The wages of sin is death, but the gift of
> God is eternal life in Christ Jesus our Lord.
>
> ROMANS 6:23 NKJV

God loves us so much that he forgives us even before we ask for forgiveness. That is what I see when I look at the cross. Even before we were born God was reconciling himself to us through the sacrifice of his Son. Why did God do this? Why did God have to die? In order to understand the forgiveness established by God we must turn to the Bible.

The Hebrew concept of forgiveness involved the shedding of blood because the penalty for sin was death. The animal that was sacrificed took the place of the person who was guilty, slaughtered for the offenses of the people.

When John the Baptist referred to Jesus as "the Lamb of God who takes away the sin of the world" (John 1:29), he was foreshadowing the fact that Jesus' death would have an effect on the way the entire world would relate to God. Sin would no longer be covered (which is what the word *atonement* means, to cover), which was temporary, but taken away, which is eternal.

---

What does it mean to you that because Jesus received the wages of death, your sins have been eternally taken away, and you've received eternal life?

*Lord Jesus Christ, Lamb of God, thank you for paying my debt so I could receive the gift of eternal life. Amen.*

AUGUST 26 ✓

# IS JESUS COMPETENT?

## Dallas Willard

*He is before all things, and in him all things hold together.*

COLOSSIANS 1:17

It is not possible to trust Jesus, or anyone else, in matters where we do not believe him to be competent. We cannot pray for his help and rely on his collaboration in dealing with real-life matters we suspect might defeat his knowledge or abilities.

And can we seriously imagine that Jesus could be Lord if he were not smart? If he were divine, would he be dumb? Or uninformed? Once you stop to think about it, how could he be what we take him to be in all other respects and not be the best-informed and most intelligent person of all, the smartest person who ever lived?

Today we think people are smart who make lightbulbs and computer chips and rockets out of "stuff" already provided! He made "the stuff"! Small wonder, then, that the first Christians thought he held within himself "all of the treasures of wisdom and knowledge" (Colossians 2:3). This confidence in his intellectual greatness is the basis of the radicalism of Christ-following in relation to the human order.

Our commitment to Jesus stands on no other foundation than a recognition that he is the one who knows everything.

*Jesus, thank you for being all-wise, all-knowing, and all-loving. Amen.*

# GOD IS HERE, THERE, AND EVERYWHERE

## A. W. Tozer

"I am with you," declares the LORD.

HAGGAI 1:13

Canon W. G. H. Holmes of India told of seeing Hindu worshipers tapping on trees and stones and whispering "Are you there? Are you there?" to the god they hoped might reside within. In complete humility the instructed Christian brings the answer to that question. He is there as he is here and everywhere, not confined to tree or stone, but free in the universe, near to everything, next to everyone, and through Jesus Christ immediately accessible to every loving heart.

This truth is to the convinced Christian a source of deep comfort in sorrow and of steadfast assurance in all the various experiences of his life. To him "the practice of the presence of God" consists not of projecting an imaginary object from within his own mind and then seeking to realize its presence; it is rather to recognize the real presence of the One whom all sound theology declares to be already there. The resultant experience is not visionary but real.

The healing balm distilled from the garments of the enfolding Presence cures our ills before they become fatal. The knowledge that we are never alone calms the troubled sea of our lives and speaks peace to our souls.

———— ❧ ————

When was a time you felt the presence of God? What was that like? What happened?

*Lord, give me a deep awareness of your presence in all times and places. Help me to know, feel, and believe that you are with me. Amen.*

# THE MYSTERY OF YOUR SELF

## Frederick Buechner

God has chosen to make known . . . the glorious riches of
this mystery, which is Christ in you, the hope of glory.

COLOSSIANS 1:27

There are mysteries you can solve by taking thought. For instance, a murder mystery whose mysteriousness must be dispelled in order for the truth to be known.

There are other mysteries that do not conceal a truth to think your way to, but whose truth is itself the mystery. The mystery of your self, for example. The more you try to fathom it, the more fathomless it is revealed to be. No matter how much of your self you are able to objectify and examine, the quintessential, living part of your self will always elude you, that is, the part that is conducting the examination. Thus you do not solve the mystery, you live the mystery. And you do that not by fully knowing yourself, but by fully being yourself.

To say that God is a mystery is to say that you can never nail him down. Even on Christ the nails proved ultimately ineffective.

---

How do you feel about being a mystery to yourself but not to God?

*Jesus, show me how to be fully myself as you were. Amen.*

# LORD, REPAY THE DESTROYERS

## Eugene Peterson

> Daughter Babylon, doomed to destruction,
> happy is the one who repays you
> according to what you have done to us.
>
> PSALM 137:8

The life of prayer carries us into difficult country, a country in which we become aware that evil is far more extensive than anything we ever guessed, where malignity has worked itself perversely and deeply into the world's ways. As Kant said, "Evil is radical."

We have been brought up, most of us, interpreting what is wrong in the world on a grid of moralism. Moralism trains us in making cool, detached judgments. Deep down, the moralist suspects that there are no, or at least not very many, real victims. People get what is coming to them. In the long run people reap what they sow. The rape victim, the unemployed, the emotionally ill, the prisoner, the refugee—if we were privy to all the details we would see that, in fact, "they asked for it."

The Psalms will have none of this. The Psalms assume a moral structure to life, but their main work is not to train us in judgmental moralism but to grapple with evil.

———— ∞ ————

How do you grapple with and pray against evil?

*Lord, at times neither my mind nor emotions are prepared to deal with evil; yet look after the destroyed. Amen.*

# GOD'S AGENT OF LOVE: THE HOLY SPIRIT

## James Bryan Smith

*When you believed, you were marked in him with a seal, the promised Holy Spirit, who is a deposit guaranteeing our inheritance until the redemption of those who are God's possession.*

EPHESIANS 1:13–14

God's love and acceptance of us is constant and never changes. How do we come to know of this love? The Holy Spirit is the agent that makes it known to us. The Holy Spirit of God enters into us and whispers his love. Flesh and blood, logic and reason will never reveal God's love to us. It is beyond our understanding; it must be revealed.

"The outpouring of the Holy Spirit is really the outpouring of his love," wrote French monk Abbé de Tourville.[14] The Holy Spirit is the continuation of the love of God seen in Jesus. The love between the Father and the Son is communicated to us through the Holy Spirit. We are temples in whom the Spirit of God dwells. God is love; love itself dwells within us. That is why John said we know we are born of God when we are able to love.

It is the voice of the Spirit within us that reminds us that we are the Beloved. If we listen closely, we will hear these words of love.

When do you find yourself doubting God's love for you? In those moments call upon the Holy Spirit, who reminds us of that love.

*Lord, give me ears to hear you whisper your love to me. Amen.*

253

# THE MEANING OF GOD'S FORGIVENESS

## James Bryan Smith

> When you were dead in your sins . . . God made you alive
> with Christ. He forgave us all our sins, having canceled the
> charge of our legal indebtedness, which stood against us and
> condemned us; he has taken it away, nailing it to the cross.
>
> COLOSSIANS 2:13-14

In Jesus' death we see God's desire to forgive us. His offer of forgiveness is extended to all people for all time. There is not a person, living or dead, for whom Jesus did not die. "I forgive you, I forgive, I forgive you" whispers the cross through all eternity. God established our forgiveness by something he did for us, even before we ever thought of turning to him. God is forgiveness.

What does this mean for you and me? It means that God, in Christ, has erased the record that stood against us, nailing it to the cross. Now we can have peace with God. There is nothing standing in the way of our relationship with God. God came to reconcile us to himself even before we turned to him. Because it is God who establishes this forgiveness and not ourselves, we are given a peace that cannot be destroyed.

---

Because of Jesus' death on the cross, there is no more need for sacrifice; his was sufficient for all time. There's nothing left for us to do other than open our hands and receive God's gift.

*Lord, thank you for offering me your forgiveness;*
*I accept it enthusiastically this day. Amen.*

September

# LET CHRIST'S MIND-SET BE IN YOU

## Dallas Willard

Do nothing from selfishness or empty conceit, but with humility of mind regard one another as more important than yourselves; do not merely look out for your own personal interests, but also for the interests of others. Have this attitude in yourselves which was also in Christ Jesus.

PHILIPPIANS 2:3–5 NASB

The leader with Christ knows that we do not exercise leadership for our own gratification. Power is not a prize. Position is not for personal gain in any respect. To get or hold onto position is simply not an objective. Leading is not something we need to make us okay. My self-esteem is not tied to success as a leader. In companionship with Jesus, I am abundantly cared for. Who leads is God's business. Fear of failing to keep our position does not cross our minds as we follow Jesus. We are entirely freed from what, in the world's way, everyone recognizes to be the number-one burden of leaders.

Paul's great "kenosis" passage in Philippians 2 lays out the path of the disciple of Jesus in leadership. The configuration of leadership is totally transformed by Jesus as we follow him into the kingdom of the heavens.

———

Jesus' leaders must be as humbles as slaves. After all, he himself didn't come to be served, but to serve (Matthew 20:28). Let Christ's same mind-set be in us.

*Lord, make me a servant, humble and meek—*
*just as you were when you suffered the cross. Amen.*

# BELIEVE WHAT GOD SAYS ABOUT HIMSELF

## A. W. Tozer

There is no one like you, Lᴏʀᴅ, and there is no God
but you, as we have heard with our own ears.

1 Cʜʀᴏɴɪᴄʟᴇs 17:20

I think it might be demonstrated that almost every heresy that has afflicted the church through the years has arisen from believing about God things that are not true, or from overemphasizing certain true things so as to obscure other things equally true. To magnify any attribute to the exclusion of another is to head straight for one of the dismal swamps of theology; and yet we are all constantly tempted to do just that.

For instance, the Bible teaches that God is love; some have interpreted this in such a way as virtually to deny that he is just, which the Bible also teaches. Others press the biblical doctrine of God's goodness so far that it is made to contradict His holiness.

We can hold a correct view of truth only by daring to believe every-thing God has said about himself. It is a grave responsibility that a man takes it upon himself when he seeks to edit out of God's self-revelation such features as he in his ignorance deems objectionable.

We'll find no conflict among God's attributes, for all that God is must coin-cide with all that God does.

*Lord, teach me more about the fullness of your character. Amen.*

# QUESTIONS MELT LIKE MIST

## Frederick Buechner

> I know that my Redeemer lives,
> and that at last he will stand upon the earth.
>
> JOB 19:25 NRSV

After Job's confrontation with God he had seen the great glory so shot through with sheer, fierce light and life and gladness, had heard the great voice raised in song so full of terror and wildness and beauty, that from that moment on, nothing else mattered. All possible questions melted like mist, and all he could say was, "I had heard of thee by the hearing of the ear, but now my eye sees thee; therefore I despise myself and repent in dust and ashes" (42:5–6).

But God didn't let him despise himself for long. He gave back to Job more riches than he had ever had before together with his health, and Job lived to have a whole new set of children.

Job never again asked for an explanation. He knew that, even if God gave him one that made splendid sense out of all the pain and suffering that had ever been since the world began, it was no longer splendid sense that he needed, because with his own eyes he had beheld, and not as a stranger, the One who in the end clothed all things, no matter how small or confused or in pain, with his own splendor.

And that was more than sufficient.

Would an encounter with God, like the one Job had, dissolve all your questions about pain and suffering?

*Lord, help me submit my questions to your glory. Amen.*

# THE ENGINE OF CHRISTIAN HOPE

## N. T. Wright

*We ourselves, who have the firstfruits of the Spirit, groan inwardly as we wait eagerly for our adoption to sonship, the redemption of our bodies.*

Romans 8:23

There is no room for doubt as to what he means: God's people are promised a new type of bodily existence, the fulfillment and redemption of our present bodily life. The rest of the early Christian writings, where they address the subject, are completely in tune with this.

The traditional picture of people going to either heaven or hell as a one-stage postmortem journey (with or without the option of some kind of purgatory or continuing journey as an intermediate stage) represents a serious distortion and diminution of the Christian hope. Bodily resurrection is not just one odd bit of that hope. It is the element that gives shape and meaning to the rest of the story we tell about God's ultimate purposes. Instead of talking vaguely about heaven and then trying to fit the language of resurrection into that, we should talk with biblical precision about the resurrection and reorganize our language about heaven around that.

Bodily resurrection, the engine of our faith, drives it and gives every other component its reason for working.

*Lord, help me refocus my hope on the resurrection of my body rather than my arrival in heaven. Amen.*

# LORD, SEARCH MY HEART

## James Bryan Smith

> Search me, O God, and know my heart;
> test me and know my thoughts.
> See if there is any wicked way in me,
> and lead me in the way everlasting.
>
> PSALM 139:23–24 NRSV

God wants to deal with sin itself, not simply get it erased. Once we have sinned it is over; nothing can change what has happened, no matter how bad we feel. What is important is that we work on what caused the sin so we do not do it again. How sad God must be when he hears us say, "I am sorry," but then we fail to let him heal us.

We are forgiven long before we repent. Experiencing that forgiveness, however, requires that we repent. Because I have been forgiven, because I have been accepted, because God loves me, I am free to walk in holiness. Repentance does not mean that we make some resolution to be morally perfect by tomorrow. Resolutions are mostly a matter of willpower, and they seldom have a positive, lasting effect. I have found that it is better to pray than to make resolutions. In our prayers we can let God examine us.

Like the psalmist, pray that God will search your heart and help you understand its depths so any unconfessed sin can be revealed and repented of, and your heart changed.

*Lord, search me and know my heart, test and know*
*my thoughts; expose any wicked ways in me and*
*lead me to walk in everlasting life. Amen.*

# HEAVEN MOVED REDEMPTIVELY

## Dallas Willard

"Blessed are the poor in spirit,
for theirs is the kingdom of heaven."

MATTHEW 5:3 NRSV

Jesus did not say, "Blessed are the poor in spirit because they are poor in spirit." He did not think, *What a fine thing it is to be destitute of every spiritual attainment or quality. It makes people worthy of the kingdom.* And we steal away the much more profound meaning of his teaching about the availability of the kingdom by replacing the state of spiritual impoverishment—in no way good in itself—with some supposedly praiseworthy state of mind or attitude that "qualifies" us for the kingdom.

In so doing we merely substitute another banal legalism for the ecstatic pronouncement of the gospel. Those poor in spirit are called "blessed" by Jesus, not because they are in a meritorious condition, but because, *precisely in spite of and in the midst of their ever so deplorable condition*, the rule of the heavens has moved redemptively upon and through them by the grace of Christ.

Those spiritually impoverished ones present before Jesus in the crowd are blessed only because the gracious touch of the heavens has freely fallen upon them.

———∞———

We are all spiritual beggars knocking at the door of God's kingdom for spiritual access, sustenance, and an audience with the King of kings.

*Lord, thank you for graciously providing all I need. Amen.*

# WHEN THE GOSPEL TAKES ROOT

## N. T. Wright

> They devoted themselves to the apostles' teaching and to
> fellowship, to the breaking of bread and to prayer.
>
> ACTS 2:42

How can the church announce that God is God, that Jesus is Lord, that the powers of evil, corruption, and death itself have been defeated, and that God's new world has begun? Doesn't this seem laughable? Well, it would be if it wasn't happening. But if a church is actively involved in seeking justice in the world, both globally and locally, and if it's cheerfully celebrating God's good creation and its rescue from corruption in art and music, and if its own internal life gives every sign that new creation is indeed happening, generating a new type of community—then suddenly the announcement makes a lot of sense.

So what account can we give, within this theology of new creation, of what happens when the gospel takes root? It happens again and again, thank God: people discover, firing up within themselves, the sense that it does make sense, that they really believe it, that they find it transforming the way they are thinking and feeling about all sorts of other things, that the presence of Jesus is suddenly a reality for them, that reading the Bible becomes exciting, that they can't get enough of Christian worship and fellowship.

———∞———

When the gospel ignites devotion to God's Word, worship, and fellowship, there's no telling what might happen!

*Lord, empower me to pursue eternal fruit. Amen.*

# SOMEONE IS LISTENING

## Frederick Buechner

Hear, LORD, and be merciful to me.

PSALM 30:10

According to Jesus, by far the most important thing about praying is to keep at it. Whatever else it may or may not be, prayer is at least talking to yourself, and that's not always a bad idea. Talk to yourself about your own life, about what you've done and what you've failed to do, and about who you are and who you wish you were and who the people you love are and the people you don't love too. Talk to yourself about what matters most to you, because if you don't, you may forget.

Believe Somebody is listening. Believe in miracles. That's what Jesus told the father who asked him to heal his epileptic son: "All things are possible to him who believes" (Mark 9:23).

What about when the boy is not healed? When, listened to or not listened to, the prayer goes unanswered? Who knows? Just keep praying, Jesus says. Even if the boy dies, keep on beating the path to God's door, because the one thing you can be sure of is that, down the path you beat with even your most half-cocked and halting prayer, the God you call upon will finally come.

When you pray, do you always believe you're being heard? How does that affect your praying?

*Father, thank you for hearing me, even when I*
*lack faith to believe that you do. Amen.*

# LOVE GOD TO EXPERIENCE HIS GENEROSITY

## Henri J. M. Nouwen

> The LORD will command the blessing on you in your storehouses and in all to which you set your hand.
>
> DEUTERONOMY 28:8 NKJV

God is a God of abundance, not a God of scarcity. Jesus reveals to us God's abundance when he offers so much bread to the people that there are twelve large baskets with leftover scraps (see John 6:5–15), and when he makes his disciples catch so many fish that their boat nearly sinks (Luke 5:1–7). God doesn't give us just enough. God gives us more than enough: more bread and fish than we can eat, more love than we dared to ask for.

God is a generous giver, but we can only see and enjoy God's generosity when we love God with all of our hearts, minds, and strength. As long as we say, "I will love you, God, but first show me your generosity," we will remain distant from God and unable to experience what God truly wants to give us, which is life and life in abundance.

---

The God we serve and love is overly generous with everything from fishes and loaves to storehouses and land. He doesn't just give us enough to get by; God pours out upon our lives more than we could ever ask or imagine.

*Lord, I love you, not only because of your generosity but because I get to extend it to others. Amen.*

# HONOR THE COST OF FORGIVENESS

## James Bryan Smith

You were bought with a price; therefore glorify God in your body.

1 CORINTHIANS 6:20 NRSV

Our forgiveness was obtained at a high price. We must never belittle sin, nor should we think of our forgiveness as a casual cleansing of the slate. It is, as Evelyn Underhill notes, "a stern and painful process" that will require "the reordering of the soul's disordered love."[15] God has forgiven us because he wants to establish a relationship with us. Within that relationship we are enabled to grow, to be healed, and to become whole.

The pain that we have caused through our sin is sometimes staggering and shocking. For years we may have run from God, afraid of his judgment and certain punishment. Off in the distance God stands alone, with a heart broken because we fail to accept his offer of forgiveness. He loves us with a furious passion. He forgives us even when we cannot forgive ourselves. Sometimes I can only sit and wonder at the thought of how much God loves us.

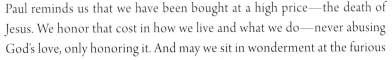

Paul reminds us that we have been bought at a high price—the death of Jesus. We honor that cost in how we live and what we do—never abusing God's love, only honoring it. And may we sit in wonderment at the furious love of God born out through his forgiveness of our sin.

*Lord, I recognize the price of my forgiveness; I confess my sin and desire to glorify you with my whole self. Amen.*

# WHEN HORRORS HAPPEN

## Frederick Buechner

> Come near to God and he will come near to you.
>
> JAMES 4:8

On the evening of the day the World Trade Center was destroyed by terrorists, a service was hastily improvised in one of the largest New York churches, where crowds of both believers and nonbelievers came together in search of whatever it is people search for at such times—some word of reassurance, some glimmer of hope.

"At times like these," the speaker said, "God is useless."

When I first heard of it, it struck me as appalling, and then it struck me as very brave, and finally it struck me as true.

When horrors happen we can't use God to make them unhappen any more than we can use a flood of light to put out a fire or Psalm 23 to find our way home in the dark. All we can do is to draw close to God and to each other as best we can, the way those stunned New Yorkers did, and to hope that, although God may well be useless when all hell breaks loose, there is nothing that happens, not even hell, where God is not present with us and for us.

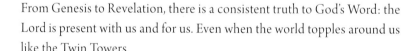

From Genesis to Revelation, there is a consistent truth to God's Word: the Lord is present with us and for us. Even when the world topples around us like the Twin Towers.

*Lord, let me feel your presence as I cling to you. Amen.*

# THE HOPE FOR LIFE BEFORE DEATH

## N. T. Wright

He will yet fill your mouth with laughter,

and your lips with shouts of joy.

JOB 8:21 NRSV

Jesus' resurrection is the foundation, I believe, for the work of hope in the day-to-day life of the church. My own vocation has taken me to an area of my country where, for many people, hope is in short supply. A nebulous sense of injustice hangs over many a community in the shape of the half-formed belief that the industrial collapse of the late twentieth century must be somebody's fault and that something should be done about it.

Part of the task of the church must be to take up that sense of injustice, to bring it to speech, to help people both articulate it and, when they are ready to do so, to turn it into prayer. And the task then continues with the church's work with the whole local community, to foster programs for better housing, schools, and community facilities, to encourage new job opportunities, and, in short, to foster hope at any and every level. When this is done, this is not something other than the surprising hope of the gospel, the hope for life after life after death. It is the direct result of that: the hope for life *before* death.

In what way do you think the gospel is hope for life now, and how can the church bring about this hope?

*Lord, thank you that salvation covers everything*
*we're involved in: life now, and life for eternity. Amen.*

# ONE FOOT IN ETERNITY

## Frederick Buechner

> For thus says the High and Lofty One
> Who inhabits eternity, whose name is Holy:
> "I dwell in the high and holy place,
> With him who has a contrite and humble spirit."
>
> ISAIAH 57:15 NKJV

As human beings we know time as a passing of unrepeatable events in the course of which everything passes away—including ourselves. As human beings, we also know occasions when we stand outside the passing of events and glimpse their meaning. Sometimes an event occurs in our lives (a birth, a death, a marriage—some event of unusual beauty, pain, joy) through which we catch a glimpse of what our lives are all about and maybe even what life itself is all about, and this glimpse of what "it's all about" involves not just the present, but the past and future too.

Inhabitants of time that we are, we stand on such occasions with one foot in eternity. God, as Isaiah says, "inhabiteth eternity" but stands with one foot in time. The part of time where he stands most particularly is Christ, and thus in Christ we catch a glimpse of what eternity is all about, what God is all about, and what we ourselves are all about too.

———

Although God dwells in the high and holy place, he is also with us.

*Lord, I praise you for your eternality;*
*I praise you for your companionship. Amen.*

# OPENHANDED GENEROSITY

## Henri J. M. Nouwen

"Give, and it will be given to you. A good measure, pressed down,
shaken together and running over, will be poured into your lap.
For with the measure you use, it will be measured to you."

LUKE 6:38

As fearful people we are inclined to develop a mind-set that makes us say, "There's not enough food for everyone, so I better be sure I save enough for myself in case of emergency," or "There's not enough knowledge for everyone to enjoy; so I'd better keep my knowledge to myself, so no one else will use it," or "There's not enough love to give to everybody, so I'd better keep my friends for myself to prevent others from taking them away from me." This is a scarcity mentality. It involves hoarding whatever we have, fearful that we won't have enough to survive. The tragedy, however, is that what you cling to ends up rotting in your hands.

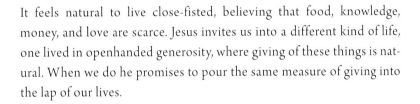

It feels natural to live close-fisted, believing that food, knowledge, money, and love are scarce. Jesus invites us into a different kind of life, one lived in openhanded generosity, where giving of these things is natural. When we do he promises to pour the same measure of giving into the lap of our lives.

*Lord, remind me to be openhanded rather than
selfish due to a perceived scarcity. Amen.*

# NEVER GROW NUMB TO YOUR DYNAMIC SALVATION

## Eugene Peterson

Praise the LORD, my soul,
and forget not all his benefits.

PSALM 103:2

The noun *g'mul*, benefit, is embedded in an action: an action of God is bringing or has brought something to a ripe finish. That, in fact, is what all of God's actions do. They work through the confused complexities of this tangled country of creation and sin to bring us and the country to a completed finish, a whole conclusion. The evidence—*g'mulim*, benefits—when we look around sharply and attentively is everywhere.

But it is easy to overlook the benefits, for very often more immediately before our eyes are projects not yet finished, the work in progress that the God of our salvation is engaged in. But if we "forget the benefits," we are only aware of our own efforts, our puny self-help efforts at making the best of a bad deal, our haphazard attempts at capitalizing on the chances available to us. If we "forget the benefits," we slip into what the psychologists label "sensory deprivation" and are deaf, dumb, and blind to the incessant, dynamic, flourishing salvation work that constitutes the dominant action in the country.

May we never become casual about all of what Christ accomplished for us.

*Lord, I marvel at all of the goodness you've rained on me. Thank you, Father. Amen.*

# WHY DO YOU WORK?

## Frederick Buechner

> What do people gain from all their labors
> at which they toil under the sun?
>
> ECCLESIASTES 1:3

Jobs are what people do for a living, many of them for eight hours a day, five days a week, minus vacations, for most of their lives. It is tragic to think how few of them have their hearts in it. They work mainly for the purpose of making money enough to enjoy their moments of not working.

If not working is the chief pleasure they have, you wonder if they wouldn't do better just to devote themselves to that from the start. They would probably end up in breadlines or begging, but even so the chances are they would be happier than pulling down a good salary as an insurance agent or a dental technician or a cabdriver and hating every minute of it.

If he's in it only for the money, the money is all he gains, and when he finally retires, he may well ask himself if it was worth giving most of his life for. If he's doing it for its own sake—if he enjoys doing it and the world needs it done—it may very possibly help to gain him his own soul.

Since we were created to work, consider your own job. Do you enjoy doing the work? Is your heart fully in it? What is your motivation for it?

*Lord, if I'm doing the wrong kind of work, lead me toward the fulfillment the right kind will bring. Amen.*

# ALL PRAYER IS PRAYED IN A STORY

## Eugene Peterson

A Psalm of David when he fled from Absalom his son.

NOTE PREFACING PSALM 3 NKJV

The life of David is full of incidents like this. Everyone's life is. Not a palace coup for most of us and, hopefully, not the treachery of a son, but conflict and failure and fear, love and betrayal, loss and salvation. Every day is a story, a morning beginning and evening ending that are boundaries for people who go about their tasks with more or less purpose, go to war, make love, earn a living, scheme and sin and believe. Everything is connected. Meaning is everywhere. The days add up to a life that is a story.

Psalm 3, its title tells us, is prayed in the middle of a story. All prayer is prayed in a story, by someone who is in the story. There are no storyless prayers. Story is to prayer what the body is to the soul, the circumstances in which it takes place. And prayer is to story what the soul is to the body, the life without which it would be a corpse. Prayers are prayed by people who live stories. Every life is a story. We are not always aware that we are living a story; often it seems more like a laundry list. But story it is.

If all prayer is prayed in story, consider your own narrative. How has it informed your prayer life?

*Lord, show me the meaning in my story. Amen.*

# THE FOCUS OF GOD'S GOSPEL PURPOSE

## N. T. Wright

> I am not ashamed of the gospel, because it is the
> power of God that brings salvation to everyone who
> believes: first to the Jew, then to the Gentile.
>
> ROMANS 1:16

Israel believed that the purposes of the creator God all came down to this question: How is God going to rescue Israel? What the gospel of Jesus revealed, however, was that the purposes of God were reaching out to a different question: How is God going to rescue the world through Israel and thereby rescue Israel itself as part of the process but not as the point of it all?

Maybe what we are faced with in our own day is a similar challenge: to focus not on the question of which human beings God is going to take to heaven and how he is going to do it but on the question of how God is going to redeem and renew his creation through human beings and how he is going to rescue those humans themselves as part of the process but not as the point of it all. If we could reread Romans and Revelation in the light of this reframing of the question, I think we would find much food for thought.

When we focus on the fullness of God's gospel purpose, the question of the church's mission is suddenly catapulted into center stage and reshaped in the process.

*Lord, remind me of your full gospel purpose: the rescue and renewal of the entire creation and human community. Amen.*

# MAGIC OR RELIGION

## Frederick Buechner

> "Yet not as I will, but as you will."
> MATTHEW 26:39

Magic is stepping on a crack to break your mother's back, or a dashboard Jesus to prevent smashups. Magic is going to church so you will get to heaven. Magic will always work if you do it by the book. Magic is manipulation and says, "My will be done." Religion is propitiation and says, "Thy will be done."

Religion is praying, and maybe the prayer will be answered and maybe it won't, at least not the way you want or when you want and maybe not at all. Even if you do it by the book, religion doesn't always work, as Jesus pointed out in one of his more somber utterances: "Not everyone who says, 'Lord, Lord,' shall enter the kingdom of heaven" (Matthew 7:21), the corollary to which would appear to be, "Not everyone who wouldn't be caught dead saying, 'Lord, Lord,' shall be blackballed from the kingdom of heaven." He softened the blow somewhat then by adding that the way to enter the kingdom of heaven is to do the will of his Father in heaven; but when religion claims that it's always sure what that will is, it's only bluffing. Magic is always sure.

If security's what you're after, try magic. If adventure is what you're after, try religion. The line between them is notoriously fuzzy.

---

When have you relied upon magic rather than religion?

*Lord Jesus, not as I will, but as you will. Amen.*

# YOU BELONG TO HIM

## Henri J. M. Nouwen

"If you belonged to the world, it would love you as its own. As it is, you do not belong to the world, but I have chosen you out of the world."

JOHN 15:19

The Beatitudes offer us a self-portrait of Jesus. At first it might seem to be a most unappealing portrait—who wants to be poor, mourning, and persecuted? Who can be truly gentle, merciful, pure in heart, a peacemaker, and always concerned about justice? Where is the realism here? Don't we have to survive in this world and use the ways of the world to do so?

Jesus shows us the way to be in the world without being of it. When we model our lives on his, a new world will open up for us. The kingdom of heaven will be ours, and the earth will be our inheritance. We will be comforted and have our fill; mercy will be shown to us. Yes, we will be recognized as God's children and truly see God, not just in an afterlife but here and now. That is the reward of modeling our lives on the life of Jesus!

Let's follow Jesus' lead in living in our earthly kingdom while pursuing his. Only then will we experience the fullness of God's life.

*Jesus, show me how to practice kingdom living while I'm waiting to go to my true home. Amen.*

# PRAYER: A LONGING FOR PRESENCE

## Brennan Manning

> Because He has inclined His ear to me,
> Therefore I will call upon Him as long as I live.
>
> PSALM 116:2 NKJV

Whatever else it may be, prayer is first and foremost an act of love. Before any pragmatic, utilitarian, or altruistic motivations, prayer is born of a desire to be with Jesus. His incomparable wisdom, compelling beauty, irresistible goodness, and unrestricted love lure us into the quiet of our hearts where he dwells. To really love someone implies a natural longing for presence and intimate communion.

Jesus prayed primarily because he loved his Father. Praise, adoration, thanksgiving, intercession, and petition emanated from his profound consciousness of being bonded to the transcendent God in filial intimacy. His personal experience of Yahweh Sabaoth as loving Father shaped not only his self-understanding but, like a knife slashing through wallpaper, brought a dramatic breakthrough into undreamed-of intimacy with God in prayer. Childlike candor, boundless trust, easy familiarity, deep reverence, joyful dependence, unflagging obedience, unmistakable tenderness, and an innate sense of belonging characterized Jesus' prayer.

———

Do you see prayer as an act of love, a necessary evil, a tired habit, a search for joy? How can you treat prayer more as a longing for God's presence?

*Lord, I come to you today seeking only you. Will you meet me here and fill me with your presence? Amen.*

# GOD'S GRACIOUS INVITATION

## James Bryan Smith

*I am writing to you, dear children, because your sins*
*have been forgiven on account of his name.*

1 JOHN 2:12

There is nothing that we have done or can do to earn this forgiveness, and this is precisely what causes many of us to reject it. We often prefer to be in control, to show that we are worthy, and to prove that we deserve to be forgiven. God's forgiveness cannot be earned, no matter how hard we try, but there is still something in us that wants to try.

Coming to believe in God's complete and final forgiveness was not an easy process for me. At first I thought it was too good to be true. I could not understand how someone could offer forgiveness without some act of contrition or promise of restitution. The major obstacle to receiving God's forgiveness is our unwillingness to accept God's offer as it is. We like to add to it, modify and adjust it, to make it more realistic. I had to come to the point where I needed to let go of my own standards and simply accept God's gracious invitation.

It is on account of Jesus that you have been forgiven. Accepting this forgiveness is humbling, because we can't do anything to earn it. All we can do is stand in awe and acceptance.

*Jesus, I simply accept the fact I am forgiven*
*because of you. Thank you, Lord. Amen.*

# WHEN YOU ARE PERSECUTED, REJOICE!

## Dallas Willard

"Blessed are you when people hate you, and when they exclude you, revile you, and defame you on account of the Son of Man. Rejoice in that day and leap for joy, for surely your reward is great in heaven."

LUKE 6:22–23 NRSV

W e see those insulted, persecuted, and lied about because they have "gone off their rocker and taken up with that Jesus." That is certainly how his disciples were viewed at the time. "They actually think this carpenter from Hicksville is the one sent to save the world!" It is almost impossible for anyone who has not received this sort of treatment to understand how degrading it is.

From the human point of view, this may be the position most removed from God's blessing, because you are, in the eyes of surrounding society, precisely offending against God. Thus, when they kill you they think they are doing God a favor (John 16:2). Yet, Jesus says, jump for joy when this happens, from the knowledge that even now you have a great and imperishable reward in God's world, in the heavens. Your reputation stands high before God the Father and his eternal family, whose companionship and love and resources are now and forever your inheritance.

———— ✿ ————

The next time you experience insults, persecution, and exclusion because you follow the Son of Man, do what Jesus said: rejoice and jump for joy. For you know your reward is secure.

*Jesus, should I ever face persecution in your name, strengthen me to praise you even as I pray for your help. Amen.*

# THE FAITHFUL, TRUE GOD

## A. W. Tozer

Know that the LORD your God, He is God, the faithful God
who keeps covenant and mercy for a thousand generations
with those who love Him and keep His commandments.

DEUTERONOMY 7:9 NKJV

The faithfulness of God is a datum of sound theology but to the believer it becomes far more than that: it passes through the processes of the understanding and goes on to become nourishing food for the soul. For the Scriptures not only teach truth, they show also its uses for mankind. The inspired writers were men of like passion with us, dwelling in the midst of life. What they learned about God became to them a sword, a shield, a hammer; it became their life motivation, their good hope, and their confident expectation. From the objective facts of theology their hearts made how many thousand joyous deductions and personal applications!

Upon God's faithfulness rests our whole hope of future blessedness. Only as he is faithful will his covenants stand and his promises be honored. Only as we have complete assurance that he is faithful may we live in peace and look forward with assurance to the life to come.

From Torah to Psalms, Gospels to Revelation, Scripture rings with the faithfulness of God. In fact, Christ's own name is Faithful and True. How has God been faithful and true in your own life?

*Lord, build in me an assurance of your steadfast love. Amen.*

# A LESSON ON FORGIVENESS

## Frederick Buechner

> "Forgive us our sins,
> for we also forgive everyone who sins against us."
>
> LUKE 11:4

To forgive somebody is to say one way or another, "You have done something unspeakable, and by all rights I should call it quits between us. Both my pride and my principles demand no less. However, although I make no guarantees that I will be able to forget what you've done, and though we may both carry the scars for life, I refuse to let it stand between us. I still want you for my friend."

To accept forgiveness means to admit that you've done something unspeakable that needs to be forgiven, and thus both parties must swallow the same thing: their pride.

This seems to explain what Jesus means. Jesus is *not* saying that God's forgiveness is conditional upon our forgiving others. In the first place, forgiveness that's conditional isn't really forgiveness at all, just fair warning; and in the second place, our unforgivingness is among those things about us that we need to have God forgive us most. What Jesus apparently is saying is that the pride that keeps us from forgiving is the same pride that keeps us from accepting forgiveness, and will God please help us do something about it.

---

When you forgive, you're spared the dismal corrosion of bitterness and wounded pride. Forgiveness means freedom.

*Lord, show me pride's secret, damaging work in my heart. Amen.*

# KNOW GOD AS PARENT

## N. T. Wright

> Those who are led by the Spirit of God are the children
> of God. . . . And by him we cry, "*Abba*, Father."
>
> ROMANS 8:14–15

Christian spirituality combines a sense of the awe and majesty of God with a sense of his intimate presence. As Jesus addressed God by the Aramaic family word *Abba*, Father, so Christians are encouraged to do the same: to come to know God in the way in which, in the best sort of family, the child knows the parent.

From time to time I have met Christians who look puzzled at this and say that they have no idea what all that stuff is about. I have to say that being a Christian without having at least something of that intimate knowledge of the God who is at the same time majestic, awesome, and holy sounds like a contradiction in terms. I freely grant that there may be conditions under which, because of wounds in the personality, or some special calling of God, or some other reason, people may genuinely believe in the gospel of Jesus, strive to live by the Spirit, and yet have no sense of God's intimate presence. But Jesus declares that the Holy Spirit will not be denied to those who ask.

One characteristic sign of the Spirit's work in our lives is a sense of the intimate presence of God. Do you experience such a presence?

*Abba, may our life together be one of intimacy in relationship. Amen.*

# PAY ATTENTION, THEN PRAISE

## Frederick Buechner

> Let everything that has breath praise the LORD.
>
> PSALM 150:6 NKJV

Maybe you are praised for some generous thing you have done. The praise handed out is a measured response, a matter of saying something to one degree or another complimentary.

The way Psalm 148 describes it, praising God is another kettle of fish altogether. It is about as measured as a volcanic eruption. The whole of creation is in on the act—the sun and moon, the sea, fire and snow, Holstein cows and white-throated sparrows, old men in walkers and children who still haven't taken their first step. Their praise is not chiefly a matter of saying anything, because most of creation doesn't deal in words. Instead, the snow whirls, the fire roars, the Holstein bellows, the old man watches the moon rise. Their praise is not something that at their most complimentary they say, but something that at their truest they are.

We learn to praise God not by paying compliments, but by paying attention. Watch how the trees exult when the wind is in them. Mark the utter stillness of the great blue heron in the swamp. Listen to the sound of the rain. Learn how to say "Hallelujah" from the ones who say it right.

---

What things do you notice today for which you can offer praise?

*Jesus, make me aware of all the*
*praiseworthy creations around me. Amen.*

# JESUS APPRECIATES YOU

## Brennan Manning

"I say these things . . . so that they may have the
full measure of my joy within them."

JOHN 17:13

A fellow Franciscan once challenged me with a set of questions: Do you ever reflect upon the fact that Jesus feels proud of you? Proud that you accepted the faith he offered you? Proud that after he chose you, you chose him for a friend and Lord? Proud that you haven't given up? Proud that you trust he can help you?

Do you ever think that Jesus appreciates you for wanting him, for wanting to say no to so many things that would separate you from him? Do you ever think that Jesus is grateful to you for pausing to smile and comfort one of his children who has a great need to see a smile, to feel a touch?

Do you ever think of Jesus being grateful to you for learning more about him so that you can speak to others more deeply and truly about him? Do you ever think that Jesus can be angry or disappointed in you for not believing that he has forgiven you totally?

Jesus said, "I do not call you servants, but friends." Therefore there is the possibility of every feeling and emotion that can exist between friends to exist here and now between Jesus and you.

<hr />

Isn't it mind-boggling to consider that Jesus could feel for us what we feel for our closest confidants? Sit with that truth for a minute!

*Lord Jesus, thank you for granting me the status of friend. Amen.*

# CULTIVATE RESURRECTION HOPE

## N. T. Wright

> We, according to His promise, look for new heavens
> and a new earth in which righteousness dwells.
>
> 2 PETER 3:13 NKJV

Creation is beautiful, but its beauty is at present transient. It is in pain, but that pain is taken into the very heart of God and becomes part of the pain of new birth. We are committed to describing the world not just as it should be, not just as it is, but as—by God's grace alone!—one day it will be.

And we should never forget that when Jesus rose from the dead, as the paradigm, first example, and generating power of the whole new creation, the marks of the nails were not just visible on his hands and his feet. They were the way he was to be identified. When art comes to terms with *both* the wounds of the world *and* the promise of resurrection and learns how to express and respond to both at once, we will be on the way to a fresh vision, a fresh mission.

---

How can you creatively cultivate new expressions of life as a foretaste of the beauty of Christ's coming resurrection?

*Lord, make me an instrument of beauty, a cultivator of redemption's hope, all in the here and now. Amen.*

# A KING YOU CAN SEE

## Frederick Buechner

Who is this King of glory?
The Lᴏʀᴅ of hosts,
He is the King of glory.

Psᴀʟᴍ 24:10 ɴʀsᴠ

This rich metaphor, here proclaimed by the psalmist, is used again and again in Scripture. Yahweh alone was King over Israel, the prophets thundered: to be feared, to be loved, above all else to be obeyed. When the people decided they wanted a king of flesh and blood like all the other nations, Samuel warned them that the consequences would be tragic (1 Samuel 8:4–18), and history proved him correct in every particular. In the long run Israel as king and kingdom vanished from history altogether.

When Jesus entered Jerusalem for the last time, it was as King and Son of David that his followers hailed him. If it was a king like David the conquering hero that they were looking for, they were of course bitterly disappointed. What they got was a king like David the father, who, when he heard of his treacherous son's death, went up to his chamber and wept. "Would I had died instead of thee, O Absalom, my son, my son!" he cried out. They were the most kingly words he ever uttered and an uncanny foreshadowing of his many-times great-grandson who some thousand years later put his money where David's mouth had been.

<hr />

Would your faith be made easier by having a Lord you could see?

*Father, give me eyes to behold your glory. Amen.*

October

# WHAT IS GOD LIKE?

## James Bryan Smith

At that time Jesus came from Nazareth in Galilee.

MARK 1:9

We often find it difficult to trust God because we know so little about God, for he is greater than we can imagine and too vast for us to comprehend. That is why Jesus is so important to us. Jesus provides for us the clearest picture of the nature of God. Even if we had never heard his words but simply watched his actions, we would know something of the character of God.

The first verb Mark used to describe Jesus' action is "came." Jesus *came* to be with us. God's first move is to be among us—Immanuel, God is with us. There is more. Mark tells of a Jesus who "taught," "cured," "took her by the hand and lifted her up," and "forgave." We see a Jesus who "sat at dinner," "had compassion," and "laid hands" on people. He "blessed," he "sang," he "cried out," he "died," and he "rose from the dead." These are verbs of compassion. If we want to know what God is like, all we have to do is look at what Jesus did.

---

We see in Jesus' actions God's compassion, tenderness, and desire to care for us. How should they impact our understanding of God's character and our trust in it?

*Lord, because of the picture of your character given through the actions of your Son, I know I can trust you. Amen.*

# REORDERED THINKING

## Dallas Willard

"Many who are first will be last, and the last first."

MARK 10:31 NKJV

Jesus knew that much of what Peter and the others thought to be important was not really so, and that what they thought to be of no importance was often of great significance before God. Their thinking would have to be rearranged before they could understand their "reward" for leaving all to follow him. So he adds his "reversal" formula to help them keep thinking.

In general, many of those thought blessed or "first" in human terms are miserable or "last" in God's terms, and many of those regarded as cursed or "last" in human terms may well be blessed or "first" in God's terms, as they rely on the kingdom of Jesus. Many, but not necessarily all. The Beatitudes are lists of human "lasts" who at the individualized touch of the heavens become divine "firsts." The gospel of the kingdom is that no one is beyond beatitude, because the rule of God from the heavens is available to all. Everyone can reach it, and it can reach everyone.

Jesus' Beatitudes remind us those who are last in our world are really first in God's world. We respond appropriately to these teachings by living as if this is so.

*Jesus, I long for the touch of heaven that*
*makes me valuable in your kingdom. Amen.*

# THE SWEET MERCY OF GOD

## A. W. Tozer

> Once you were not a people, but now you are the people of God;
> once you had not received mercy, but now you have received mercy.
>
> 1 PETER 2:10

When through the blood of the everlasting covenant we children of the shadows reach at last our home in the light, we shall have a thousand strings to our harps, but the sweetest may well be the one tuned to sound forth most perfectly the mercy of God.

For what right will we have to be there? Did we not by our sins take part in that unholy rebellion which rashly sought to dethrone the glorious King of creation? And did we not in times past walk according to the course of this world, according to the evil prince of the power of the air, the spirit that now works in the sons of disobedience?

But we who were onetime enemies and alienated in our minds through wicked works shall then see God face-to-face and his name shall be in our foreheads. And all through the tender mercy of our God, whereby the Dayspring from on high hath visited us.

We who once lived in the flesh and were by nature the children of wrath, we who deserved hell will one day know the bliss of heaven—all because of the sweet mercy of God.

> *Lord, thank you for your rich mercy, which brought
> me from darkness into your marvelous light. Amen.*

# BEHOLD GOD'S GLORY IN CREATION

## Frederick Buechner

The firmament proclaims his handiwork.

PSALM 19:1 NRSV

Glory is to God what style is to an artist. A painting by Vermeer, a sonnet by Donne, a Mozart aria—each is so rich with the style of the one who made it that to the connoisseur it couldn't have been made by anybody else, and the effect is staggering. The style of artists brings you as close to the sound of their voices and the light in their eyes as it is possible to get this side of actually shaking hands with them.

In the words of Psalm 19:1, "The heavens are telling the glory of God." It is the same thing. To the connoisseur, not just sunsets and starry nights, but dust storms, rain forests, garter snakes, and the human face are all unmistakably the work of a single hand. Glory is the outward manifestation of that hand in its handiwork just as holiness is the inward. To behold God's glory, to sense God's style, is the closest you can get to God this side of paradise, just as to read *King Lear* is the closest you can get to Shakespeare.

Glory is what God looks like when for the time being all you have to look at him with is a pair of eyes.

When have you beheld the glory of God in creation? How did it impact your experience of God and his character?

*Lord, thank you for unveiling your glory*
*before me through all you have made. Amen.*

# A LOVABLE GOD

## Dallas Willard

> O love the LORD, all you His godly ones!
>
> PSALM 31:23 NASB

The acid test for any theology is this: Is the God presented one that can be loved, heart, soul, mind, and strength? If the thoughtful, honest answer is "Not really," then we need to look elsewhere or deeper. It does not really matter how sophisticated intellectually or doctrinally our approach is. If it fails to set a lovable God—a radiant, happy, friendly, accessible, and totally competent being—before ordinary people, we have gone wrong. We should not keep going in the same direction; we should turn around and take another road.

Theologians on both the left and the right, and those on no known scale of comparison, are all loved by God, who has great things in mind for every one of them. They are our neighbors, and we are to share God's vision and love for them. They need to love God. The theologian who does not love God is in great danger, and in danger of doing great harm, for he or she needs to know him and believe with assurance concerning him.

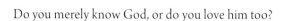

Do you merely know God, or do you love him too?

*My Father, I receive your love and offer you mine. Amen.*

# THE SURPRISE OF EVANGELISM

## N. T. Wright

*Always be prepared to give an answer to everyone who asks*
*you to give the reason for the hope that you have.*

1 PETER 3:15

Evangelism will always come as a surprise. You mean there is more? There is a new world, and it has already begun, and it works by healing and forgiveness and new starts and fresh energy? Yes, answers the church, and it comes about as people worship the God in whose image they are made, as they follow the Lord who bore their sins and rose from the dead, as they are indwelt by his Spirit and thereby given new life, a new way of life, a new zest for life.

It is often pointed out that some of the places most lacking in hope are not the industrial wastelands or the bleak landscapes shorn of beauty but the places where there is too much money, too much high culture, too much of everything except faith, hope, and love. To such places, and to the sad people who live in them as well as to those who find themselves battered by circumstances beyond their control, the message of Jesus and his death and resurrection comes as good news from a far country, news of surprising hope.

---

Evangelism flourishes when we give ourselves to works of justice and beauty, for they loudly proclaim the good news of God's new world.

*Lord, empower me to be always prepared to live, speak, and*
*bring the gospel into reality through surprising acts. Amen.*

# DO NOT BE AFRAID

## James Bryan Smith

> "Do not be afraid, Abram, I am your shield;
> your reward shall be very great."
>
> GENESIS 15:1 NRSV

O f all the words God has spoken to me over the years, "Do not be afraid" have to be the most frequent. I know that it is God when I hear those words in the depths of my soul. Perfect love casts out fear, so I have come to recognize that it is God who is speaking when those words calm me down.

I usually fear something in my life. Planes, trains, and automobiles seem to crash all around us. People I know and love get sick and die. Friends get divorced. Children are abused. It is a dark and frightening world. "Do not be afraid" echoes in my soul. Though fear frequently overtakes me, I am usually not afraid for long. I know that God is in control. Even if I should make a mess of things, even if something terrible occurs, I know that God is able to accomplish his ends.

God will never forget me. Like a mother whose child is nursing at her breast, God could never forget me. I am not trusting in myself, nor in my government, to protect me; I am learning to trust God, and therefore I am at peace.

What in life do you fear most? Can you let the compassionate care of God be the foundation of your trust and peace? How?

*Lord, I turn to you with my fears, trusting you as my shield. Amen.*

# YOUR NATURAL, GOD-CLOTHED BEAUTY

## Dallas Willard

"Not even Solomon in all his splendor was dressed like one of these flowers. If that is how God clothes the grass of the field . . . will he not much more clothe you—you of little faith?"

MATTHEW 6:29-30

The sad truth is that many people around us drift into a life in which being thin and correctly shaped, having "glorious" hair, appearing youthful, and so forth, are the only terms of blessedness or woe for their existence. It is all they know. They have heard nothing else. Many people today really are in this position.

Instead, Jesus took time in his teaching to point out the natural beauty of every human being. He calls attention to how the most glamorous person you know ("Solomon in all his splendor") is not as ravishingly beautiful as a simple field flower. Just place a daffodil side by side with anyone at the president's inaugural ball or at the motion-picture Academy Awards, and you will see. But the abundant life of the kingdom flowing through us makes us of greater natural beauty than the plants.

While all forms of media insist the most unfortunate people in the world are overweight, homely, and old, God's kingdom says otherwise. For as he bestows natural beauty on a simple flower, so he bestows the same beauty on every person on the planet.

*Lord, spark in me an understanding of my natural beauty, in which you yourself have clothed me. Amen.*

# THE JUSTIFYING HEART OF GOD

## A. W. Tozer

[God is] just and the one who justifies those who have faith in Jesus.

ROMANS 3:26

God's compassion flows out of his goodness, and goodness without justice is not goodness. God spares us because he is good, but he could not be good if he were not just. This is reason seeking to understand, not that it may believe but because it already believes.

A simpler and more familiar solution for the problem of how God can be just and still justify the unjust is found in the Christian doctrine of redemption. It is that, through the work of Christ in atonement, justice is not violated but satisfied when God spares a sinner. The just penalty for sin was exacted when Christ our Substitute died for us on the cross. However unpleasant this may sound to the ear of the natural man, it has ever been sweet to the ear of faith. Millions have been morally and spiritually transformed by this message, have lived lives of great moral power, and died at last peacefully trusting in it.

———— ✦ ————

What compassion and goodness we find at Christ's cross! For it is there Christ paid the price in our place; it is there the sinner is declared "Not guilty!"

*Lord, I rejoice in your compassion and goodness made evident in my salvation from sins through Christ's cross. Amen.*

# IT'S TIME TO WAKE UP!

## N. T. Wright

> Awake, sleeper,
> And arise from the dead,
> And Christ will shine on you.
> EPHESIANS 5:14 NASB

Living at the level of the nonheavenly world around you is like being asleep; worse, it's like that for which sleep is a metaphor—being dead. Lying, stealing, sexual immorality, bad temper, and so on (Paul lists them all in a devastating short passage) are forms of death, both for the person who commits them and for all whose lives are touched by their actions. They are ways of sleeping a deadly sleep.

It's time to wake up, he says. Come alive to the real world, the world where Jesus is Lord, the world into which your baptism brings you, the world you claim to belong to when you say in the creed that Jesus is Lord and that God raised him from the dead. What we all need from time to time is for someone (a friend, a spiritual director, a stranger, a sermon, a verse of Scripture, or simply the inner prompting of the Spirit) to say, "It's time to wake up! You've been asleep long enough! The sun is shining and there's a wonderful day out there! Wake up and get a life!"

---

Are you awake or asleep? What's one step you can take in your spiritual journey to wake up and live the life God has called you to in Christ?

> Lord, awaken me to the real world, where you are Lord,
> where I'm called to live your kind of life. Amen.

# BLESSED ARE GOD'S GRUBBY PEOPLE

## Dallas Willard

God has chosen the foolish things of the world to put to shame the wise.

1 CORINTHIANS 1:27 NKJV

W e must see from our heart that:

Blessed are the physically repulsive,
Blessed are those who smell bad,
The twisted, misshapen, deformed,
The too big, too little, too loud,
The bald, the fat, and the old—
For they are all riotously celebrated in the party of Jesus.

These are God's grubby people. Any spiritually healthy congregation of believers in Jesus will more or less look like these.

Among them there indeed are a few of the humanly wise, the influential, and the socially elite. They belong here too. God is not disturbed by them. But the Beatitudes is not a list of spiritual giants. Often you will discern a peculiar nobility and glory on and among these "blessed" ones. But it is not from them. It is the effulgence of the kingdom among them.

Rejoice that the heart of God is big enough to embrace and bless us all.

*Lord, thank you for blessing me by counting*
*me among your grubby people. Amen.*

# THE BOUNDLESS MERCY OF GOD

## A. W. Tozer

In his great mercy he has given us new birth into a living hope
through the resurrection of Jesus Christ from the dead, and
into an inheritance that can never perish, spoil or fade.

1 PETER 1:3–4

Could our failure to capture the pure joy of mercy consciously experienced be the result of our unbelief or our ignorance, or both? To receive mercy we must first know that God is merciful. We must believe that God's mercy is boundless, free, and through Jesus Christ our Lord, available to us now in our present situation.

We may plead for mercy for a lifetime in unbelief, and at the end of our days be still no more than sadly hopeful that we shall somewhere, sometime receive it. This is to starve to death just outside the banquet hall into which we have been warmly invited. Or we may, if we will, lay hold on the mercy of God by faith, enter the hall, and sit down with the bold and avid souls who will not allow difference and unbelief to keep them from the feast of fat things prepared for them.

Do you believe that God's forgiveness is boundless, free, and available to you now? Have you taken hold of it by faith?

*Lord, I want to join your banquet. Show me how to grasp your compassion in a life-altering way. Amen.*

# A TRANSFORMED HEART

## Dallas Willard

"When you give to the needy, do not announce it with trumpets, as the hypocrites do in the synagogues and on the streets, to be honored by others. Truly I tell you, they have received their reward in full."

MATTHEW 6:2

When Jesus spoke of "the hypocrites," he was utilizing a very vivid image that effectively seized the minds of his hearers because of their familiarity with stage characters. They were thus able to see much of the most obvious religious behavior of their day as the sham it in fact was.

But we must never forget that Jesus points *beyond* action to the source of action in character. This is a general principle that governs all he says. The kind of people who have been so transformed by their daily walk with God that good deeds naturally flow from their character are precisely the kind of people whose left hand would not notice what their right hand is doing. These are people who do not have to invest a lot of reflection in doing good for others. Their deeds are "in secret" no matter who is watching, for they are absorbed in love of God and of those around them. They hardly notice their own deed, and they rarely remember it.

When people have internalized Jesus' teachings, their behavior is almost as natural as speaking their native language.

*Lord, transform my heart that loving deeds may become my natural response to the needs I see around me. Amen.*

# THE GOOD-NEWS, HOLY-TERROR GOSPEL

## Frederick Buechner

> In the gospel the righteousness of God is revealed—
> a righteousness that is by faith from first to last.
>
> ROMANS 1:17

What is both good and new about the good news is the wild claim that Jesus did not simply tell us that God loves us even in our wickedness and folly and wants us to love each other the same way and to love God too, but that if we will allow it to happen, God will actually bring about this unprecedented transformation of our hearts himself.

What is both good and new about the good news is the mad insistence that Jesus lives on among us not just as another haunting memory but as the outlandish, holy, and invisible power of God working not just through the sacraments, but in countless hidden ways to make even slobs like us loving and whole beyond anything we could conceivably pull off by ourselves.

Thus the gospel is not only good and new but, if you take it seriously, a holy terror. Jesus never claimed that the process of being changed from a slob into a human being was going to be a Sunday school picnic. On the contrary. Childbirth may occasionally be painless, but rebirth, never.

The good news about Jesus is that God loves us, that God forgives us of our sinful slobbery, that Jesus works in and through us to make us righteous.

*Lord, thank you for the good news of Jesus—*
*a gospel of transformation and righteousness. Amen.*

# BECOMING FOOD FOR THE WORLD

## Henri J. M. Nouwen

*While they were eating, Jesus took bread, and when he had given thanks,
he broke it and gave it to his disciples, saying, "Take it; this is my body."*

MARK 14:22

When Jesus took bread, blessed it, broke it, and gave it to his disciples, he summarized in these gestures his own life. Jesus is chosen from all eternity, blessed at his baptism in the Jordan River, broken on the cross, and given as bread to the world. Being chosen, blessed, broken, and given is the sacred journey of the Son of God, Jesus the Christ.

When we take bread, bless it, break it, and give it with the words "This is the body of Christ," we express our commitment to make our lives conform to the life of Christ. We too want to live as people chosen, blessed, and broken, and thus become food for the world.

Symbolically in giving of his life in service on earth, and literally in giving of his body in death on the cross, Jesus Christ offered himself as food for the world. He has invited us to break ourselves in the same way. In what way might Jesus want you to open yourself to become food for the world?

*Lord Jesus Christ, show me how to "break" in order to
become nourishment for those around me. Amen.*

# CELEBRATE WITH RECKLESS GRATITUDE

## James Bryan Smith

"I tell you, there is joy in the presence of the angels
of God over one sinner who repents."

LUKE 15:10 NASB

Jesus forgave many people, and with few exceptions, these people all rejoiced and celebrated their freedom. Mary Magdalene, Zaccheus, Matthew, Peter—all of them were found out and forgiven. Jesus said when a soul is reconciled to God the angels rejoice. If the angels are celebrating, shouldn't we?

Celebrations help us acknowledge the goodness of God. They provide visible, concrete reminders of what God has done for us, and they allow us to revel in it. God became one of us because he loves us: let us feast and call it Christmas. God died and rose in order to save us: let us rejoice and call it Easter. God loves it when we celebrate his goodness.

I am suggesting that we consecrate and confirm our reconciliation with a celebration of reckless gratitude. Why not have a party? What about a feast? Perhaps we could take time out and spend a day in solitude simply basking in the gift of forgiveness.

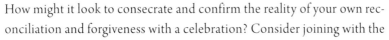

How might it look to consecrate and confirm the reality of your own reconciliation and forgiveness with a celebration? Consider joining with the angels by reveling in your own God-given redemption.

*Lord, today I join in the angels' joy over my repentance. Amen.*

# THE INFINITE GRACE OF GOD

## A. W. Tozer

> By grace you have been saved through faith, and this
> is not your own doing; it is the gift of God.
>
> EPHESIANS 2:8 NRSV

No one was ever saved other than by grace, from Abel to the present moment. And wherever grace found any man it was always by Jesus Christ. Grace indeed came by Jesus Christ, but it did not wait for his birth in the manger or his death on the cross before it became operative. Christ is the Lamb slain from the foundation of the world. The first man in human history to be reinstated in the fellowship of God came through faith in Christ. In olden times men looked forward to Christ's redeeming work; in later times they gazed back upon it, but always they came and they come by grace, through faith.

Instead of straining to comprehend this as a theological truth, it would be better and simpler to compare God's grace with our need. We can never know the enormity of our sin, neither is it necessary that we should. What we can know is that "where sin abounded, grace did much more abound."

Where you have need for God's unmerited favor, he is ready to give—and give abundantly.

*Lord, I recognize my ongoing need for your abundant grace to cover the multitude of my sins. May it increase where I have need. Amen.*

# HEALTHY GUILT, GRATUITOUS GRACE

## Brennan Manning

*If we confess our sins, he is faithful and just and will forgive
us our sins and purify us from all unrighteousness.*

1 JOHN 1:9

Healthy guilt adds not a single paragraph to the script for self-hatred. To the contrary, the conviction of personal sinfulness leads to realistic confrontation, ruthless honesty, and self-knowledge; it stimulates compunction, contrition, the desire for reconciliation, and inner peace.

As in any lovers' quarrel, the making-up not only absolves the past but brings a new depth of trust and security to the relationship. There is more power in sharing our weaknesses than in sharing our strengths. The forgiveness of God is gratuitous and unconditional, offering liberation from the domination of guilt. God overlooks our past, takes away present or future consequences of past transgressions, and causes us to cry out, "O happy fault!" The sinful and repentant prodigal son experienced an intimacy and joy with his Father in his brokenness that his sinless self-righteous brother would never know.

The sharing of healthy guilt is purgative and cathartic, introduces objectivity, banishes self-hatred, and becomes the occasion of gracious encounter with the merciful love of the redeeming God.

When have you experienced healthy guilt and then God's grace and forgiveness?

*Lord, I'm grateful that the simple step of confession
always leads to the monumental result of forgiveness. Amen.*

# SEND ME

## Frederick Buechner

> In the year that King Uzziah died, I saw the
> Lord sitting on a throne, high and lifted up.
>
> ISAIAH 6:1 NKJV

There were banks of candles flickering in the distance and clouds of incense thickening the air with holiness and stinging his eyes, and high above him there was the Mystery Itself, whose gown was the incense and the candles a dusting of gold at the hem. Winged creatures shouted back and forth the way excited children shout to each other, and the whole vast, reeking place started to shake beneath his feet, and he cried out, "O God, I am done for! I am foul of mouth. With my own two eyes I have seen him. I'm a goner." Then one of the winged things touched his mouth with fire and the Mystery said, "Who will it be?" and with charred lips he said, "Me," and Mystery said "Go."

Mystery said, "Go give the deaf hell till you're blue in the face and go show the blind heaven till you drop in your tracks. Go do it."

Isaiah said, "Do it till when?"

Mystery said, "Till hell freezes over."

Mystery said, "Do it till the cows come home."

And that is what a prophet does for a living and, starting from the year that King Uzziah died, when he saw and heard all these things, Isaiah went and did it.

If you were in Isaiah's shoes the day he saw the Lord, would you have said "Send me"?

*Father, please use me as you will. Amen.*

# HAVE SPIRITUAL COURAGE

## Henri J. M. Nouwen

"Be strong and courageous."

JOSHUA 1:6 NASB

Have courage," we often say to one another. Courage is a spiritual virtue. The word *courage* comes from the Latin word *cor*, which means "heart." A courageous act is an act coming from the heart. A courageous word is a word arising from the heart. The heart, however, is not just the place our emotions are located. The heart is the center of our being, the center of all thoughts, feelings, passions, and decisions.

A courageous life, therefore, is a life lived from the center. It is a deeply rooted life, the opposite of a superficial life. "Have courage" therefore means "Let your center speak."

Courage is connected with taking risks. Jumping the Grand Canyon on a motorbike, coming over Niagara Falls in a barrel, or crossing the ocean in a rowboat are called courageous acts because people risk their lives by doing these things. But none of these daredevil acts comes from the center of our being. They all come from the desire to test our physical limits and to become famous and popular.

Spiritual courage is completely different. It is following the deepest desires of our hearts at the risk of losing fame and popularity. It asks our willingness to lose our temporal lives in order to gain eternal life.

Be strong, be courageous. For what reasons might the Lord be calling you to have spiritual courage?

*Lord, embolden me to speak and live from my heart. Amen.*

# RECLAIM THE WORLD AS SACRED SPACE

## N. T. Wright

> "The hour is coming, and is now here, when the true
> worshipers will worship the Father in spirit and truth, for
> the Father seeks such as these to worship him."
>
> JOHN 4:23 NRSV

The renewal and reclaiming of space has recently involved, among other things, a fresh grasp of the Celtic tradition of "thin places," places where the curtain between heaven and earth seems almost transparent. We urgently need to recapture this theology before, to use an obvious metaphor, all the ancient trees are cut down to make room for a shopping center and parking lot just when people are starting to realize how much shade those trees provide in summer, how much fruit they bear in autumn, and how beautiful they look in spring. Jesus does indeed declare that God calls all people everywhere to worship him in spirit and truth rather than limiting worship to this or that holy mountain. But this doesn't undercut a proper theology of God's reclaiming of the whole world, which is anticipated in the claiming of space for worship and prayer.

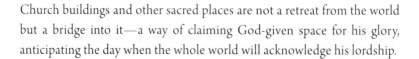

Church buildings and other sacred places are not a retreat from the world but a bridge into it—a way of claiming God-given space for his glory, anticipating the day when the whole world will acknowledge his lordship.

*Lord, help us reclaim every ounce of the world for*
*the glory, honor, and worship of your name. Amen.*

OCTOBER 22

# JESUS' DEFINITION OF PEACE

## Frederick Buechner

Let the peace that comes from Christ rule in your hearts.

<small>COLOSSIANS 3:15 NLT</small>

*P*eace has come to mean the time when there aren't any wars or even when there aren't any major wars. Beggars can't be choosers; we'd most of us settle for that. But in Hebrew *peace*, *shalom*, means fullness, means having everything you need to be wholly and happily yourself.

One of the titles by which Jesus is known is Prince of Peace, and he used the word himself in what seem at first glance to be two radically contradictory utterances. On one occasion he said to the disciples, "Do not think that I have come to bring peace on earth; I have not come to bring peace, but a sword" (Matthew 10:34). And later on, the last time they ate together, he said to them, "Peace I leave with you; my peace I give to you" (John 14:27).

The contradiction is resolved when you realize that, for Jesus, peace seems to have meant not the absence of struggle, but the presence of love.

———

When have you experienced peace in the midst of struggle?

*Lord Jesus, remind me that your love is present even when circumstances try to tell me otherwise. Amen.*

# MORE THAN JUST FORGIVEN

## Dallas Willard

> He has rescued us from the power of darkness and
> transferred us into the kingdom of his beloved Son,
> in whom we have redemption, the forgiveness of sins.
>
> COLOSSIANS 1:13–14 NRSV

The bumper sticker gently imposes its little message: Christians Aren't Perfect, Just Forgiven. Just forgiven? And is that really all there is to being a Christian? The gift of eternal life comes down to that? Quite a retreat from living an eternal kind of life now!

Christians certainly aren't perfect. There will always be need for improvement. But there is a lot of room between being perfect and being "just forgiven" as that is nowadays understood. You could be much more than forgiven and still not be perfect.

It certainly needs to be said that Christians are forgiven. And it needs to be said that forgiveness does not depend on being perfect. But is that really what the slogan communicates?

Unfortunately, it is not. What the slogan really conveys is that forgiveness alone is what Christianity is all about, what is genuinely essential to it. It says that you can have a faith in Christ that brings forgiveness, while in every other respect your life is no different from that of others who have no faith in Christ at all.

―⦿―

Consider all we've received through Christ: rescue, redemption, forgiveness, and a kingdom. Clearly we are more than "just forgiven."

*Jesus, thank you for all I have through all you've done. Amen.*

# BETWEEN ACTS AND REVELATION

## N. T. Wright

All Scripture is inspired by God and profitable for teaching, for reproof, for correction, for training in righteousness; so that the man of God may be adequate, equipped for every good work.

2 TIMOTHY 3:16–17 NASB

Scripture—the Old and New Testaments—is the story of creation and new creation. Within that, it is the story of covenant and new covenant. When we read Scripture as Christians, we read it precisely as people of the new covenant and of the new creation. We do not read it, in other words, as a flat, uniform list of regulations or doctrines. We read it as the narrative in which we ourselves are now called to take part. We read it to discover the story so far and also how it's supposed to end. To put it another way, we live somewhere between the end of Acts and the closing scene of Revelation. If we want to understand Scripture and to find it doing its proper work in and through us, we must learn to read and understand it in the light of that overall story.

As we do this, we must allow the power of God's promised future to have its way with us.

———◦◦◦———

How does God's promised future affect you today?

*Lord, help me understand your story better so it can do its proper work in and through me. Amen.*

# GRACE IS A GIVEN

## Frederick Buechner

> How much more did God's grace and the gift that came by the
> grace of the one man, Jesus Christ, overflow to the many!
>
> ROMANS 5:15

Grace is something you can never get but can only be given. There's no way to earn it or deserve it or bring it about any more than you can deserve the taste of raspberries and cream or earn good looks or bring about your own birth.

A good sleep is grace and so are good dreams. Most tears are grace. The smell of rain is grace. Somebody loving you is grace. Loving somebody is grace. Have you ever tried to love somebody?

A crucial eccentricity of the Christian faith is the assertion that people are saved by grace. There's nothing *you* have to do. There's nothing you *have* to do. There's nothing you have to *do*.

The grace of God means something like: "Here is your life. You might never have been, but you are, because the party wouldn't have been complete without you. Here is the world. Beautiful and terrible things will happen. Don't be afraid. I am with you. Nothing can ever separate us. It's for you I created the universe. I love you."

To receive this gift you must accept it. Will you go to God with outstretched hands?

> *Lord, thank you for your grace-gift.*
> *I receive it willingly and joyfully. Amen.*

# DON'T REJECT THE WORLD—RENEW IT

## N. T. Wright

"My prayer is not that you take them out of the world
but that you protect them from the evil one."

JOHN 17:15

If the church is to be renewed in its mission precisely in and for the world of space, time, and matter, we cannot ignore or marginalize that same world. We must rather claim it for the kingdom of God, for the lordship of Jesus, and in the power of the Spirit so that we can then go out and work for that kingdom, announce that lordship, and effect change through that power.

The mission of the church must therefore include, at a structural level, the recognition that our present space, time, and matter are all subject not to rejection but to redemption. Living between the resurrection of Jesus and the final coming together of all things in heaven and earth means celebrating God's healing of his world, not his abandoning of it; God's reclaiming of space as heaven and earth intersect once more; God's redeeming of time as years, weeks, and days speak the language of renewal; and God's redeeming of matter itself, in the sacraments, which point in turn to the renewal of the lives that are washed in baptism and fed with the Eucharist.

Jesus prayed that his Father wouldn't remove us from the world but instead protect us as we reclaim, redeem, and renew it.

*Lord, help me see how you are redeeming this world even now; show me how to be an agent of that change. Amen.*

# REMEMBER YOUR SIN REDEMPTIVELY

## James Bryan Smith

> They shall all know me, from the least of them to the greatest, says the
> LORD; for I will forgive their iniquity, and remember their sin no more.
>
> JEREMIAH 31:34 NRSV

The Bible declares that God remembers our sin no more. I am not certain as to what that means. God, being God, could certainly do anything, even forget something, despite being all-knowing. If we take Jeremiah literally, then we can say that God actually chooses to forget our sins. What I am certain about is this: God treats me exactly as if he did not remember. God never brings up past sins, and he regards me as if they had never happened at all.

We are not capable of forgetting. The memory of a difficult event will always be with us. But we can choose to remember in a redemptive manner. We can remember the event as a time of real pain but also as a testimony of God's forgiveness and grace. We will always remember our mistakes, but we can also remember that they led to healing.

---

Through honesty, faith, and reconciliation, we can live our lives free of past sin. We can acknowledge it happened, but we've been forgiven. While that past remains, let's join with God in letting go of it. In this way we redeem even the memory of our pain.

*Lord, I'm so grateful you offer complete forgiveness;*
*may I offer it to myself and others as well. Amen.*

# CATCH LOVE, DWELL IN LOVE, DO LOVE

## Dallas Willard

Love is patient; love is kind; love is not envious or boastful or arrogant or rude. It does not insist on its own way; it is not irritable or resentful; it does not rejoice in wrongdoing, but rejoices in the truth. It bears all things, believes all things, hopes all things, endures all things.

1 Corinthians 13:4–7 nrsv

People usually read this passage and are taught to read it as telling them to be patient, kind, free of jealousy, and so on—just as they read Jesus' Discourse as telling them to not call others fools, not look on a woman to lust, not swear, to go the second mile, and so forth.

But Paul is plainly saying—look at his words—that it is love that does these things, not us, and that what we are to do is to "pursue love" (1 Corinthians 14:1). As we "catch" love, we then find that these things are after all actually being done by us. These things, these godly actions and behaviors, are the result of dwelling in love. We have become the kind of person who is patient, kind, free of jealousy, and so on.

———

If you want to be patient and kind, hopeful and enduring, then get love. It's when we dwell in love that we do love, for it is love itself that is at work in us and works through us.

> Lord, show me how to catch love and
> dwell in it so I become loving. Amen.

# A LESSON IN GOD'S GRACE AND MERCY

## A. W. Tozer

> Because of his great love for us, God, who is rich in mercy,
> made us alive with Christ even when we were dead in
> transgressions—it is by grace you have been saved.
>
> EPHESIANS 2:4–5

In God mercy and grace are one; but as they reach us they are seen as two, related but not identical.

As mercy is God's goodness confronting human misery and guilt, so grace is his goodness directed toward human debt and demerit. It is by his grace that God imputes merit where none previously existed and declares no debt to be where one had been before.

Grace is the good pleasure of God that inclines him to bestow benefits upon the undeserving. It is a self-existent principle inherent in the divine nature and appears to us as a self-caused propensity to pity the wretched, spare the guilty, welcome the outcast, and bring into favor those who were before under just disapprobation. Its use to us sinful men is to save us and make us sit together in heavenly places to demonstrate to the ages the exceeding riches of God's kindness to us in Christ Jesus.

We benefit eternally by God's being just what he is—a merciful, gracious God who has released us from prison, exchanged our prison clothes for royal robes, and offers us sustenance all the days of our lives.

*Heavenly Father, thank you for your goodness and grace made manifest through sparing me, welcoming me, blessing me. Amen.*

# THE FUTURE SAMPLED NOW

## N. T. Wright

Jesus took bread, blessed and broke it, and gave it to the disciples and said, "Take, eat; this is My body." Then He took the cup, and gave thanks, and gave it to them, saying, "Drink from it, all of you."

MATTHEW 26:26–27 NKJV

What happens in the Eucharist is that through the death and resurrection of Jesus Christ, God's future dimension is brought sharply into play. We break this bread to share in the body of Christ; we do it in remembrance of him. Yet if we stop there we've only said the half of it.

To make any headway in understanding the Eucharist, we must see it as the arrival of God's future in the present, not just the extension of God's past (or of Jesus' past) into our present. We do not simply remember a long-since-dead Jesus; we celebrate the presence of the living Lord. And he lives, through the resurrection, precisely as the one who has gone on ahead into the new creation, the transformed new world, as the one who is himself its prototype. The Jesus who gives himself to us as food and drink is himself the beginning of God's new world.

At communion we are like the Israelites in the wilderness, tasting fruit plucked from the promised land. It is God's future sampled in the present.

*Lord, thank you for gifting me with samples of your promised future: the bread of your body, the cup of your blood. Amen.*

# ALL IS HOLY

## Frederick Buechner

> The Word became flesh and made his dwelling among us.
>
> JOHN 1:14

John 1:14 is what *incarnation* means. It is untheological. It is unsophisticated. It is undignified. But according to Christianity, it is the way things are.

All religions and philosophies that deny the reality or the significance of the material, the fleshly, the earthbound, are themselves denied. Moses at the burning bush was told to take off his shoes because the ground on which he stood was holy ground (Exodus 3:5), and incarnation means that all ground is holy ground because God not only made it but walked on it, ate and slept and worked and died on it. If we are saved anywhere, we are saved here. And what is saved is not some diaphanous distillation of our bodies and our earth, but our bodies and our earth themselves. Jerusalem becomes the New Jerusalem coming down out of heaven like a bride adorned for her husband (Revelation 21:2). Our bodies are sown perishable and raised imperishable (1 Corinthians 15:42).

One of the blunders religious people are particularly fond of making is the attempt to be more spiritual than God.

What does it mean to you that all ground is holy because Jesus came?

*Lord, thank you for saving all of me, body and soul. Amen.*

# November

# GIVEN IN FAITH FOR THE WORLD

## Henri J. M. Nouwen

> All these people earned a good reputation because of their faith.
>
> HEBREWS 11:39 NLT

Jesus is given to the world. He was chosen, blessed, and broken to be given. Jesus' life and death are a life and death for others. The beloved Son of God, chosen from all eternity, was broken on the cross so that this one life could multiply and become food for people of all places and all times.

As God's beloved children we have to believe that our little lives, when lived as God's chosen and blessed children, are broken to be given to others. We too have to become bread for the world. When we live our brokenness under the blessing, our lives will continue to bear fruit from generation to generation. That is the story of the saints—they died, but they continue to be alive in the hearts of those who live after them—and this can be our story too.

---

The accounts in Hebrews 11 show us what it means to live a life given in faith for the world. Christ wants your story to be like their stories: lives given to others.

*Lord, the world was not worthy of the saints' stories;*
*empower me to give my life in faith for the world. Amen.*

# BURIED IN HIS DEATH, RAISED IN HIS RESURRECTION

## N. T. Wright

Do you not know that all of us who have been baptized into Christ Jesus were baptized into his death? Therefore we have been buried with him by baptism into death . . . so we too might walk in newness of life.

ROMANS 6:3–4 NRSV

In the simple but powerful action of plunging someone into the water in the name of the triune God, there is a real dying to the old creation and a real rising into the new—with all the dangerous privileges and responsibilities that then accompany the new life as it sets out in the as-yet-unredeemed world. Baptism is not magic, a conjuring trick with water. But neither is it simply a visual aid. It is one of the points, established by Jesus himself, where heaven and earth interlock, where new creation, resurrection life, appears within the midst of the old. Just as for many Christians the truth of Easter is something they glimpse occasionally rather than grasp and act on, so, for many, baptism remains in the background, out of sight, whereas it should be the foundational event for all serious Christian living, all dying to sin and coming alive with Christ.

Buried to sin in Christ's death, raised to new life in his resurrection: these words, spoken during baptism, are a reminder of our new-life Christian reality.

*Lord, thank you for the tangible reminder of baptism.*
*Help me live out my new life in all its fullness. Amen.*

# GOD'S ONE SUPREME LAW REVEALED

## Frederick Buechner

> "All the Law and the Prophets hang on these two commandments."
> MATTHEW 22:40

Jesus said the one supreme law is that we are to love God with all our hearts, minds, and souls, and our neighbors as ourselves. In any given situation, the lesser law is to be obeyed if it is consistent with the law of love and superseded if it isn't.

The Mosaic law against murder is an example of precisely the opposite kind. In this case, far from setting it aside as a lesser law, you radicalize it. That is to say, if we are above all else to love our neighbors, it is not enough simply not to kill them. We must also not lose our tempers at them, insult them, or call them fools, Jesus says (Matthew 5:21–22).

A legalistic religion like the Pharisees' is in some ways very appealing. All you have to do in any kind of ethical dilemma is look it up in the book and act accordingly. Jesus, on the other hand, says all you have to do is love God and your neighbors. That may seem more appealing still until, in dilemma after dilemma, you try to figure out just how to go about doing it.

Whether or not any feeling is involved, loving God means honoring, obeying, and staying in constant touch with God; loving your neighbor means acting in his or her best interests no matter what.

*Lord, show me when I can radicalize
your love to help my neighbor. Amen.*

# DIGGING INTO OUR SPIRITUAL RESOURCES

## Henri J. M. Nouwen

Make sure that nobody pays back wrong for wrong, but always strive to do what is good for each other and for everyone else.

1 THESSALONIANS 5:15

When someone hurts us, offends us, ignores us, or rejects us, a deep inner protest emerges. It can be rage or depression, desire to take revenge, or even an impulse to harm ourselves. We can feel a deep urge to wound those who have wounded us or to withdraw in a suicidal mood of self-rejection. Although these extreme reactions might seem exceptional, they are never far away from our hearts. During the long nights we often find ourselves brooding about words and actions we might have used in response to what others have said or done to us.

It is precisely here that we have to dig deep into our spiritual resources and find the center within us, the center that lies beyond our need to hurt others or ourselves, where we are free to forgive and love.

———

Whenever you feel the impulse to pay back wrong for wrong, consider how Jesus responded: when he was beaten and bruised, crushed and crucified, he did not strike back. Instead he forgave and loved. May we dig deep into the same well of love to respond without offense, rejection, or hurt.

*Lord Jesus Christ, Son of God, show me how to follow your lead by digging into the well of spiritual resources so I can forgive as you forgave, love as you loved. Amen.*

# FORGIVENESS: GOD'S WAY OF LIFE

## N. T. Wright

> "Shouldn't you have had mercy on your fellow
> servant just as I had on you?"
>
> MATTHEW 18:33

Forgiveness is not a moral rule that comes with sanctions attached. God doesn't deal with us on the basis of abstract codes and rules like that. Forgiveness is a way of life, God's way of life, God's way *to* life; and if you close your heart to forgiveness, why, then you close your heart to forgiveness. That is the point of the terrifying parable in Matthew 18, about the slave who had been forgiven millions but then dragged a colleague into court to settle a debt of a few pence. If you lock up the piano because you don't want to play to somebody else, how can God play to you?

Not to forgive is to shut down a faculty in the innermost person, which happens to be the same faculty that can receive God's forgiveness. It also happens to be the same faculty that can experience real joy and real grief. Love bears all things, believes all things, hopes all things, endures all things.

Jesus' prayer, "Forgive us our trespasses, as we forgive those who trespass against us" isn't a bargain we make with God. It's a fact of human life. So how (and whom) can you forgive, as God has forgiven you?

*Lord, teach me forgiveness as my way of life. Amen.*

# GOD CALLING

## Frederick Buechner

God called to him from the middle of the bush, "Moses! Moses!"

EXODUS 3:4 NLT

After Moses learned he would not enter the promised land with the Israelites, he died in his one hundred and twentieth year. The figure of Moses breathing his last in the hills around Mount Pisgah, with his sore feet and aching back, serves as a good example of the fact that when God puts the finger on people, their troubles have just begun.

And yet there's no doubt that Moses wouldn't have had it any different. Hunkered down in the cleft of a rock, once he had been allowed to see the Glory, and it was something to hold on to for the rest of his life. And one other thing was even better. Way back when out of the burning bush God had collared him, he had asked God what God's name was, and God had told him, so that from then on he could get in touch with God anytime he wanted. Nobody had ever known God's name before Moses did, and nobody would ever have known it afterward except for his having passed it on; and with that thought in his heart up there on Pisgah, and with that name on his lips, and with the sunset in his whiskers, he became in the end a kind of burning bush himself.

Has the Lord ever spoken to you in an unexpected way or through a surprising source? What happened?

*Lord, help me recognize your voice every time you speak.*

# OUR WORK IS LINKED WITH GOD'S

## Eugene Peterson

> The LORD God took the man and put him in the
> garden of Eden to tend and keep it.
>
> GENESIS 2:15 NKJV

God is first presented to us in our Scriptures as a Worker, a Maker. In the beginning, God went to work. In the second creation story, man and woman are placed in the garden as workers, employed at tasks assigned by their Maker. Work is the primary context for our spirituality. The spiritual life begins—seriously begins—when we get a job and go to work.

Work is our Spirit-anointed participation in God's work. When Jesus stood up in the Nazareth synagogue to announce that he was going to work, and how he was going to go about it, he said, "The Spirit of the LORD is upon Me because He has *anointed* Me" (Luke 4:18).

In our biblical texts being anointed means being given a job by God. It means employment. We're told, in effect, that there's a job to be done and that we're assigned to do it—and that we *can* do it. Anointing is the sacramental connection linking God's work with our work.

God is a Worker, a Maker; so are we. We are his handiwork, called and commissioned to co-create works of goodness along with him in this world. How does God want you to tend and keep the garden of earth?

*Lord, as one called and commissioned to be your coworker,*
*I ask you to show me how my work is linked with yours. Amen.*

# NO FEAR EXISTS IN THE ARMS OF OUR BELOVED

## A. W. Tozer

There is no fear in love, but perfect love casts out fear; for fear has to do with punishment, and whoever fears has not reached perfection in love.

1 JOHN 4:18 NRSV

Fear is the painful emotion that arises at the thought that we may be harmed or made to suffer. This fear persists while we are subject to the will of someone who does not desire our well-being. The moment we come under the protection of one of goodwill, fear is cast out.

The world is full of enemies, and as long as we are subject to the possibility of harm from these enemies, fear is inevitable. The effort to conquer fear without removing the causes is altogether futile. As long as we are in the hands of chance, as long as we look for hope to the law of averages, as long as we must trust for survival to our ability to outthink or outmaneuver the enemy, we have every good reason to be afraid. And fear hath torment.

To know that love is of God and to enter into the secret place leaning upon the arm of the Beloved—this and only this can cast out fear.

God is both love and sovereign. In his love he desires our everlasting welfare; in his sovereignty he secures it. His perfect love casts out fear perfectly.

*Lord, I seek your loving sovereignty to eliminate my fear and secure my safety from my enemies. Amen.*

# THE PRAYER PROMISE OF GOD

## James Bryan Smith

> "When you are praying, do not heap up empty phrases
> as the Gentiles do; for they think that they will be heard
> because of their many words. Do not be like them, for your
> Father knows what you need before you ask him."
>
> MATTHEW 6:7–8 NRSV

Jesus promised us that God would respond to our needs. If we come to God in faith, we will not be turned away. When we ask we will receive, but the answer may not come as we thought it would. God is too gracious to answer all of our prayers.

Martin Luther said that we should never prescribe measure, manner, time, or place in our prayers because he believed that we should trust in God's wisdom, which is higher than ours. Jesus said something similar. God looks in our heart and sees what we really need. The answer may not come as we anticipate, but I have learned that it will come.

I keep a prayer journal, writing down each person or situation I am praying for, as well as the request I make to God. When I look back over the journal I am stunned by three things: one, God eventually answers all my prayers; two, the answers rarely resemble my requests; and three, the answers are always better.

---

Consider keeping a prayer journal yourself. It is an exercise that will reveal and teach you to trust in God's wisdom.

> *Lord, when your answers are confusing, I trust you are doing something even better than I could imagine. Amen.*

# WALK IN PURITY

## Dallas Willard

How can a young person stay on the
path of purity?
By living according to your word.

Psalm 119:9

Job is protesting his integrity on all fronts. "I made a covenant with my eyes," he says (Job 31:1). He had, as it were, an understanding with them that they would not engage in lusting. "How," he asks, "could I ogle a young woman," a "virgin"? The salacious gaze would be seen by God. And it would certainly lead into deceitful actions (v. 5). But God knows that none of this is a part of his life (v. 6).

Job is so emphatic about his purity in this area that he goes into great detail concerning the all-too-familiar course of wrong sexual involvement and its consequences. Obviously he knew exactly what goes on.

To be right sexually before God is to be precisely as Job was. It is to be the kind of person who has a detailed and established practice of not engaging his or her bodily parts and perceptions, thoughts, and desires in activities of sexual trifling, dalliance, and titillation.

Let's strive to be persons whose feet, eyes, hands, hearts, and all the rest simply walk within the godly policy of sexual purity, knowing that it is good and right.

*Lord, like Job, I make a covenant to walk in sexual purity. Amen.*

# THE FRIENDSHIP OF GOD

## A. W. Tozer

> "I no longer call you servants, because a servant does not know his master's business. Instead, I have called you friends, for everything that I learned from my Father I have made known to you."
>
> JOHN 15:15

God's love tells us that he is friendly and his Word assures us that he is our Friend and wants us to be his friends. No man with a trace of humility would first think that he is a friend of God, but the idea did not originate with men. The disciples might well have hesitated to claim friendship with Christ, but Christ said to them, "Ye are my friends." Modesty may demur at so rash a thought, but audacious faith dares to believe the Word and claim friendship with God. We do God more honor by believing what he has said about himself and having the courage to come boldly to the throne of grace than by hiding in self-conscious humility among the trees of the garden.

It is a beautiful, remarkable reality that the God of the universe has freely chosen to extend to us his friendship, that he has offered his heart to us in emotional, relational attachment. He wants our love and will not be satisfied until he gets it. Does he have your love? Do you have his friendship?

*Heavenly Father, I receive your loving friendship*
*this day and offer you my love in return. Amen.*

# BE STILL

## Frederick Buechner

"Be still, and know that I am God!"

PSALM 46:10 NRSV

In our minds we are continually chattering with ourselves, and the purpose of meditation is to stop it. To begin with, maybe we try to concentrate on a single subject—the flame of a candle, the row of peas we are weeding, our own breath. When other subjects float up to distract us, we escape them by simply taking note of them and then letting them float away without thinking about them. We keep returning to the in-and-out of our breathing until there is no room left in us for anything else. To the candle flame until we ourselves start to flicker and burn. To the weeds until we become only a pair of grubby hands pulling them. In time we discover that we are no longer chattering.

If we persist, every once and so often we may find ourselves entering the suburbs of a state where we are conscious but no longer conscious of anything in particular, where we have let go of almost everything.

The end of meditation is to become empty enough to be filled with the kind of stillness the psalmist has in mind.

Use this time to meditate and be still, reciting the following: *Be still, and know that I am God. Be still, and know that I am. Be still, and know. Be still. Be.*

*Lord, enable me to be still in your presence,*
*trusting that you are God of my world. Amen.*

# SPIRITUAL DRYNESS AND DIVINE INTIMACY

## Henri J. M. Nouwen

> As the deer pants for the water brooks,
> So my soul pants for You, O God.
>
> PSALM 42:1 NASB

Sometimes we experience a terrible dryness in our spiritual lives. We feel no desire to pray, don't experience God's presence, get bored with worship services, and even think that everything we ever believed about God, Jesus, and the Holy Spirit is little more than a childhood fairy tale.

Then it is important to realize that most of these feelings and thoughts are just feelings and thoughts, and that the Spirit of God dwells beyond our feelings and thoughts. It is a great grace to be able to experience God's presence in our feelings and thoughts, but when we don't, it does not mean that God is absent. It often means that God is calling us to a greater faithfulness. It is precisely in times of spiritual dryness that we must hold on to our spiritual discipline so we can grow into new intimacy with God.

When have you longed for God during a time of spiritual dryness? How did you grow closer to God through it?

*Lord, when my spiritual life grows dry, show yourself present, help me be faithful, grow me into a deeper relationship with you. Amen.*

# THE COMPANIONSHIP OF THE LORD

## James Bryan Smith

> Even though I walk through the darkest valley,
>
> I fear no evil;
>
> for you are with me.
>
> PSALM 23:4 NRSV

The psalmist could make this bold statement because he believed that God's presence is all that we need in life. Because God is with us we can lie down in peace, find sustenance for our souls, and even walk through death's dark valley with courage.

The Bible is full of stories of God being *with* people. Enoch walked *with* God for three hundred years; God was *with* Ishmael when he was alone in the wilderness; Jacob was promised by God, "I am *with* you and will keep you wherever you go"; and God promised to help Moses overcome his fear of speaking to Pharaoh, saying, "Now therefore go, and I will be *with* your mouth and teach you what you are to speak."

Finally, Jesus told his followers, "And behold, I am *with* you always, to the end of the age" (Matthew 28:20). It is the promise of God's presence that makes us able to say with the author of Hebrews, "The Lord is my helper; I will not be afraid. What can anyone do to me?" (Hebrews 13:6).

Whatever dark valley you're facing in life, the Lord is with you. You'll never face a situation without the presence and care of God.

*Lord, I trust that I can walk through any dark valley—for you are with me. Amen.*

# CULTIVATE A KINGDOM-DIRECTED HEART

## Dallas Willard

*"If your hand causes you to stumble, cut it off; it is better*
*for you to enter life maimed than to have two hands*
*and to go to hell, to the unquenchable fire."*

MARK 9:43 NRSV

Of course being acceptable to God is so important that, if cutting bodily parts off could achieve it, one would be wise to cut them off. Jesus seems to have made this very point on some occasions. But so far from suggesting that any advantage before God could actually be gained in this way, Jesus' teaching in this passage is exactly the opposite. The mutilated stump could still have a wicked heart. The deeper question always concerns who you are, not what you did do or can do. What would you do if you could? Eliminating bodily parts will not change that.

If you dismember your body to the point where you could never murder or even look hatefully at another, never commit adultery or even look to lust, your heart could still be full of anger, contempt, and obsessive desire for what is wrong, no matter how thoroughly stifled or suppressed it may be.

———∞———

In contrast to the many forms of evil that our hearts churn out, the goodness of a kingdom-directed heart crowds out such sins. From that heart come deeds of respect and purity that characterize holiness as God meant it to be.

> *Lord, cultivate within me a kingdom-directed*
> *heart so it doesn't cause me to stumble. Amen.*

# WOE TO ME!

## A. W. Tozer

"Woe to me!" I cried. "I am ruined! For I am a man of
unclean lips, and I live among a people of unclean lips, and
my eyes have seen the King, the LORD Almighty."

ISAIAH 6:5

The moral shock suffered by us through our mighty break with the high will of heaven has left us all with a permanent trauma affecting every part of our nature. There is disease both in ourselves and in our environment.

The sudden realization of his personal depravity came like a stroke from heaven upon the trembling heart of Isaiah at the moment when he had his revolutionary vision of the holiness of God. His painful cry expresses the feeling of every man who has discovered himself under his disguises and has been confronted with an inward sight of the holy whiteness that is God. Such an experience cannot but be emotionally violent.

Until we have seen ourselves as God sees us, we are not likely to be much disturbed over conditions around us as long as they do not get so far out of hand as to threaten our comfortable way of life. We have learned to live with unholiness and have come to look upon it as the natural and expected thing.

When have you been faced with the stark reality of your own depravity in the face of God's holiness?

*Lord Jesus Christ, Son of God, don't let
me settle for unholiness in my life. Amen.*

# JESUS: PHYSICIAN AND HEALER

## Frederick Buechner

Jesus said, "It is not the healthy who need a doctor, but the sick."

MATTHEW 9:12

We go to physicians with whatever ails us. Who knows what the examination will reveal, but we try to prepare ourselves for the worst. It is not just our bodies that we are putting on the line, but maybe even our chance for survival. We are no longer in control of our future but, like children, can only wait for a grown-up to determine it. Stripped of our dignity and self-confidence no less than of most of our clothes, we perhaps don't feel quite so vulnerable anywhere else on earth.

When physicians finally step through the door and start checking us over, we hang not just on every word they speak but on the look in their eyes and the tone of their voices for some clue to what they make of us. When they finally tell us, we listen as though our lives depend on it, which quite possibly they do. If they know their business, in just the touch of their hand there is healing.

Several times in the Gospels, Jesus indirectly refers to himself as a physician. It is a richly touching and suggestive image.

———— ❦ ————

What might the image of Jesus as Physician suggest about the character of God? What might that mean for every dimension of our lives?

*Jesus, I come to you as my Physician, seeking to be examined and understood, to find healing for what ails me. Amen.*

# CHOOSING LIFE CALLS FOR DISCIPLINE

## Henri J. M. Nouwen

I have set before you life and death . . . therefore choose life,
that both you and your descendants may live.

DEUTERONOMY 30:19 NKJV

Choose life." That's God's call for us, and there is not a moment in which we do not have to make that choice. Life and death are always before us. In our imaginations, our thoughts, our words, our gestures, our actions—even in our nonactions. This choice for life starts in a deep interior place. Underneath very life-affirming behavior I can still harbor death-thoughts and death-feelings. The most important question is not *Do I kill*? but *Do I carry a blessing in my heart or a curse*?

When we look critically at the many thoughts and feelings that fill our minds and hearts, we may come to the horrifying discovery that we often choose death instead of life, curse instead of blessing. Jealousy, envy, anger, resentment, greed, lust, vindictiveness, revenge, hatred—they all float in that large reservoir of our inner life. Often we take them for granted and allow them to be there and do their destructive work.

But God asks us to choose life and to choose blessing.

―――― ∞ ――――

This choice of life requires a great attentiveness to what's within us. We can't always do this on our own, but it's important that we make the inner effort and find support to help us choose life.

*Lord, you have set before me life and death, blessing
and curse; help me choose life and blessing. Amen.*

# SELF-LOVE FOR NEIGHBOR-LOVE

## Frederick Buechner

> "Love your neighbor as yourself."
>
> MATTHEW 22:39

Cleanse the thoughts of our hearts by the inspiration of the Holy Spirit," the collect goes, "that we may perfectly love" if not thee, because we are such a feckless and faithless crowd most of us, then at least ourselves, at least each other. If, as someone has said, we are as sick as our secrets, then to get well is to air those secrets if only in our own hearts, which the prayer asks God himself to air and cleanse.

When our secrets are guilty secrets we can start to make amends, to change what can be changed; we can start to heal. When they are sad and hurtful secrets, like my father's death, we can in a way honor the hurt by letting ourselves feel it as we never let ourselves feel it before, and then, having felt it, by laying it aside; we can start to take care of ourselves the way we take care of people we love. To love our neighbor as we love ourselves means also to love ourselves as we love our neighbors. It means to treat ourselves with as much kindness and understanding as we would the person next door who is in trouble.

---

How good are you at loving yourself? How might your level of self-love impact how you love your neighbor?

> Lord, cleanse my heart by your Spirit so I
> can heal; heal my heart so I can love. Amen.

# FREE FROM ANXIETY

## James Bryan Smith

Be anxious for nothing, but in everything by prayer and supplication
with thanksgiving let your requests be made known to God.

PHILIPPIANS 4:6 NASB

Anxiety is the great sickness in our society. Paul's words seem like an impossible command for most of us, who do well not to worry about *everything*. The looming national debt, the sputtering economy, the presence of guns in our schools, the spread of AIDS, and the rapidly changing job market create a people who are frightened and anxious about the future.

The only reason Paul was able to tell the Philippians not to worry was because he knew that God was alive and present and caring for them. He finishes the verse by saying, "but in everything by *prayer* . . . let your requests be made known to God." Do not worry, Paul says, but instead turn to God in prayer.

Peter did the same when he said, "Cast all your anxiety on him because he cares for you" (1 Peter 5:7). God actually wants us to bring our cares to him. It is God's design that we take whatever is bothering us, whatever concerns we have, whatever needs we would like to see filled, to him in prayer.

Regardless of worries over wars and the economy, our jobs, and our health, we can be free from anxiety. Why? Because we can bring all issues to God in prayer, and he will tend them.

*Lord, I want to exchange my anxiety for your peace. Amen.*

# THE LAW OF RETALIATION
# vs. THE LAW OF LOVE

## Dallas Willard

> "You have heard that it was said, 'Eye for eye, and tooth for
> tooth.' But I tell you, do not resist an evil person. If anyone slaps
> you on the right cheek, turn to them the other cheek also."
>
> MATTHEW 5:38–39

The old rightness for the cases in question was that injurers should be injured in *exactly the same way*, so far as possible, as they had injured. This was a completely general statement to cover any kind of injury done, even to cover intended evil and property damage. The intent of the *lex talionis*, or law of retaliation, as it came to be called, was that reciprocity would be achieved through equalization.

So what, in the situation of personal injury, is the rightness of the kingdom heart? Here we must once again recall the point about order: that we have *already* heard and received the word of the kingdom, and that anger, contempt, and absorbing desire have been dealt with so that our lives are not being run by them. If they occasionally test us still, that is very natural. But they do not control us and leave us unable to reliably and happily carry through with our sober intention to do what is good and avoid what is evil.

———— ∞ ————

Do you subscribe to the world's law of retaliation or to the kingdom's law of love? Ask Jesus to let his wisdom guide you.

*Jesus, help me put aside the so-called wisdom
of the world and follow your lead instead. Amen.*

# THE SPIRIT OF TRUTH AND THE HOLINESS OF GOD

## A. W. Tozer

"When the Spirit of truth comes, he will guide you into all the truth."

JOHN 16:13 NRSV

We know nothing like the divine holiness. It stands apart, unique, unapproachable, incomprehensible, and unattainable. The natural man is blind to it. He may fear God's power and admire his wisdom, but his holiness he cannot even imagine.

Only the Spirit of the Holy One can impart to the human spirit the knowledge of the holy. Yet as electric power flows only to a conductor, so the Spirit flows through truth and must find some measure of truth and the mind before he can illuminate the heart. Faith wakes at the voice of truth that responds to no other sound.

Theological knowledge is the medium through which the Spirit flows into the human heart, yet there must be humble penitence in the heart before truth can produce faith. The Spirit of God is the Spirit of truth. It is possible to have some truth in the mind without having the Spirit in the heart, but it is never possible to have the Spirit apart from truth.

None can comprehend or appreciate the holiness of God unless the Spirit of truth awakens our minds. How can you seek such truth by actively seeking the Spirit?

*Lord, give me your Spirit to awaken my mind to your holiness. Amen.*

# OPERATION SANCTIFICATION

## Frederick Buechner

> You were washed, you were sanctified, you were justified in the
> name of the Lord Jesus Christ and in the Spirit of our God.
>
> 1 CORINTHIANS 6:11 NRSV

In "Beauty and the Beast," it is only when the Beast discovers that Beauty really loves him in all his ugliness that he himself becomes beautiful. In the experience of Saint Paul, it is only when we discover that God really loves us in all our unloveliness that we ourselves start to become godlike. Paul's word for this gradual transformation is *sanctification*, and he sees it as the second stage in the process of salvation.

Being sanctified is a long and painful stage because with part of themselves sinners prefer their sin, just as with part of himself the Beast prefers his glistening snout and curved tusks. Many drop out with the job hardly more than begun, and among those who stay with it there are few if any who don't drag their feet most of the way.

But little by little—less by taking pains than by taking it easy—the forgiven person starts to become a forgiving person, the healed person to become a healing person, the loved person to become a loving person. God does most of it. The end of the process, Paul says, is eternal life.

---

From what has God been gradually transforming you, sanctifying you, saving you? What has that process been like?

> *Lord, continue your work of sanctification;*
> *transform me day by day. Amen.*

# RECEIVE BLESSING AND PASS IT ALONG

## Henri J. M. Nouwen

I am setting before you today a blessing and a curse—the blessing if
you obey the commands of the Lord your God that I am giving you
today; the curse if you disobey the commands of the Lord your God.

DEUTERONOMY 11:26-28

To *bless* means to say good things. We have to bless one another constantly. Parents need to bless their children, children their parents, husbands their wives, wives their husbands, friends their friends. In our society, so full of curses, we must fill each place we enter with our blessings. We forget so quickly that we are God's beloved children and allow the many curses of our world to darken our hearts. Therefore we have to be reminded of our belovedness and remind others of theirs.

It is an ongoing temptation to think of ourselves as living under a curse. The loss of a friend, an illness, an accident, a natural disaster, a war, or any failure can make us quickly think that we are no good and are being punished. This temptation to think of our lives as full of curses is even greater when all the media present us day after day with stories about human misery.

Jesus came to bless us, not to curse us. But we must choose to receive that blessing and hand it on to others.

---

The Lord always places in front of us blessings and curses. We are free to choose.

*Lord, I recognize the choice I have to bless or curse.*
*Show me where I can pass your blessing to others. Amen.*

# DOES GOD CARE ABOUT ME?

## James Bryan Smith

> Where can I go from your Spirit?
> Where can I flee from your presence?
> If I go up to the heavens, you are there;
> if I make my bed in the depths, you are there.
>
> PSALM 139:7-8

Most of us have difficulty believing that God really cares for us. We have trouble believing that God is always present, always gracious, and always providing for our needs. Surely God must be busy with things like the troubles in the Middle East, or the poverty in Bangladesh, or the destruction of the environment. Our small troubles—and even some of our big ones—seem inconsequential.

The Bible describes a God who is so in love with us that he never leaves us. According to Psalm 139, there is no place we can go where God is not. If we go to the top of the mountain, God is there; if we go to the deepest valley, God is there; if we descend even into hell itself, God would follow us there.

If God is concerned about making the grass green, and about feeding the birds, who are here today and gone tomorrow, how much more is God concerned about you?

———

Nothing in our lives goes unseen. God cares for it all.

*Lord, I can never escape your care. Thank you! Amen.*

# HOW ARE YOU AT ENEMY-LOVE?

## Dallas Willard

*Do not be overcome by evil, but overcome evil with good.*

ROMANS 12:21

There is a standard list of "enemies" in the daily news, which in fact hardly scratches the surface of the reality of standing hatreds that define people as enemies over against one another in this world. Jesus tells us to love our enemies and to carry that love through with the highest act of love, prayer.

Loving those who love us and lavishing care and honor on those of our own group is something that traitorous oppressors, the Mafia, and terrorists do. How, then, could that serve to distinguish the goodness of someone born into God's family or the presence of a different kind of reality and life? Even those with no knowledge of God at all do it.

But, Jesus says to his disciples, because you are living from God as citizens of the kingdom, have the kind of wholeness, of full functionality, that he has.

———

Few of us manage to go through life without enemies. Jesus calls on us, as citizens of his Father's kingdom, to respond to them by taking on the nature of God, who himself loves them. How are you at enemy-love?

*Lord, empower me to love my enemies*
*with your same perfect love. Amen.*

# BECAUSE GOD IS HOLY, FOLLOW IN HIS HOLINESS

## A. W. Tozer

> Just as he who called you is holy, so be holy in all you do;
> for it is written: "Be holy, because I am holy."
>
> 1 Peter 1:15–16

God is holy with an absolute holiness that knows no degrees, and this he cannot impart to his creatures. But there is a relative and contingent holiness which he shares with angels and seraphim in heaven and with redeemed men on earth as their preparation for heaven. This holiness God can and does impart to his children. He shares it with them by imputation and by impartation, and because he has made it available to them through the blood of the Lamb, he requires it of them.

Caught in this dilemma, what are we Christians to do? We must hide our unholiness in the wounds of Christ as Moses hid himself in the cleft of the rock while the glory of God passed by. We must take refuge from God in God. Above all we must believe that God sees us perfect in His Son while he disciplines and chastens and purges us that we may be partakers of his holiness.

———❧———

God did not say "Be holy *as* I am holy" but "*because* I am holy." No one can say "I am holy" as God is holy, but neither can we ignore God's instructions to pursue his holiness.

> *Lord, set me apart for yourself, cultivate within me your wholeness—so I can partake of your holiness. Amen.*

# THE TRUTH OF CHRISTIANITY WRITTEN IN OUR LIVES

## Frederick Buechner

*You show that you are a letter from Christ, the result of our ministry, written not with ink but with the Spirit of the living God, not on tablets of stone but on tablets of human hearts.*

2 Corinthians 3:3

The truth that Christianity claims to be true is ultimately to be found, if it's to be found at all, not in the Bible, or the church, or theology—the best they can do is point to the truth—but in our own stories. If the God you believe in as an idea doesn't start showing up in what happens to you in your own life, you have as much cause for concern as if the God you don't believe in as an idea does start showing up.

It is absolutely crucial, therefore, to keep in constant touch with what is going on in your own life's story and to pay close attention to what is going on in the stories of others' lives. If God is present anywhere, it is in those stories that God is present. If God is not present in those stories, then they are scarcely worth telling.

The ancient creeds of the Christian faith are not a theological idea or a religious system, but a series of largely flesh-and-blood events that happened, are happening, will happen in time and space—in the letters of our lives.

> *Lord, may my story show the truth of your presence and activity in the world. Amen.*

# RECEIVE GOD'S SACRED HANDIWORK

## Henri J. M. Nouwen

> Everything created by God is good, and nothing is to
> be rejected, provided it is received with thanksgiving;
> for it is sanctified by God's word and by prayer.
>
> 1 Timothy 4:4–5 nrsv

How do we live in creation? Do we relate to it as a place full of "things" we can use for whatever need we want to fulfill and whatever goal we wish to accomplish? Or do we see creation first of all as a sacramental reality, a sacred space where God reveals to us the immense beauty of the divine?

As long as we only use creation, we cannot recognize its sacredness because we are approaching it as if we were its owners. But when we relate to all that surrounds us as created by the same God who created us and as the place where God appears to us and calls us to worship and adoration, we are able to recognize the sacredness of all God's handiwork.

---

Given that God formed every ounce of creation, and that God's word and prayer have sanctified it, how should we live in it? If we do what Paul encourages—receive it with thanksgiving—then we we are able to see it for what it is: good and sacred.

*Lord, I receive your creation with thanksgiving,*
*recognizing it as holy. Amen.*

# BETWEEN GOD'S PROMISE AND PROVISION

## James Bryan Smith

*Against all hope, Abraham in hope believed and*
*so became the father of many nations.*

ROMANS 4:18

Sometimes, despite our best intentions, we fail to let God provide for us, and instead we assume control of our destiny. When Abraham and Sarah were promised to be the parents of many nations they assumed that they would have children right away. When Sarah did not get pregnant for many years, they began to doubt God and tried to find a solution of their own. They decided that Abraham should try to have a child with their servant, Hagar. Soon after, Hagar got pregnant and gave birth to a son, Ishmael.

It was not until they were in their nineties that God fulfilled the original promise, as Sarah gave birth to Isaac. God gave them a promise, but in between the promise and the provision they had to be patient. Many of us know what this is like. God has said that he will care for us, but when we run into a problem we may be tempted to create an Ishmael.

God promises that he will provide for us, but that promise often comes with a challenge. This is not because God wants to be cruel but because he wants us to grow.

❧

Although the process of waiting may seem painful, God molds and shapes us, increasing our faith.

*Lord, as I wait for your fulfillment, please deepen my faith. Amen.*

December

# A TREMBLING ANGEL

## Frederick Buechner

> Mary was greatly troubled at his words. . . . But the angel said
> to her, "Do not be afraid, Mary; you have found favor with God.
> You will conceive and give birth to a son." . . . "I am the Lord's
> servant," Mary answered. "May your word to me be fulfilled."
>
> LUKE 1:29-31, 38

She struck the angel Gabriel as hardly old enough to have a child at all, let alone this child, but he'd been entrusted with a message to give her, and he gave it.

He told her what the child was to be named, and who he was to be, and something about the mystery that was to come upon her. "You mustn't be afraid, Mary," he said.

As he said it, he only hoped she wouldn't notice that beneath the great, golden wings he himself was trembling with fear to think that the whole future of creation hung now on the answer of a girl.

———

What does it mean to you that Mary submitted her will to the angel's announcement? Do you think you could have participated in such a shocking and all-encompassing plan?

> *Lord, thank you for young Mary's acceptance of*
> *your will, and all that it means to my life. Amen.*

# GOD'S FOREVER-STANDING PLANS

## A. W. Tozer

The plans of the LORD stand firm forever,
the purposes of his heart through all generations.

PSALM 33:11

We know that God will fulfill every promise made to the prophets; we know that sinners will someday be cleansed out of the earth; we know that a ransomed company will enter into the joy of God, and that the righteous will shine forth in the kingdom of their Father; we know that God's perfections will yet receive universal acclamation, that all created intelligences will own Jesus Christ as Lord to the glory of God the Father, that the present imperfect order will be done away, and a new heaven and a new earth be established forever.

Toward all this God is moving with infinite wisdom and perfect precision of action. No one can dissuade him from his purposes, nothing turn him aside from his plans. Since he is omniscient, there can be no unforeseen circumstances, no accidents. As he is sovereign, there can be no countermanded orders, no breakdown in authority; and as he is omnipotent, there can be no want of power to achieve his chosen ends. God is sufficient unto himself for all these things.

---

How should this realization that the plans, purposes, and promises of God stand forever shape your experience of his heart?

*Lord, I acknowledge that all of your works are executed with infinite wisdom, and I await their being fulfilled with perfect precision. Amen.*

# THIS DAY IS GOD'S

## Frederick Buechner

> This is the day the LORD has made;
> We will rejoice and be glad in it.
>
> PSALM 118:24 NKJV

It is a moment of light surrounded on all sides by darkness and oblivion. In the entire history of the universe, let alone in your own history, there has never been another just like it and there will never be another just like it again. It is the point to which all your yesterdays have been leading since the hour of your birth. It is the point from which all your tomorrows will proceed until the hour of your death. If you were aware of how precious it is, you could hardly live through it. Unless you are aware of how precious it is, you can hardly be said to be living at all.

"This is the day which the Lord has made," says Psalm 118. "Let us rejoice and be glad in it." Or weep and be sad in it for that matter. The point is to see it for what it is, because it will be gone before you know it. If you waste it, it is your life that you're wasting. If you look the other way, it may be the moment you've been waiting for always that you're missing.

---

All other days have either disappeared into oblivion or have not yet emerged from it. Today is God's day. What are you going to do with it?

*Lord, I rejoice in this day that you*
*have made and given—to me. Amen.*

# ALLOW GOD TO CARE FOR YOU

## James Bryan Smith

I keep the LORD always before me;
because he is at my right hand, I shall not be moved.

PSALM 16:8 NRSV

I have come to realize that a lot of our religious behavior is actually designed to keep God at a distance. That is why it is so crucial for us to find ways to invite God's presence into our lives.

God invites us to integrate his presence, his resources, his wisdom, and his power into our lives. We are invited to go through our day and watch this happen. God wills that we solicit his help in every aspect of our lives, particularly those we find difficult. God suffers when he sees us try to work through strained relationships, painful memories, and family trials on our own. Caring for ourselves as God would have us do will mean allowing God to be a part of our lives.

David made an effort to keep his attention fixed on the presence of God. God is here. God is present, even now as you read. David knew that by keeping God before him he was being strengthened, so much so that he could say, "I shall not be moved." The foundation of caring for ourselves is the fact that God is with us.

---

How are you at integrating your life with the Lord's presence, resources, wisdom, and power? What might happen if you kept him always before you, being consciously aware of his presence?

*Lord, keep my attention fixed on your presence. Amen.*

# HOLINESS HAPPENS

## Frederick Buechner

> God sent the angel Gabriel to Nazareth . . . to a virgin pledged to
> be married to a man named Joseph, a descendant of David.
>
> LUKE 1:26-27

The earliest of the four Gospels makes no reference to the virgin birth, and neither does Paul, who wrote earlier still. On later evidence, however, many Christians have made it an article of faith that it was the Holy Spirit rather than Joseph who got Mary pregnant. If you believe God was somehow in Christ, it shouldn't make much difference to you how he got there. If you don't believe, it should make less difference still. In either case, life is complicated enough without confusing theology and gynecology.

In one sense anyway, the doctrine of the virgin birth is demonstrably true. Whereas the villains of history can always be seen as the products of heredity and environment, the saints always seem to arrive under their own steam. Evil evolves. Holiness happens.

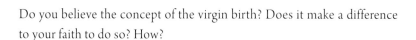

Do you believe the concept of the virgin birth? Does it make a difference to your faith to do so? How?

*Father, thank you for the miracle that produced your Son in human form. Thank you for the love that act represented. Amen.*

# ACQUAINT YOURSELF WITH GOD

## A. W. Tozer

In the wilderness prepare the way for the LORD;
make straight in the desert a highway for our God. . . .
And the glory of the LORD will be revealed,
and all people will see it together.

ISAIAH 40:3, 5

When viewed from the perspective of eternity, the most critical need of this hour may well be that the church should be brought back from her long Babylonian captivity and the name of God be glorified in her again as of old. The matter is for each of us a personal one. Any forward step in the church must begin with the individual.

What can we plain Christians do to bring back the departed glory? Is there some secret we must learn? Is there a formula for personal revival we can apply to the present situation, to our own situation? The answer to these questions is yes.

Yet the answer may easily disappoint some persons, for it is anything but profound. It is simply the old and ever-new counsel: *acquaint thyself with God*. To regain her lost power the church must see heaven opened and have a transforming vision of God.

The secret to God's returning glory is found in individuals having a transforming vision of God once again—making straight paths for him in their lives, in their churches.

*Lord, I open up for you a path in my life so I can know you better, so your glory will be fully revealed. Amen.*

# THE ANTICIPATION OF ADVENT

## Frederick Buechner

> The holy one to be born will be called the Son of God.
>
> Luke 1:35

In the silence of a midwinter dusk there is far off in the deeps of it somewhere a sound so faint that for all you can tell it may be only the sound of the silence itself. You hold your breath to listen. You walk up the steps to the front door. The empty windows at either side of it tell you nothing, or almost nothing. For a second you catch a whiff in the air of some fragrance that reminds you of a place you've never been and a time you have no words for. You are aware of the beating of your heart.

The extraordinary thing that is about to happen is matched only by the extraordinary moment just before it happens. Advent is the name of that moment.

If you concentrate just for an instant, far off in the deeps of yourself somewhere you can feel the beating of your heart. For all its madness and lostness, not to mention your own, you can hear the world itself holding its breath.

---

Anticipation has its own beauty aside from the actual event you're waiting for. Does waiting for something you really want enhance your enjoyment of it?

*Thank you, God, that we didn't wait in vain.*
*Your Word never fails. Amen.*

# AS CLOSE AS OUR VERY BREATH

## Henri J. M. Nouwen

*"The virgin will conceive and give birth to a son, and they will call him Immanuel" (which means "God with us").*

MATTHEW 1:23

Jesus is God-with-us, Immanuel. The great mystery of God becoming human is God's desire to be loved by us. By becoming a vulnerable child, completely dependent on human care, God wants to take away all distance between the human and the divine.

Who can be afraid of a little child who needs to be fed, to be cared for, to be taught, to be guided? We usually talk about God as the all-powerful, almighty God on whom we depend completely. But God wanted to become the all-powerless, all-vulnerable God who completely depends on us. How can we be afraid of a God who wants to be "God-with-us" and wants us to become "Us-with-God"?

God made a covenant with us. The word *covenant* means "coming together." God wants to come together with us. God wants to be as close to us as our breath.

In many stories from the Old Testament, we see God appearing as our Defender against enemies, Protector against dangers, and Guide into freedom. God does all of this *for* us, because the birth of his Son revealed how much he loves us and wants to be *with* us.

*Lord, thank you for the truth of your covenant,*
*which reveals your desire to stay near us. Amen.*

# PEACE ON EARTH

## Frederick Buechner

> "In this world you will have trouble.
> But take heart! I have overcome the world."
>
> JOHN 16:33

Peace has come to mean the time when there aren't any wars or even when there aren't any major wars. Beggars can't be choosers; we'd most of us settle for that. But in Hebrew peace, *shalom*, means fullness, means having everything you need to be wholly and happily yourself.

One of the titles by which Jesus is known is Prince of Peace, and he used the word himself in what seem at first glance to be two radically contradictory utterances. On one occasion he said to the disciples, "Do not think that I have come to bring peace to the earth; I have not come to bring peace, but a sword" (Matthew 10:34). And later on, the last time they ate together, he said to them, "Peace I leave with you; my peace I give to you" (John 14:27).

The contradiction is resolved when you realize that, for Jesus, peace seems to have meant not the absence of struggle, but the presence of love.

In the midst of great trial it is possible to know deep peace. Has this been your experience? How has peace helped you in different situations?

*Lord Jesus, thank you for peace that's available in the most unlikely times. Amen.*

# LOVE AS GOD LOVES

## James Bryan Smith

Concerning love of the brothers and sisters, you do not
need to have anyone write to you, for you yourselves
have been taught by God to love one another.

1 THESSALONIANS 4:9 NRSV

God has created a world in which we are the ones who care for one another. To put it another way, God cares for us through one another. But before God can begin using us to care for one another he does two things: first, God instills in us the desire to care, and second, he provides an example of how to care for one another.

The motive to care for one another comes from the care God has shown us. The apostle John wrote, "Beloved, since God loved us so much, we also ought to love one another. . . . By this we know that we abide in him and he in us, because he has given us of his Spirit" (1 John 4:11, 13). God's love for us becomes the source of our desire to love one another. We love, says John, because we have been loved *first* (1 John 4:19).

God's love for us—as seen in his acceptance, forgiveness, and care—penetrates our hearts and begins a journey outward to the people around us. If we fail to love others, we have most likely failed to know that God loves and cares for us.

*Lord, recognizing your love and care for me,*
*I resolve to love as you love, to care as you care. Amen.*

# MEDITATE UPON THE MAJESTY OF GOD

## A. W. Tozer

> On the glorious splendor of your majesty,
> and on your wondrous works, I will meditate.
>
> PSALM 145:5 NRSV

We must practice the art of long and loving meditation upon the majesty of God. This will take some effort, for the concept of majesty has all but disappeared from the human race. The focal point of man's interest is now himself. Humanism in its various forms has displaced theology as the key to the understanding of life. All this must be reversed by a deliberate act of the will and kept so by a patient effort of mind.

God is a Person and can be known in increasing degrees of intimate acquaintance as we prepare our hearts for the wonder. It may be necessary for us to alter our former beliefs about God as the glory that gilds the sacred Scriptures dawns over our interior lives. We may also need to break quietly and graciously with a lifeless textualism that prevails among the gospel churches, and to protest the frivolous character of much that passes for Christianity among us. By this we may for the time lose friends and gain a passing reputation for being holier-than-thou; but no man who permits the expectation of unpleasant consequences to influence him in a matter like this is fit for the kingdom of God.

What steps can you take to practice the art of meditating upon the majesty of God?

*Lord, sift my beliefs for errors so I can freely meditate upon your majesty, delighting in your wonder. Amen.*

# LORD, FORGIVE ME

## Dallas Willard

Hear from heaven, your dwelling place, and when you hear, forgive.

1 KINGS 8:30

A s a father pities his children, so the Lord pities us. He knows what we are made of and remembers that we are dust. He does not deal with us according to our sins, nor does he reward us in proportion to our wrongdoings (Psalm 103:10–14). That is the wonderful, healing nature of the kingdom among us.

Once we step into this kingdom and trust it, pity becomes the atmosphere in which we live. Of course it is his pity for us that allows us in to start with, and then it patiently bears with us. "The Lord is bursting with compassion and full of pity" (James 5:11). But we also are to be "of one mind, having compassion one of another, love as brethren, be pitiful, be courteous" (1 Peter 3:8 KJV).

It is not psychologically possible for us really to know God's pity for us and at the same time be hardhearted toward others. So we are "forgiving of others in the same manner as God forgives us." That is a part of our prayer.

We cannot forgive without God's help; he's the one who showed us the way by forgiving us.

*Lord, thank you for the healing nature of your kingdom.*
*Help me to participate in it by practicing the*
*same mercy you bestow on me. Amen.*

# WHY ARE WE HERE?

## James Bryan Smith

> It was you who formed my inward parts;
> you knit me together in my mother's womb.
>
> PSALM 139:13 NRSV

Why is God with us? Why are we even here? We are here because God is preparing us to be something so special that through all of the ages we will be the primary testimony of his love. Our life is about what God is making us. Human life, from God's perspective, is meant to be dramatic and exciting. We were built to be God-inhabited, created to live on bread that this world knows nothing of.

Each of us came into this world for a single purpose: to glorify God and enjoy him forever. We were uniquely created, each different and distinct from one another, but we were all created so that one day we would stand before the heavenly host as an eternal trophy of God's goodness, grace, and tender mercy.

We did not make ourselves. Our existence is not due to anything we have done. God has created us out of love, and through his ongoing presence and desire to be among us, he intends that each one of us would stand as a witness to that love.

Remarkably, God created us because God loves us. We were created to experience that love and stand as a symbol of that love. That's why we are here; that's the meaning of life.

> *Lord, I praise you because I am wonderfully made in love;*
> *empower me to glorify you and enjoy that love forever. Amen.*

# HAVE A VERY TAME CHRISTMAS?

## Frederick Buechner

Praise be to the Lord, the God of Israel,
because he has come to his people and redeemed them.

LUKE 1:68

Rudolph, the Red-Nosed Reindeer," the plastic tree, the cornball crèche, the Hallmark Virgin: yet for all our efforts, we've never quite managed to ruin it. That in itself is part of the miracle, a part you can see. Most of the miracle you can't see, or don't.

Christmas itself is by grace. It could never have survived our own blindness and depredations otherwise. It could never have *happened* otherwise. Perhaps it is the very wildness and strangeness of the grace that has led us to try to tame it.

But if the Christmas event in itself is indeed—as a matter of cold, hard fact—all it's cracked up to be, then even at best our efforts are misleading. The Word become flesh. Ultimate Mystery born with a skull you could crush one-handed. Incarnation. "God of God, Light of Light, very God of very God . . . who for us . . . and for our salvation," as the Nicene Creed puts it, "came down from heaven."

*Came down.* Only then do we dare uncover our eyes and see what we can see. It is the Resurrection and the Life she holds in her arms. It is the bitterness of death he takes at her breast.

───

How can you bolster a sense of worship in your celebration?

*Lord Jesus, thank you for coming,*
*and thank you, God, for giving. Amen.*

365

# LOVE YOUR WORLD

## James Bryan Smith

> We love because he first loved us.
>
> 1 JOHN 4:19

When we grasp the magnitude of God's love for us, we will begin to feel it flow out of our hands and feet and mouths and into the lives of others. God has given us his Spirit, a Spirit of love that will drive us to care for one another.

God provides for us the *example* of how to care for one another. How does God care for us? God cares for our spiritual life, God cares for the health of our soul, and God provides for our physical needs. God is available, God listens, and God never abandons us. This is how we are to care for one another.

Jesus also left us a clear picture of how to care for one another. He never discouraged people, he spoke the truth in love, and he gave of his time and energy to meet the needs of those around him. He received the poor and the sinful in the same manner as he welcomed the rich and the righteous. He loved all people and wept for their pain. We are given the model of how we are to treat one another in the example of Jesus.

---

We follow God's lead when we care for the world around us in tangible ways and treat others as Jesus treats us.

*Lord, empower me to follow your lead and love my world well. Amen.*

# THE ETERNAL KIND OF LIFE

## Dallas Willard

It is for freedom that Christ has set us free.

GALATIANS 5:1

Jesus entered human history through the life of an ordinary family. But then he inducts us into the eternal kind of life that flows through himself. He first brings that life to bear upon our needs, then diffuses it throughout our deeds—deeds done with expectation that he and his Father will act with and in our actions.

Jesus came among us to show and teach the life for which we were made. He came very gently, opened access to the governance of God with him, and set afoot a conspiracy of freedom in truth among human beings. Having overcome death he remains among us. By relying on his word and presence we are enabled to reintegrate the little realm that makes up our life into the infinite rule of God. And that is the eternal kind of life. Caught up in his active rule, our deeds become an element in God's eternal history. They are what God and we do together, making us part of his life and him a part of ours.

The reality of God's rule, and all of the instrumentalities it involves, is present in action and available with and through the person of Jesus.

---

The human person of Jesus introduced a life shot through with eternity.

*Father, where I am hung up on earthly problems,*
*help me to become caught up in your rule instead. Amen.*

# THE CENTER OF CHRISTIAN SPIRITUALITY

## N. T. Wright

> The twenty-four elders fall before the one who is seated on the throne and worship the one who lives forever and ever."
>
> REVELATION 4:10–11 NRSV

Worship is at the very center of all Christian living. One of the main reasons theology (trying to think straight about who God is) matters is that we are called to love God with all our heart, mind, soul, and strength. It matters that we learn more about who God is so we can praise him more appropriately.

Perhaps one of the reasons why so much worship, in some churches at least, appears unattractive to so many people is that we have forgotten, or covered up, the truth about the one we are worshiping. But whenever we even glimpse the truth, we are drawn back. Like groupies sneaking off work to see a rock star who's in town for just an hour or so, like fans waiting all night for a glimpse of a football team returning in triumph—only much more so!—those who come to recognize the God we see in Jesus, the Lion who is also the Lamb, will long to come and worship him.

---

We will praise him appropriately only when we've encountered the one true God!

*Lord, I pray first for a real encounter with you,*
*that I may fully worship you. Amen.*

# DAILY NEEDS, DAILY REQUESTS

## Dallas Willard

"Give us this day our daily bread."

MATTHEW 6:11 NRSV

Food, of course, is symbolically central, but whatever else we really need to live in a functional manner is included in this request. Paul speaks of being at peace if we have "foods and clothings" (1 Timothy 6:8). And that, you may recall, fits in exactly with what we found in Jesus' discussion of birds and flowers in Matthew 6:25–34 and with what God provided in the desert wanderings of his covenant people (Deuteronomy 8:3–5).

Of course this request embodies that confidence in our Father that relieves us from all anxiety. The emphasis is on *provisions today* of what we need *for today*. This is because God is always present today, no matter which day it is. His reign is the Eternal Now. So we do not ask him to provide today what we will need for tomorrow. Today I have God, and he has the provisions. Tomorrow it will be the same. So I simply ask today for what I need for today or ask now for what I need now.

Whether food or clothing, housing or health, we need the Lord to provide for the immediate sustenance of our bodies—today and every day. Are you confident that he meets these needs?

*Lord, give me this day my daily bread—*
*whether food or clothes, housing or health. Amen.*

# IMAGINE A WORLD WITHOUT CONDEMNATION

## Dallas Willard

> "Do not judge so that you will not be judged."
>
> MATTHEW 7:1 NASB

If we would really help those close to us and dear, and if we would learn to live together with our family and "neighbors" in the power of the kingdom, we must abandon the deeply rooted human practice of condemning and blaming. This is what Jesus means when he says, "Judge not." He is telling us that we should, and that we can, become the kind of person who does not condemn or blame others. As we do so, the power of God's kingdom will be more freely available to bless and guide those around us into his ways.

But what is it, exactly, that we do when we condemn someone? When we condemn another we really communicate that he or she is, in some deep and just possibly irredeemable way, bad—bad as a whole, and to be rejected. In our eyes the condemned is among the discards of human life. He or she is not acceptable. We sentence that person to exclusion. Surely we can learn to live well and happily without doing that.

Although when we first hear Jesus' words to "judge not" we may disbelieve their necessity. Condemning and being condemned seem so "normal." And yet Jesus invites us to imagine something different: a world without them.

*Jesus, I join you in creating a world without condemnation by refusing to condemn. Amen.*

# CHRIST'S COMMITMENT IS TO US

## James Bryan Smith

I am convinced that neither death, nor life, nor angels, nor principalities,
nor things present, nor things to come, nor powers, nor height,
nor depth, nor any other created thing, will be able to separate
us from the love of God, which is in Christ Jesus our Lord.

ROMANS 8:38–39 NASB

For most of my Christian life I related to God on the basis of what I did for him. If I prayed well, studied hard, served much, and sinned little, then I felt reasonably sure God was pleased with me. I was living in a kind of fear that was paralyzing my ability to love God, love myself, and ultimately, love others.

I was afraid God would look at my faults and withdraw his love. I was afraid my weaknesses would separate me from the love of Christ. Now I see they cannot. I was afraid my sinfulness would separate me from the love of Christ. Now I am certain that nothing will ever separate me from the love God has made visible in Jesus.

I see now how foolish it was to think that my feeble attempts at righteousness had anything to do with how God feels about me. For too long I was impressed with my "commitment" to Christ; now I am impressed only with Christ's commitment to me.

What things do you fear will build a wall between you and God's love?
Can you see how impossible that is?

*Lord, I receive the truth that I am my
Beloved's and he is mine. Amen.*

# THE EARTHINESS OF SAINTS

## Frederick Buechner

> Golden bowls full of incense . . . are the prayers of the saints.
>
> REVELATION 5:8 NKJV

In his holy flirtation with the world, God occasionally drops a pocket handkerchief. These handkerchiefs are called saints.

Many people think of saints as plaster saints, men and women of such paralyzing virtue that they never thought a nasty thought or did an evil deed their whole lives long. As far as I know, real saints never even come close to characterizing themselves that way. The feet of saints are as much of clay as everybody else's, and their sainthood consists less of what they have done than of what God has for some reason chosen to do through them.

When you consider that Saint Mary Magdalene was possessed by seven devils, that Saint Augustine prayed, "Give me chastity and continence, but not now," that Saint Francis started out as a high-living young dude in downtown Assisi, you figure that maybe there's nobody God can't use as a means of grace, including even ourselves.

The Holy Spirit has been called "the Lord, the giver of life" and, drawing their power from that source, saints are essentially life-givers. To be with them is to become more alive.

See if you can spot a saint in the next week. What criteria will you use?

> *Lord, today I bless the beauty of your saints*
> *and all they accomplish in your name. Amen.*

# PRAY ABOUT WHAT MATTERS TO YOU

## Dallas Willard

Trust in Him at all times, you people;

Pour out your heart before Him;

God is a refuge for us.

PSALM 62:8 NKJV

Prayer is never just asking, nor is it merely a matter of asking for what I want. God is not a cosmic butler or fix-it man, and the aim of the universe is not to fulfill my desires and needs. On the other hand, I am to pray for what concerns me, and many people have found prayer impossible because they thought they should only pray for wonderful but remote needs they actually had little or no interest in or even knowledge of.

Prayer simply dies from efforts to pray about "good things" that honestly do not matter to us. The way to get to meaningful prayer for those good things is to start by praying for what we are truly interested in. The circle of our interests will inevitably grow in the largeness of God's love.

―――⚬⚬⚬―――

What are the things that matter to you? The picture of prayer emerging from the teachings of Jesus is one of asking, requesting things from God. When we do, we will receive and find, and the door to our requests will be opened to us.

*Lord, I come to you with the issues that I'm most concerned about. Thank you for caring about these things too. Amen.*

# BETWEEN CHRIST'S ASCENSION AND APPEARING

## N. T. Wright

[We look] for the blessed hope and glorious appearing
of our great God and Savior Jesus Christ.

TITUS 2:13 NKJV

Like the Jewish worldview, the Christian worldview is a story with a beginning, a middle, and an end. Not to have closure at the end of the story—to be left with a potentially endless cycle, round and round with either the same things happening again and again or simply perhaps the long outworking of karma—would be the very antithesis of the story told by the apostles and by the long line of their Jewish predecessors. And precisely because Jesus is not collapsed into the church, or indeed the world, we can renounce both the triumphalism that conveniently makes his sovereign lordship an excuse for its own and the despair that comes when we see such hopes dashed, as they always will be, in the follies and failings of even the best and greatest Christian organizations, structures, leaders, and followers. Because we live between ascension and appearing, joined to Jesus Christ by the Spirit but still awaiting his final coming and presence, we can be *both* properly humble and properly confident.

———— ∞ ————

How do you think it looks to live between Christ's ascension and appearing with proper humility and confidence?

> *Lord, may I live well as I await your appearing on the other side of your life, death, resurrection, and ascension. Amen.*

# THE POWER OF A BABE

## Frederick Buechner

Magi from the east came to Jerusalem and asked,
"Where is the one who has been born king of the Jews?
We saw his star when it rose and have come to worship him."

MATTHEW 2:1-2

The foolishness of the wise is perhaps nowhere better illustrated than by the way the three Magi went to Herod the Great, king of the Jews, to find out the whereabouts of the holy child who had just been born king of the Jews to supplant him. It did not even strike them as suspicious when Herod asked them to be sure to let him know when they found him so he could hurry on down to pay his respects.

Luckily for the holy child, after the three Magi had followed their star to the manger and left him their presents, they were tipped off in a dream to avoid Herod like the plague on their way home.

Herod was fit to be tied when he realized he'd been had and ordered the murder of every male child two years old and under in the district. For all his enormous power, he knew there was somebody in diapers more powerful still. The wisdom of the foolish is perhaps nowhere better illustrated.

When have you seen wisdom rise from an unlikely source? Have you ever uttered words you knew reflected more insight than you were capable of?

*Lord, thank you for all the startling truths we see played out
in history, such as the confounding of Herod. I praise you,
knowing none of your plans can be thwarted. Amen.*

# HOW MUCH DO YOU LOVE ME?

## Brennan Manning

[I pray] that you, being rooted and grounded in love, may be able to comprehend with all the saints what is the width and length and depth and height—to know the love of Christ which passes knowledge.

EPHESIANS 3:17–19 NKJV

I went to pray in the parish church in Tamarac, Florida, at two in the afternoon. The usual tenor of my prayer life is dryness, longing, and experiencing the absence of God in the hope of communion. But the moment I knelt down my mind was filled with the image of a three-year-old boy playing on the rug in his living room. Off in the corner his mother sat on the floor in the lotus position, knitting. Suddenly she dropped her work and beckoned to him. He toddled over and climbed up on her lap. She smiled down at him and asked softly, "How much do you love me?" He extended his tiny arms as far as they would go and exclaimed, "*This much* I love you."

In an instant, it was thirty-some years later; the little boy in the fullness of manhood hung nailed to a crossbeam. His mother looked up and said, "How much do you love me?" His arms were stretched out to the ends of the universe. "*This much* I love you."

When have you experienced the "love of Christ which passes knowledge"? How did it affect you?

*Lord, thank for loving me "this much." I love you too. Amen.*

# A PAINFUL PROCLAMATION

## Frederick Buechner

*This child is destined to cause the falling and rising of many in Israel.*

LUKE 2:34

Jesus was still in diapers when his parents brought him to the temple in Jerusalem "to present him to the Lord" (Luke 2:22), as the custom was, and offer a sacrifice, and that's when old Simeon spotted him. Years before, he'd been told he wouldn't die till he'd seen the Messiah with his own two eyes, and time was running out. When the moment finally came, one look through his cataract lenses was all it took.

"Lord, now lettest thou thy servant depart in peace, according to thy word, for mine eyes have seen thy salvation," he said (Luke 2:29), the baby playing with the fringes of his beard. The parents were pleased as punch, and so he blessed them too for good measure. Then something about the mother stopped him, and his expression changed.

What he saw in her face was a long way off, but it was there so plainly he couldn't pretend. "A sword will pierce through your soul," he said (Luke 2:35). He would rather have bitten off his tongue than said it, but in that holy place he felt he had no choice. Then he handed her back the baby and departed in something less than the perfect peace he'd dreamed of all the long years of his waiting.

Sometimes the truth won't just set you free—it will pierce your soul. When has hearing truth been a painful experience for you? What was the result?

*Lord, when the truth is crushing, strengthen me to accept it. Amen.*

# LORD, LEAD ME NOT INTO TRIALS

## Dallas Willard

> "Do not bring us to the time of trial,
> but rescue us from the evil one."
>
> MATTHEW 6:13 NRSV

This request is not just for evasion of pain and of things we don't like, though it frankly is that. It expresses the understanding that we can't stand up under very much pressure, and that it is not a good thing for us to suffer. It is a vote of "no confidence" in our own abilities.

God expects us to pray that we will escape trials, and we should do it. The bad things that happen to us are always challenges to our faith, and we may not be able to stand up under them. They are dangerous. To know this, one has only to watch how quickly people begin to attack God when bad things start to happen to them. The popularity of the book on why bad things happen to good people is explicit testimony to how "bad things" tend to undermine faith.

As we attentively make this prayer a part of our constant bearing in life, we will see how God indeed does keep us from trials and deliver us from evil. Constantly.

―――∞―――

We are utterly feeble, and we are utterly dependent on God for deliverance. Thankfully with God there is a continuous provision for all of our needs, no matter how dire. How has God delivered you from trials, from evil?

*Lord, you know how weak I am, how prone to collapse when my world crumbles. Strengthen me to face whatever I must, in a way that brings you glory. Amen.*

# JOURNEY TO GOD'S HEART

## Henri J. M. Nouwen

The LORD your God . . . goes before you on your way, to seek
out a place for you to encamp, in fire by night and cloud
by day, to show you the way in which you should go.

DEUTERONOMY 1:32-33 NASB

Even though our emotional and spiritual lives are distinct, they do influence one another profoundly. Our feelings often give us a window on our spiritual journeys. When we cannot let go of jealousy, we may wonder if we are in touch with the Spirit in us that cries out "Abba." When we feel very peaceful and "centered," we may come to realize that this is a sign of our deep awareness of our belovedness.

Likewise our prayer lives, lived as a faithful response to the presence of the Spirit within us, may open a window on our emotions, feelings, and passions and give us some indication of how to put them in the service of our long journey into the heart of God.

When do you feel most in touch with God's Spirit? What are the outward signs of his presence within?

*Lord, please continue to be my close companion*
*as I make my way into your heart. Amen.*

# AN ESSENTIAL CONDITION

## Dallas Willard

> "Follow me," Jesus told him, and Levi got up and followed him.
>
> MARK 2:14

If I am to be someone's apprentice, there is one absolutely essential condition. I must be with that person. And it is precisely what it meant to follow Jesus when he was here in human form. To follow him meant, in the first place, to be with him.

If I am Jesus' disciple that means I am with him to learn from him how to be like him. To take cases from ordinary life, a child learning to multiply and divide numbers is an apprentice to its teacher. Children are with their teachers, learning from them how to be like them in a certain respect—similarly for a student of the piano or voice, of the Spanish language, of tennis, and so forth. The "being with," by watching and by hearing, is an absolute necessity.

And provision has been made for us to be with Jesus, as one person to another, in our daily life. But it is also necessary that we have a practical—though not a metaphysical or even a theological—understanding of this arrangement in order to carry on our side of the apprenticeship relation.

How do you practice following Jesus on a day-to-day basis? How are you with him, and he with you?

> *Jesus, remind me of your presence near me all day*
> *every day, so I can learn to be like you. Amen.*

# SUBMIT TO GOD

## Dallas Willard

> "You have been faithful over a few things,
> I will make you ruler over many things."
>
> MATTHEW 25:23 NKJV

When we submit what and where we are to God, our rule or dominion then increases. For God is unlimited creative will and constantly invites us, even now, into an ever larger share in what he is doing. Like Jesus, we can enter into the work we see our Father doing.

In accord with his original intent, the heavenly Father has in fact prepared an individualized kingdom for every person, from the outset of creation. That may seem impossible to us. But we do have a very weak imagination toward God, and we are confused by our own desires and fears, as well as by gross misinformation. It is a small thing for him.

As we learn through increasing trust to govern our tiny affairs with him, the kingdom he had all along planned for us will be turned over to us, at the appropriate time. Accordingly, in the last chapter of the Bible we see God's purposes in creation come round full circle in eternity: "The Lord God will be their light, and they will reign for ever and ever" (Revelation 22:5).

What might God be calling you to rule in increasing measure?

*Lord, I submit myself fully to you,*
*so I may fully participate in your work. Amen.*

# DO ALL AS JESUS WOULD

## Dallas Willard

> So, whether you eat or drink, or whatever you do,
> do everything for the glory of God.
>
> 1 CORINTHIANS 10:31 NRSV

The specific work to be done—whether it is making ax handles or tacos, selling automobiles or teaching kindergarten, performing in the arts or teaching English as a second language—is of central interest to God. It is work that should be done, and it should be done as Jesus himself would do it. Nothing can substitute for that. In my opinion, at least, as long as one is on the job, all peculiarly religious activities should take second place to doing "the job" in sweat, intelligence, and the power of God. That is our devotion to God.

Our intention with our job should be the highest possible good in its every aspect, and we should pursue that with conscious expectation of a constant energizing and direction from God. Although we must never allow our job to become our life, we should, within reasonable limits, routinely sacrifice our comfort and pleasure for the quality of our work, whether it be ax handles, tacos, or the proficiency of a student we are teaching.

Following Jesus means doing every job well, because that is what Jesus himself would do. And because we admire and love him, we do everything to God's glory.

*Lord, I lift up my work and commit to doing it
to the best of my ability—to your glory. Amen.*